D1091721

THE BEAUHARNOIS SCANDAL

T.D. REGEHR

The Beauharnois Scandal: A Story of Canadian Entrepreneurship and Politics

UNIVERSITY OF TORONTO PRESS
Toronto Buffalo London

Toronto Buffalo London
Printed in Canada

ISBN 0-8020-2629-X

Printed on acid-free paper

Canadian Cataloguing in Publication Data

Regehr, T.D.
The Beauharnois scandal

Bibliography: p.
Includes index.
ISBN 0-8020-2629-X

1. Beauharnois Scandal, 1931.* 2. Beauharnois Power Corporation. 3. Canada – Politics and government – 1930–1935.* 4. Campaign funds – Canada. 5. Corruption (in politics) – Canada. I. Title.

FC573.B4R43 1990 971.062'3 C89-094681-7
F1034.R43 1990

This book has been published with the help of a grant from the Canadian Federation for the Humanities, using funds provided by the Social Sciences and Humanities Research Council of Canada.

Contents

Acknowledgments

The writing of this history would have been impossible without the assistance and guidance of archivists who have responded willingly to my many requests for information and materials. Those at the Hydro-Quebec Archives, the National Archives of Canada, the Manuscript Department of the William R. Perkins Library at Duke University, the Ontario Hydro Archives, the Ontario Archives, the Archive Nationale du Québec, and Queen's University were particularly helpful.

Financial assistance to undertake the necessary research was received from the Social Sciences and Humanities Research Council of Canada through a Sabbatical Leave Fellowship and a research grant. The research at Duke University in North Carolina was made possible through a small research grant from the College of Arts and Science, University of Saskatchewan.

Many colleagues have provided relevant information and advice, but the assistance of Professor J. Michael Hayden, who read the entire manuscript and made many useful suggestions, was particularly helpful, as were the comments from the several anonymous assessors. My wife, Sylvia, exhibited much patience and later proofread the entire manuscript, while my daughter Sonya assisted with the research.

A final word of thanks is due to the editorial and production staff at the University of Toronto Press. Gerald Hallowell and Catherine Frost helped to improve the manuscript and transform it into a book.

Picture credits

Unless otherwise stated, illustrations are from the Williams States Lee Papers, Duke University, including the map of the Beauharnois project from *Physical Facts and Financial Figures on Beauharnois* and the profile of the new canal from *Down the Canal: A Pictorial Presentation of the Beauharnois Power and Navigation Development*, both published in Montreal by the Beauharnois Power Corporation, 1930 and 1931, respectively. Queen's University Archives R.O. Sweezey; *Who's Who in Canada, 1932–33* (Toronto: International Press 1933) W.L. McDougald; National Archives of Canada Raymond PA48899, Henry C6713, Haydon C6716; *Visites des installations d'Hydro-Québec* (Montreal: Hydro-Québec 1982) powerhouse in 1961.

Beauharnois chronology

1845	First Beauharnois Canal is completed.
1899	Soulanges Canal is completed.
1902	Beauharnois Light, Heat & Power Co. is incorporated
1913	R.O. Sweezey investigates Beauharnois site.
1914	N. Cantin incorporates Great Lakes and Atlantic ... Co.
1921	Robert family grant option to N. Cantin.
1921	Newman, Sweezey & Co. is incorporated.
4 April 1925	Sweezey begins work for N. Cantin.
Nov. 1926	Joint Board of Engineers files its report.
31 Dec. 1926	Sweezey resigns position with Cantin.
3 Feb. 1927	Sweezey signs deal with Robert family.
Summer 1927	The first Beauharnois syndicate is organized.
27 Sept. 1927	F.P. Jones is named president, Beauharnois.
Sept. 1927	Winfield Sifton begins work for Beauharnois.
29 Dec. 1927	McDougald contributes $10,000 to L.H. Trust fund
17 Jan. 1928	Beauharnois application to the federal government is filed.
4 April 1928	Second Beauharnois syndicate is organized.
13 June 1928	Winfield Sifton dies.
23 June 1928	Quebec amends Beauharnois charter and lease.
October 1928	McDougald contributes $15,000 to L.H. Trust fund
11 Dec. 1928	King meets with Haydon, McLachlan, and Henry.
13 Dec. 1928	Deputy minister of railways and canals dies.
18 Dec. 1928	Beauharnois and Sterling Industrial Corp. are merged.
15 Jan. 1929	Public Hearings in J.C. Elliott's office.
5 Feb. 1929	Supreme Court rules on federal powers in streams.

14 Feb. 1929	Henry becomes deputy minister of railways and canals.
8 March 1929	Federal cabinet approves PC 422.
30 March 1929	R.A.C. Henry resigns as deputy minister.
10 June 1929	Tentative agreement with Ontario Hydro
July 1929	Beauharnois attempts to file detailed plans.
26 July 1929	F.P. Jones resigns as president of Beauharnois.
26 July 1929	Corporate reorganization with Montreal Power
12 Oct. 1929	Official beginning of Beauharnois construction
13 Oct. 1929	Banks threaten to stop advances to Beauharnois.
28 Oct. 1929	Contract with Ontario Hydro is signed.
29 Oct. 1929	Worst day of the Wall Street stock market crash
30 Oct. 1929	Ontario general election
31 Oct. 1929	Beauharnois Power Corporation is organized.
30 Nov. 1929	Final contract with Ontario Hydro is signed.
March 1930	Sweezey is forced to give evidence in Cantin suit.
7 April 1930	Garland asks for Beauharnois documents in House of Commons.
22 May 1930	Gardiner motion re Beauharnois is introduced.
19 June 1930	Frank Regan contacts Ontario Attorney-General W.H. Price.
28 July 1930	Canadian federal election
15 Jan. 1931	Beauharnois first mortgage bonds are authorized.
22 May 1931	Gardiner and Garland ask questions in House of Commons.
19 May 1931	First major attack in the House of Commons
10 June 1931	Special Select Committee, House of Commons, is appointed.
15 June 1931	Special Select Committee begins its work.
1 July 1931	Special Select Committee visits Beauharnois.
28 July 1931	Official report of parliamentary committee is filed.
1 Aug. 1931	Federal legislation to assist project completion
1 Aug. 1931	Banks refuse further loans to Beauharnois.
Sept. 1931	Bennett rejects proposed Montreal Power offer and agrees to guarantee Beauharnois bank loans.
16 Nov. 1931	King returns trust money to McDougald.
19 Nov. 1931	Sweezey, McDougald, and Henry resign.
Jan. 1932	Bennett suggests arrangements be made with some other power company or Beauharnois be liquidated.

11 Feb. 1932	Special Senate Committee is appointed.
1 April 1932	Beauharnois defaults on bond interest payments.
22 April 1932	Temporary committee of bondholders is organized.
28 April 1932	Montreal Power proposes scheme of reorganization.
10 June 1932	Disputed bondholders meeting in Montreal
11 June 1932	Toronto bondholders' committee is organized.
31 Oct. 1932	Ontario royal commission report is presented.
1 Oct. 1932	Beauharnois begins power deliveries.
10 Nov. 1932	Andrew Haydon dies.
16 March 1933	New Montreal Power scheme of reorganization is accepted.
10 July 1934	Mitch Hepburn is elected premier of Ontario.
14 Oct. 1935	Mackenzie King wins federal election.
25 Nov. 1935	Quebec provincial election reduces Taschereau to minority government.
6 Dec. 1935	Ontario Hydro's Beauharnois contract is repudiated.
17 Aug. 1936	Liberals are defeated in Quebec election.
16 Feb. 1937	Modified contract with Ontario Hydro is ratified.
21 April 1938	New Montreal Power scheme of reorganization is accepted.
May 1941	Quebec legislature authorizes nationalization of Montreal Power and subsidiaries.
14 May 1944	Quebec Hydro Electric Commission is created and takes over Beauharnois and Montreal Power works.
17 March 1961	Construction of last Beauharnois phase is completed.

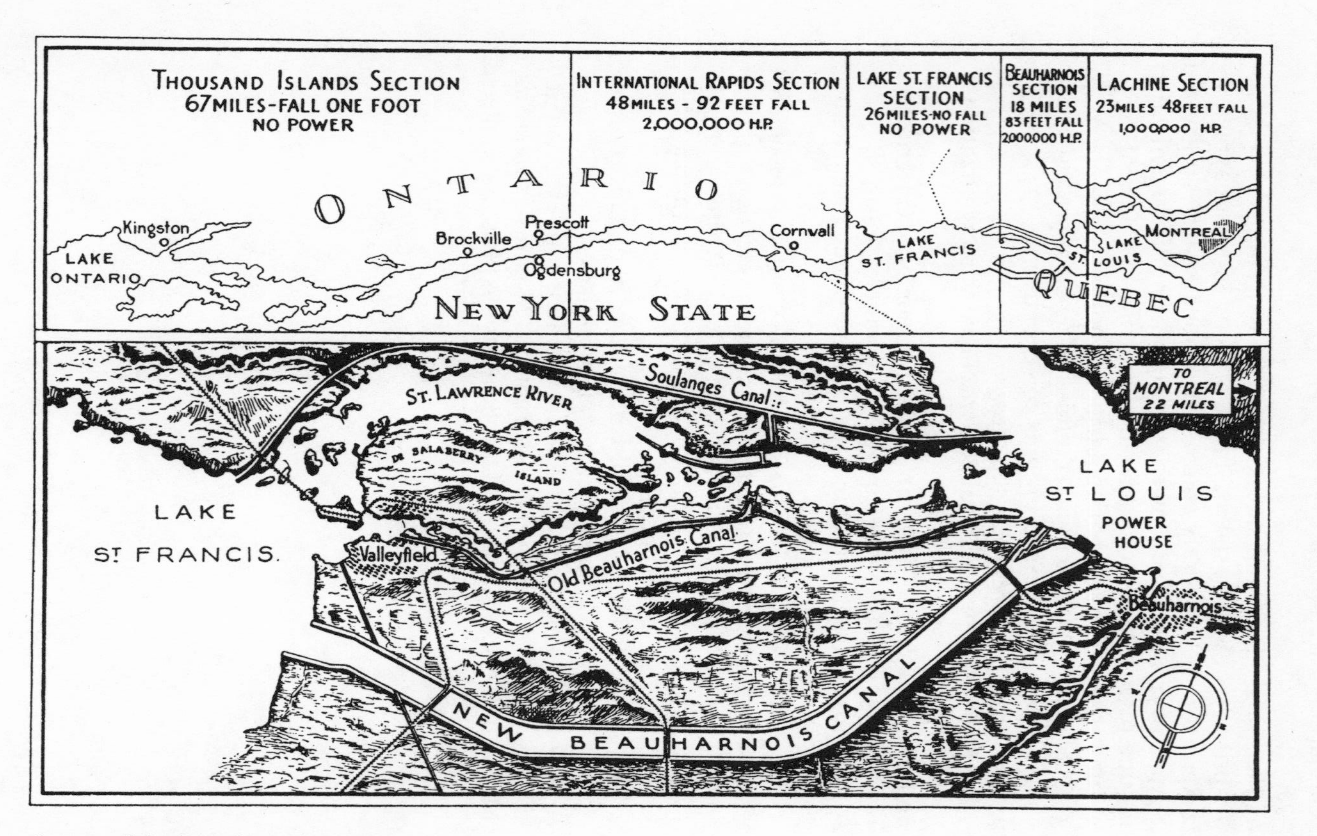

A map of the Beauharnois project

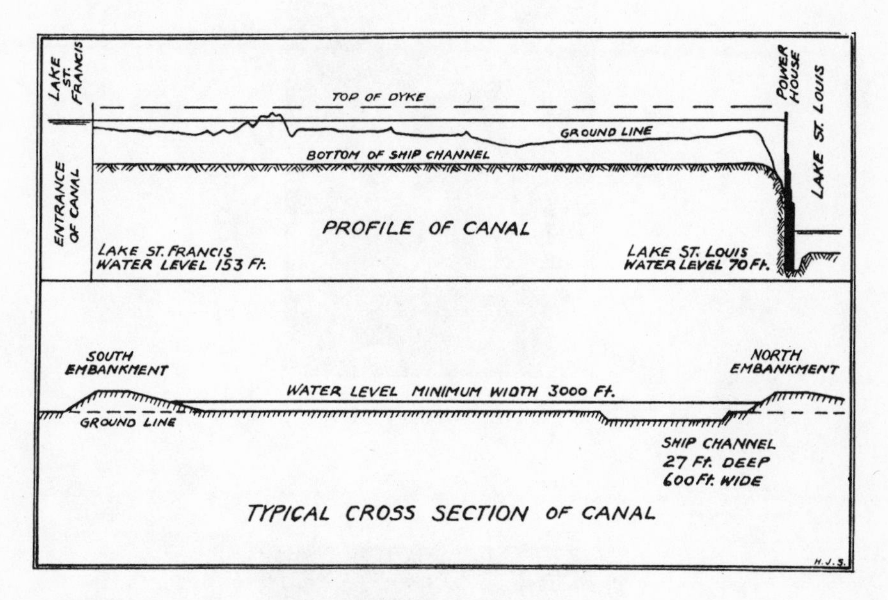

A profile of the new Beauharnois canal

Robert Oliver Sweezey, 1883–1968

Senator Wilfrid Laurier McDougald, 1881–1940

RIGHT
Senator Donat Raymond, 1880–1963

BELOW RIGHT
Robert Alexander Cecil Henry, 1884–1962

BELOW LEFT
Senator Andrew Haydon, 1867–1932

The dredge 'R.O. Sweezey' cutting through the New York Central Railroad, 14 October 1930

The discharge pipes mounted on pontoons, 5 May 1930

Discharge from the dredge 'R.O. Sweezey,' 5 May 1930

The Marion-type electric shovel, 29 March 1930

The dipper of the Marion shovel, 8 February 1930

Bankers and insurance men at Beauharnois, 16 October 1930

Members of the Montreal Board of Trade at Beauharnois, 23 September 1930

The Beauharnois powerhouse on 13 March 1931

The Beauharnois powerhouse as completed in 1961

THE BEAUHARNOIS SCANDAL

Introduction

The Beauharnois Power Corporation and its subsidiary companies are scarcely remembered today. Those who have heard of these companies probably associate them in some vague way with a political scandal that happened a long time ago. A few well-informed Canadians might even know that the affair seriously embarrassed William Lyon Mackenzie King, the long-time leader of the Liberal party of Canada. In their day, however, the Beauharnois companies were the subject of exciting technological, entrepreneurial, and political developments. They also revealed some dubious relationships between Canadian enterprise and politics. As a result, the Beauharnois affair became one of the biggest scandals in Canadian history.

The Beauharnois promoters wanted to build an enormous canal and powerhouse, through which the entire flow of the mighty St Lawrence River would one day be diverted. The engineering designs were daring, innovative, and competent. Financing seemed readily available, and the project, once completed, was expected to provide cheap hydroelectric power which would attract many new industries to the Montreal area. It would also stimulate competition and bring lower costs to Montreal consumers of power. Projected as one of the most significant developments in Canadian history, it was frequently compared to the construction of the transcontinental railways.

There were, however, serious obstacles. The unimaginative monopolists who controlled the Montreal Light, Heat and Power Consolidated strongly opposed the project. So did many politicians and bureaucrats, whose cautious procedures and obstructionist tactics threatened fatal delays. Attempts by the Beauharnois promoters to circumvent these delays led to dubious activities, which when revealed, created much political and entrepreneurial excitement but few major changes or fundamental reforms.

The Beauharnois companies fulfilled some of their pledges but failed in others. The engineering and technical features, all designed by American engineers, were as good and as innovative as promised by the promoters. The new works were able to generate large amounts of inexpensive hydroelectric power. That did not, however, lead to increased competition in the Montreal market. Once construction of the Beauharnois works was assured, the rival Montreal Light, Heat and Power took effective steps to retain control of the situation, and the Beauharnois story provides a compelling illustration of how Canadian monopolists dealt with potential competitors.

The Beauharnois companies, despite the early promises, never attracted much new industry to Canada. Here the disastrous economic conditions of the 1930s played a major role, as did the financial and political embarrassments of the original promoters following the very damaging revelations of the summer of 1931. Instead of encouraging new industries, the companies sought and obtained permission to export much, and ultimately all, of the power generated at Beauharnois to the United States to provide power for new industrial developments there. Yet another Canadian staple resource was exported to the United States.

The political scandal revealed in 1931 had little effect on Canadian business practices, despite the fact that it was, at least briefly, a sensation. The Beauharnois companies and their early promoters were removed from the scene, but that action was largely the result of the great depression. Even Canada's strongest companies experienced considerable difficulty raising capital in the 1930s. The original Beauharnois promoters probably could not have completed the project on their own, even if there had been no scandal. Only substantial assistance by the federal government, and later by Montreal Light, Heat and Power Consolidated, ensured completion of the first phase of the project. The scandal certainly weakened the credibility of the early promoters, but the reorganizations followed fairly typical Canadian governmental and business practices.

The scandal also revealed, but did not significantly change, several sordid aspects of Canadian politics and political campaign contributions. Members of the Progressive party, who received few campaign contributions from big business, were eager to reveal the details of huge donations made by the Beauharnois promoters to Liberal fund-raisers. The Conservatives were quite content to see their political opponents embarrassed, provided there were no investigations of the way the Tory party raised campaign funds. Neither Canadian businessmen nor the politicians in the two main parties were genuinely interested in major reforms in regard to political campaign contributions. The scandal forced both parties to establish some greater distance between the elected leaders and their campaign funds, but it did not lead to fundamental changes.

In all these respects the Beauharnois story is typical of Canadian politics and enterprise, and the relationship between the two. What was unusual, aside from the size of the project and hence of the quantity of campaign funds, was the fact that the matter became public. When it did, Canadians had a view of affairs most politicians and businessmen would prefer to keep hidden. Beauharnois is a story of Canadian entrepreneurship and politics.

1

A spectacular beginning, 12 October 1929

Boom went the great explosion; the echos resounded far down the St. Lawrence Valley; cameras clicked; the crowd cheered; movie men cranked furiously; one old lady fainted; and the band struck up 'O Canada'.[1]

The great explosion marked the official beginning of construction of an enormous new hydroelectric power project. The time was exactly 4:00 o'clock in the afternoon on Saturday, 12 October 1929. The site was a quiet rural pasture some twenty-five miles upstream from downtown Montreal. Here the promoters and contractors of the Beauharnois Power Corporation promised to build Canada's largest hydroelectric powerhouse. Their plans called for the ultimate diversion and utilization of the entire flow of the St Lawrence River.

The highest place of honour on this festive occasion went to Lord Willingdon, governor-general of Canada, who had been asked to press an appropriate button to detonate the first dynamite blast. The dynamite had been placed around a large rock which was blown up in plain view of a group of dignitaries, who were seated on a raised platform 800 feet from the blast site.

Lord Willingdon loved these ceremonies. He shared the optimism and confidence of Canadian entrepreneurs in those last days before the devastating Wall Street crash. In his brief speech he referred proudly to his participation in similar ceremonies which had marked the beginning of construction of the new parliament buildings in Ottawa, the opening of the Royal York Hotel in Toronto, and the laying of the cornerstone of a new university near Hamilton. He proclaimed that 'whether it be in medicine, whether in administration, or whether in commerce or industry, this country is going ahead in the most amazing way.' He thought himself fortunate to experience 'the beginning of a new era of prosperity, the nature of which no one can foresee.' He praised Canadian capitalists who were making all these developments possible and expressed the hope that they would derive profit and value from their enterprise. It was, he said, 'the wish of the government to encourage such noble initiative of capital as the present one.'[2]

The optimism of the governor-general on that sunny October afternoon in 1929 may have been misplaced, but the size and significance of the proposed new hydroelectric power development were impressive. About twenty-five miles upstream from Montreal the St Lawrence widens into a stretch of water known as Lake St Louis, and some fifteen miles further upstream, the river expands again into Lake St Francis. Between these two 'lakes,' or broad sections of the St Lawrence, there is a series of four rapids – the Coteau, Cedars, Split Rock, and Cascades. The drop over these four rapids, and hence the difference in altitude between the two lakes, is eighty-three feet. The entire fifteen-mile section between the two lakes was referred to as the Soulanges Section of the St Lawrence. Several small hydroelectric powerhouses had already been built along the rapids or on one of the two navigation canals which had been built to circumvent them and link water transport between Lake St Francis and Lake St Louis.

The Beauharnois plans called for the construction of a new power and navigation canal, with appropriate high embankments where necessary, covering the fifteen miles between the two lakes. The water was to flow on a level course from Lake St Francis until it reached Lake St Louis. There a new powerhouse would be built to take advantage of the full eighty-three-foot drop. The project was to be built in stages, the first stage utilizing a flow of 40,000 cubic feet of water per second and generating 500,000 horsepower of electricity. Ultimately the entire flow of the St Lawrence was to be diverted, generating 2 million horsepower,[3] substantially more than all the hydroelectric power then generated at Niagara Falls.

The new power canal would be 3,000 feet wide, its ship channel 27 feet deep and 600 feet wide. If the federal government chose to install appropriate locks, it could also serve as an improved navigation link in a deep waterway from the Atlantic to the Great Lakes. The peaceful rural fields and pastures around the small villages of Beauharnois and Valleyfield at the two ends of the project were thus to be transformed into 'the centre of a power and navigation development remarkable for its magnitude and for what it will contribute to the growth of Canadian industry, trade and population.'[4]

The governor-general and the other civil and religious authorities present pledged their 'sympathy and protection to works which were destined to play a very important part in the growth of Canada.'[5] Notable among those with whom the governor-general shared the platform and prominence of place were two high-ranking Roman Catholic church leaders. Mgr Andrea Cassulo, apostolic delegate to Canada and Newfoundland, and Archbishop Gauthier of Montreal, both resplendent in colourful ecclesiatical garb, were invited platform guests.

The organizers of the official ceremony marking the beginning of construction of the new powerhouse had in fact been confronted with a rather delicate problem. How could they give first place and the most important function to the governor-general without in any way slighting their high-ranking ecclesiatical guests. But they had found an admirable solution. Since the entire project covered approximately fifteen miles, Mgr Cassulo had been invited to bless the works and invoke divine protection for the workmen on the canal at Valleyfield near the western end of the project. This ceremony was completed two hours before the first blast of dynamite was detonated at the Beauharnois powerhouse site at the eastern end of the project.

At Valleyfield the apostolic delegate had warmly commended entrepreneurs and workmen alike to the care, protection, and blessings of God, before he traversed the length of the project to participate in the Beauharnois ceremony. Later, at a banquet, the archbishop offered his good wishes. The support of these and other Catholic leaders had been eagerly sought by the Beauharnois promoters and contractors. On an earlier hydroelectric power project on Quebec's Saguenay River, the senior Beauharnois contractor had encountered considerable opposition from the local Catholic clergy. The rural clergy were not sure that such developments would prove beneficial to their people, particularly if construction was to continue uninterrupted twenty-four hours a day, seven days a week. This timetable made it impossible for many of the workmen to attend regularly scheduled mass, and the local priest seemed willing to make an issue of the matter. But careful inquiries were made regarding the local priest's preferences in wine or brandy and, as it turned out, a particular and rather expensive brand of imported Belgian chocolates. A suitable supply of these items was procured and subsequent discussions, aided and lubricated by chocolates and brandy, ended in a mutually satisfactory arrangement whereby the times of masses were arranged to accommodate the men working Sunday shifts. Similarly astute presentations of flowers and gifts and substantial contributions to the struggling local Catholic college played a role in negotiations between the Beauharnois promoters and Archbishop Gauthier and the apostolic delegate.[6] In their dealings with both politicians and ecclesiastics, the promotors and contractors of the Beauharnois project were men who got things done.

The support that the promoters and contractors were particularly eager to obtain from the church officials was clearly spelled out by Mgr Cassulo in his address at Valleyfield. He referred to 'the harmony which existed between capital and labour in Canada.' It was obvious, he said, that 'capital and labour were animated by the best intentions in working for the progress of Canada.' He went on to describe the promoters as 'men who had shown intelligence and wise financial spirit in the task they had undertaken.' Then, turning directly to the workmen, the apostolic delegate said he was confident that they 'were animated only with the desire to give the best of their help and co-operation in bringing the task to successful fruition.'[7] With such encouragement from the Catholic hierarchy the promoters could confidently assure prospective investors that a 'sane' labour policy would be implemented. They were proud to point out that, 'In the history of the Beauharnois Area, there has never been a strike or labour trouble of any kind ... The labour situation in Quebec is regarded by employers as the most satisfactory in all America ... As the region is still largely agricultural, and living costs below those of large cities, wages in the entire territory are substantially below the level prevailing in the larger towns of the province.'[8] This was Mgr Cassulo's vision of 'Glory to God in the Highest, peace and good will on earth,'[9] in what the promoters cheerfully described as 'the happiest section of the whole Dominion.'[10] As a souvenir of the occasion both the governor-general and the apostolic delegate were presented with large silver trays on which was engraved a map of the entire Beauharnois project.[11]

The governor-general and the apostolic delegate were the keynote speakers at the official ceremonies, which were followed by a reception in the recently refurbished assembly hall of Beauharnois College. Approximately 2,000 people, including more than 500 local citizens and company workers, attended the ceremonies and the ensuing sumptuous entertainment. In all these activities Robert

Sweezey, president of the Beauharnois Power Corporation, and of its four subsidiary companies, was prominent.

The Beauharnois project was Sweezey's. He had dreamed and planned, negotiated and promoted it for years. Much preliminary work had already been done, for which Sweezey and other company officials were profusely praised at the banquet. Sweezey responded with due humility:

He felt a deep sense of responsibility upon him as president of the company as it proceeds with the present function to carry out in the St. Lawrence river the greatest water power development in Canada.

We quite realize as administrators of this company that we are but trustees in the development of the country, and we feel that this is a beginning of a wonderful new era of development in Canada, the greatest ever known, and we trust that as trustees we will deserve the confidence of the governments of Ottawa and Quebec, and can gain the goodwill of the people at large.[12]

The company had already gained the support of the two governments named by Sweezey. Once construction was under way, the youthful, energetic, and aggressive Robert Sweezey would dominate the often stormy and controversial history of the Beauharnois companies. His background and personality therefore merit some detailed attention.

Robert Oliver Sweezey was born on 8 December 1883 in Three Rivers, Quebec.[13] His father, Robert Ruben Sweezey, was the superintendent or agent of a succession of lumber companies and spent much of his time 'in the bush.' The family moved to the small community of Chicoutimi on the Saguenay River five years after young Robert's birth. Chicoutimi, then a frontier resource community in the middle of the wilderness, provided an atmosphere of high adventure for growing boys, which Sweezey later described with great feeling: 'The proximity of the forest primeval, the rivers, the mountains and the exhilarating grandeur of the entire region were enough to awaken the keenest and most eager desire to penetrate those mysterious forests and follow their trout filled streams and lakes into the north as far as the Ungava and the arctic.'[14]

Robert Sweezey received his early education at Chicoutimi, and in numerous summer camps. A biographical sketch by a friendly journalist portrays his early youth thus:

Sweezey, *père*, was a timber operator of high standing and, since those were the days when even the boss stayed pretty near to the job, it was only natural for young Bob to spend long months in the bush with his dad. The family limits were in the Saguenay country and there the youngster was hardened to toil at the working end of a paddle, learned to love nature by living in the open and sleeping under the stars, grew to love the back of beyond by living with it, and came outside at last, a competent woodsman who liked the country for its own sake.[15]

Those early experiences left an indelible mark on the young Sweezey. What impressed him most, he wrote many years later, was 'the illimitable expanse of her [Canada's] hinterland – the great undeveloped natural resources of forests, water powers and minerals ... Gazing daily across the country at the far away mountains my own imagination was easily stimulated with the desire to penetrate those unknown and unexplored forests and adapt them to the needs of mankind.'[16]

In 1900 Robert Sweezey left school in Chicoutimi at the age of sixteen and got a job as a field assistant on a survey crew which examined the Chute-à-Caron on the Saguenay River for possible hydroelectric development. The legendary Thomas L. Willson, widely known as Carbide Willson, planned to establish large electro-chemical and electro-metallurgical factories on this site, using electricity developed at the falls to power them. The site was not developed for another twenty years, but young Sweezey was deeply impressed by Willson's dreams, energy, and inventive genius. Inexpensive electricity could power major industrial developments, and Canada had many excellent sites where electrical power could be developed.

In the years after 1900 Sweezey worked at a series of jobs, including a stint with a survey team of the aborted Trans Canada Railway. He participated in several timber drives, operated boats and tugs, and even spent a summer with a telephone crew in Alberta. It soon became evident, however, that such stimulating and enjoyable frontier work outdoors would not lead to senior management positions, or to opportunities to participate in a substantial way in the development of Canada's natural resources.

In those frontier camps consulting or construction engineers held the positions of greatest esteem and influence. Many also became active participants and shareholders in resource development companies. To get ahead an ambitious youth could hardly do better than attain the requisite qualifications as a professional engineer. Sweezey's schooling in Chicoutimi however, had been only rudimentary; it did not qualify him for admission to a respectable engineering course at a university or technical college. He therefore took a series of correspondence courses to improve his academic qualifications. Then followed a winter of more intensive study at Erie, Pennsylvania, after which Sweezey wrote and passed university entrance examinations.

On the strength of this unusual schooling, Sweezey was admitted to the prestigious engineering school at Queen's University in Kingston, Ontario. At Queen's Sweezey earned a rather mixed reputation. Like other youngsters from frontier communities who were adept at rough living, Sweezey was contemptuous of the effete life-styles of the city. But he was also deeply impressed by the influence and power of the wealthy. At Queen's he was the perpetrator of a number of practical jokes and an enthusiastic and imaginative participant in freshman intitiation and hazing incidents. He paid his own way through university and generally earned enough money on summer jobs to live fairly comfortably. There is strong evidence that, even in his youth, he was willing to spend his money freely. He certainly did not manifest an excessively parsimonious and money-pinching attitude, as did a surprising number of other Canadians who subsequently achieved great success in Canadian business undertakings. Sweezey had a good time at Queen's and was popular as an undergraduate. He was also, however, a student who adapted himself easily to the staid and conservative society of Kingston's elite.

He was most interested in applied engineering. He had already been on many major work sites and knew many of the practical problems that arose. Theoretically correct engineering designs often had to be modified to meet the realities of local conditions. Sweezey often expressed disdain for designers and planners who did not know the site, and he spoke contemptuously of the 'tenderfoot methods' of some development companies which relied too much on plans drawn by desk-bound city engineers. On construction and development sites the most important consideration was to get the job done. The work must prove durable and the plant had to function satisfactorily – rules and specifications be damned if they stood in the way. In his university assignments and later as a professional engineer Sweezey was one of those dynamic and innovative individuals who was always looking for better ways to get things done, even if that meant disregarding the orthodox prescriptions of city planners, designers, and bureaucrats.

Sweezey's engineering training at Queen's was a great success, even though he sometimes disagreed with professors who knew their factual material and theories, but not the real conditions and problems likely to arise on large projects on Canada's development frontier. In his fourth year at the university he was sometimes regarded more as a colleague than as a student by his professors. Throughout his later life, Sweezey retained close connections with and deep affections for Queen's, which became the recipient of his generosity on a number of occasions. The links with Queen's were further strengthened in 1911, three years after his graduation, when he married Harriet Watson, daughter of John Watson, a well-known and highly esteemed Queen's professor.

Robert Sweezey's university education in engineering gave him the technical and professional competence to pursue his dream of developing Canada's natural resources, adapting them to the needs of mankind, and enhancing the profits of developers.

After graduation from university Sweezey returned to the bush and worked for a time as a timber cruiser and prospector. His propensity for roughing it got him into at least one serious scrape when he, an Indian assistant, and two huskie dogs pulling a toboggan, tried to make their way across frozen northern Quebec lakes and tundra in temperatures that dipped as low as 55 degrees Fahrenheit below zero. On the way, the two huskies found and ate the bread and bacon the two men had taken along. A campers' shack where they expected to obtain additional provisions had been accidentally burned to the ground before they got there. To make matters worse, the Indian assistant became seriously ill, and the huskies became exhausted and were unable to proceed further. In this dire situation Sweezey, who had been in the area during the previous summer, decided to strike out across the lake to a point where he believed there was a small Indian camp. He too became utterly exhausted and only by the narrowest of margins reached the camp before collapsing. The Indian men of the camp were away hunting, but one woman looked after Sweezey while the others fetched his assistant and the huskies. In later years Sweezey was proud to tell, and no doubt enlarge upon, this story and other tales of how he and others of his generation had grown up on the wild resource frontier of northern Quebec.

After his marriage in 1911 Sweezey took a slightly more conventional job, while at the same time substantially broadening his education. He became an employee of the Royal Securities Corporation, then owned and controlled by Max Aitkin, later Lord Beaverbrook. It was Aitkin's speciality to organize and finance new hydroelectric and traction companies.[17] Sweezey, a professional engineer, was hired to investigate various water power sites in western Canada. He specifically reported to Aitkin on possible power developments at Medicine Hat and Prince Albert, but his responsibilities were more general. He was to be on the look-out for any promising new development projects, which would then be financed through the Royal Securities Corporation. This more general responsibility led to an investigation and report on possible new hydroelectric developments on the St Lawrence, which Sweezey believed offered far better prospects than anything he saw in the west. 'The farther I got away from Montreal,' he said later, 'the more I realized the importance of the Montreal water powers as compared with the water powers in other parts of Canada.'[18]

In 1913 Sweezey reported on the hydroelectric development potential of the St Lawrence River generally, but he concentrated particularly on what he believed was the most attractive stretch – the Soulanges Section between Lake St Francis and Lake St Louis. But Max Aitkin had moved to London in 1912, and the Canadian economy entered an economic recession in 1913. Several other larger hydroelectric projects were also being planned in 1913, and it was feared that the market could not absorb all the new electricity that would be generated if a major development in the Soulanges Section also went ahead. The outbreak of war in 1914 ended any remaining prospect of immediate development of the Soulanges water power by the Royal Securities Corporation.

Sweezey's association with Max Aitkin and the Royal Securities Corporation had, nevertheless, been valuable and instructive. First, he had become intimately acquainted with, and enthusiastic about, the site on which, in 1929, construction of the powerhouse of the Beauharnois Power Corporation would begin. Equally important were the lessons Sweezey learned about the financing of large and very expensive projects. Max Aitkin and his Royal Securities Corporation salesmen were masters at organizing development companies and then issuing and selling the stocks and bonds of these companies to eager though often unwary and gullible investors on both sides of the Atlantic.[19] It would be as an exceptionally able engineer and as a shrewd investment wholesaler and banker that Sweezey would make his mark.

Sweezey returned to Kingston during World War I, but this time to the Royal Military College where he served on the staff. Engineering was a vital aspect of wartime planning and operations. In 1914 there was, however, great consternation about the technical backwardness of the armed forces, and about outdated teaching methods at the Royal Military College. Sweezey was appointed acting professor of survey and served in that capacity from 1914 through 1916. He introduced instruction in the newest survey methods, including hydroelectric developments. Sweezey was also during that time a consultant on a wide range of applied military projects.[20]

After the war Sweezey was eager to get back into private business. The newsprint industry was in the middle of a phenomenal expansion. It was a business Sweezey, the son of a timber agent and a former timber cruiser himself, knew well. He became a director of several newsprint companies, including the aggressively expansionist Belgo Canadian Paper Company which had a big new mill at Three Rivers. The newsprint mills used enormous amounts of hydroelectric power, and most built their own generating plants to meet their requirements. For Sweezey the construction of large power sites was always ancillary to the growth and development of new processing and manufacturing ventures.

Sweezey's enthusiasm for such Canadian development projects led him, in 1921, to establish his own securities firm, Newman, Sweezey and Company. It was modelled on Max Aitkin's Royal Securities Corporation. It dealt in many securities, but Sweezey's primary interests were in newsprint and hydroelectric projects. He became actively involved in the rapid expansion and the various mergers and take-overs which swept the pulp and paper industry in the late 1920s.

In order to create a more expansionist developmental hydroelectric policy Sweezey returned in 1925 to the power site he had first explored for Max Aitkin in 1913. He encountered many difficulties and fierce opposition from the established power interests. Those problems are discussed in greater detail in later chapters of this book. In October 1929 the issues had apparently been resolved and success seemed assured. Construction on the great project had begun. Newspaper reporters were enthusiastic.

Two million horse-power, neither pushing nor pulling; wasted energy, enough to turn every wheel in this vast Dominion. Wasted for want of what? This is the question! Not want of money! Not want of experience! What then? Does it not bring us back to that magic word Youth, with its pushful vigor and dreadnought ardour?

What but comparative youth could conceive and daringly put into effect a 14 mile canal, 3000 feet in width to bring lake to lake in liquid contact over just that number of miles of cultivated fields?[21]

Great projects, even though they originate in the mind of a single creative individual, cannot be realized without the support and work of many, and the guests at the Beauharnois ceremonies in October 1929 included many who had already done much to promote the project, and who would play important roles in its subsequent history. Three Canadian senators occupied a special place of honour on that platform. They were Wilfrid Laurier McDougald of Montreal, Andrew Haydon of Ottawa, and Donat Raymond of Montreal. All three were Liberals who were personally interested in the project.

Senator McDougald was particularly active and prominent in the ceremonies. He was immaculately dressed with a distinguished and impressive appearance, appropriate to his position as chairman of the board of directors of the Beauharnois Power Corporation. He was a proud and sometimes vain man who placed great stock in appearances. He made a short speech at the official ceremonies and later engaged in much hand-shaking and conversation with the numerous guests invited to witness the historic event.

This occasion, in fact, marked the high point of McDougald's business and political career.[22] He was born at Alexandria, Ontario, on 9 August 1881, into a family of modest means, and he attended separate schools at Alexandria and Cornwall, Ontario, before completing his secondary education at the Cornwall Collegiate Institute. From there he went to Queen's University to study medicine, which he then practised in Montreal for several years. In 1908 McDougald married Mary Hannan of Ogdensburg, New York. The Hannan family owned the prosperous Ogdensburg Coal and Towing Company, whose service McDougald entered after his marriage. He quickly rose in the ranks and reorganized the company as a firm importing and transporting American coal to Canada. With the reorganization he became president and soon involved himself in many other Montreal business ventures. He quickly earned a reputation as a determined and sometimes ruthless man, who, in the view of some of his friends, 'was too ambitious for money.'[23] He amassed a considerable fortune, but, alas, his methods antagonized many in the Montreal business community. As a result he was repeatedly refused membership in that citadel of the Montreal establishment, the Mount Royal Club. An attempt to gain a seat on the board of directors of the Bank of Montreal was also unsuccessful.

Failure to achieve in the Montreal business community the respect and acceptance he desperately craved led McDougald into politics and a close friendship with Prime Minister William Lyon Mackenzie King. McDougald's Christian names hardly left any doubt about the political awareness and sentiments of the McDougald family, and Wilfrid Laurier McDougald became active in and made substantial financial contributions to the local Liberal organization in Montreal. This brought him into contact with leading Liberals, including the prime minister.

The relationship between McDougald and King was in part based on lavish entertainment and expensive gifts given by the businessman to an appreciative political leader. In 1922, for example, Mackenzie King accepted an invitation from McDougald to spend a holiday at the Hannan family's luxurious retreat in the Adirondack Mountains.[24] It was a vacation that the prime minister enjoyed very much, and the friendship between the two men grew. Thereafter McDougald dined with King on a number of occasions at which he also gave the leader expensive personal gifts.[25] On at least one occasion in 1927, McDougald also paid a New York City hotel bill for the prime minister. The following entry in Mackenzie King's diary accurately describes the relationship that developed between the two men: 'At 7 Dr. & Mrs. McDougald, Senator and Mrs. Haydon arrived for dinner. Godfroy and I took the Doctor down to the stream in Godfroy's motor. We all dined in the sunroom. The McDougald's brought me two exquisite Venetian glasses, long stems (for lunch) from Venice, a wonderful gift. We had a pleasant evening, but a little too hurried, house a little cold.'[26]

As a friend and confidant of the prime minister, McDougald gained the influence and respectability that had eluded him as a businessman in Montreal. The prime minister, despite some misgivings about McDougald's business reputation, enjoyed his company and appointed him first to the prestigious position of Chairman of the Montreal Harbours Board in 1921 and then, in 1926, to the Senate. The recommendation in this case came before the federal election of that year but was confirmed only after the resignation and re-election of the King government. McDougald did what he could, financially and otherwise, to help re-elect the Liberals in 1926.

After the election and the confirmation of his Senate appointment, McDougald devoted much of his time and energy to the promotion of hydroelectric developments in the Soulanges Section of the St Lawrence. He became interested in a very controversial company called the Sterling Industrial Corporation which was merged with the Beauharnois Company. Much more will be said about this subject in later chapters.

The second Canadian senator prominently involved in the Beauharnois project was Andrew Haydon. Haydon, like McDougald, was a native of the Ottawa Valley, having been born at Pakenham, Ontario, on 28 June 1867.[27] He received his primary and secondary education in Pakenham and Almonte before going to Queen's University and then to Osgoode Hall to study history and law. At Queen's, Haydon was a double medallist, graduating with first-class honours in English and in history and political science. He was greatly influenced by several professors, including John Watson, later the father-in-law of Robert O. Sweezey; Dr Adam Shortt; and O.D. Skelton. The last two also became intimately involved with the Beauharnois companies.

Haydon established his first law firm at Lanark, but he soon moved to Ottawa. There he became one of the senior partners in the firm of McGivern, Haydon and Ebbs, later McGivern, Haydon and Gregg, and then Haydon and Ebbs.

When his law partner H.B. McGivern became a Liberal candidate in the 1908 federal election, Haydon acted as his campaign manager. This position brought him into close contact with Sir Wilfrid Laurier, and a friendship between the two men developed. Haydon quickly demonstrated great skill in political organization and was named the Liberal party's national secretary in 1919. In that capacity he made most of the arrangements for Canada's first major party leadership conference or convention, at which William Lyon Mackenzie King was chosen to succeed Laurier. King was also impressed with Haydon's work. A close professional relationship, and a deep personal friendship, grew between the new leader and the very capable national secretary. Haydon, at King's urging, served as the head of the Liberal organization throughout the 1920s, although he possessed no official title after 1922. His style was later described thus: 'As head of the Liberal organization in Canada Senator Haydon shunned all personal publicity, preferring to direct affairs with the spotlight focused elsewhere than on him.'[28]

Haydon was appointed to the Senate in 1924, on the recommendation of the prime minister. He was an eminently likeable and cultured man, keenly interested in the arts and in history. He wrote a local history of his native Lanark County. Mackenzie King felt great affection for Haydon, which he frequently expressed in his diaries. His tribute at the time of Haydon's death accurately expressed his feelings:

During the many years in which he practiced his profession and was actively interested in public affairs, Senator Haydon enjoyed in exceptional measure the confidence of all with whom he was associated. He had friends in every walk of life, and towards all he was loyalty itself. That he was held in the highest esteem by those with whom he was most closely associated and, without exception, beloved as well as honoured by those who knew him best, is only too apparent from the many tributes which today are being paid his memory.[29]

As head of the Liberal party organization, one of Haydon's tasks throughout the 1920s included the raising of campaign funds. That role is always controversial, but Haydon was widely regarded as 'one of the most honourable, upright, generous and withal one of the most loveable men that I have ever known.'[30] His law partner, John Ebbs, thought Haydon was 'the essence of honour itself, sincere, kindly and charitable.'[31] The firm of Haydon and Ebbs served as a legal representative and agent of the Beauharnois Power Corporation and its subsidiaries. It was this legal involvement that earned Senator Haydon and John Ebbs a place of honour at the October 1929 ceremonies, and much criticism two years later.

The third Canadian senator prominent in the affairs of the Beauharnois companies was Donat Raymond. The Raymond family was a political power in the Beauharnois district. Donat's younger brother, Maxime, was the local member of parliament. Donat was probably best known as a co-founder and president of the Canadian Arena Company of Montreal, which built, owned, and operated the Montreal Forum and owned the famous Canadiens hockey team.

Donat Raymond was born at St-Stanislas de Kostka, Quebec, in 1880 and received his education at nearby Valleyfield College.[32] He went to Montreal as a youth and found 'a very minor position' with the Queen's Hotel in that city. Raymond, like his colleague, Senator McDougald, gained his entrance into the Montreal business community through a fortunate marriage; his wife was Graziella Timmins, daughter of L.H. Timmins, the fabulously wealthy promoter of the Hollinger mines in northern Ontario.

Donat Raymond and his brothers enjoyed the hotel business and purchased both the Queen's and the Windsor hotels in Montreal. It was in the smoke-filled rooms of these hotels that the most controversial Beauharnois transactions were consummated.

Donat Raymond's business activities, however, extended far beyond hotels and hockey. He later became chairman of the boards of the Trust

Général du Canada, the Canadian Imperial Bank of Commerce, and the Fire Insurance Company of Canada, and a director of many other large Montreal companies. He was also active in racing, and his horses won the coveted King's Plate at the Blue Bonnets track three times – in 1914, 1923, and 1930. Raymond was a major shareholder in the Beauharnois Power Corporation.

Donat Raymond had been called to the Senate in December 1926, recommended by Prime Minister Mackenzie King, who had acted on the advice of the Quebec provincial premier, Louis-Alexandre Taschereau. Raymond had earned this appointment by his work as a provincial Liberal organizer and fund-raiser. He was also regarded as one of Quebec's most successful 'gentlemen farmers.' His main land holdings were in Vaudreuil County. If the Beauharnois project attracted many new industries to the region, some would certainly be located on land owned by the Raymond brothers.

Another person very active at the ceremonies in October 1929 and prominent in the affairs of the Beauharnois company was Robert Alexander Cecil Henry, the general manager of the Beauharnois companies.[33] Henry was born at Montreal in 1884 and received his BA and BSC degrees from McGill University. He worked for several years for the Canadian Pacific Railway and then served with the Department of the Interior, Water Powers Branch, as superintendent of various construction sites. Henry joined the Department of Railways and Canals in 1920 but left that department in 1922 to establish a Bureau of Economics for the newly nationalized and amalgamated Canadian National Railways. In the course of that work he also served as a member of a committee which investigated allegations of irregularities and wrongdoing by the Montreal Harbours Board and its chairman, Wilfrid Laurier McDougald. In 1929, following the death of the incumbent deputy minister of railways and canals, Henry was appointed to his position. He served in that capacity for only three months, after which he became general manager of the Beauharnois Light, Heat and Power Company.

Henry was an exceptionally able construction engineer and civil servant. He first took an interest in the hydroelectric potential of the Soulanges Section of the St Lawrence in the early 1920s when, together with Wilfrid Laurier McDougald, he organized the Sterling Industrial Corporation. That corporation, and its engineering plans and developmental application to the federal government, later became the subject of much controversy. It had gained for R.A.C. Henry and W.L. McDougald a large block of Beauharnois shares.

Two men who would also figure prominently in the affairs of the Beauharnois companies were not at the ceremonies marking the beginning of construction. Prime Minister Mackenzie King had received an invitation, but declined to come. He felt uncomfortable at such lavish and flamboyant ceremonies and was somewhat peeved when the governor-general and the papal delegate agreed to attend. He thought both men had better and more important things that they should be doing. King had, studied the plans and proposals of the Beauharnois promoters carefully, however, and his government had approved a critically important order in council which made development possible. King believed the project would serve the best interests of the country, but the style and manner of the promoters did not impress him. He had to deal with these businessmen, but he did not like most of them. Senator Haydon, and for a time Senator McDougald, were exceptions. King enjoyed their company but not that of their corporate friends.

The second prominent Canadian conspicuously absent from the ceremonies on 12 October 1929 was Sir Herbert Samuel Holt. Holt was president of Montreal Light, Heat and Power Consolidated (Montreal Power).[34] He had come to Canada from Ireland as an impoverished youngster in the early 1870s. Two of his maternal uncles had operated a water-powered flour mill near Dublin. Herbert Holt and his older brother Thomas had lived for a time with these uncles following the early death of their father, owing to the inability of their mother to provide adequately for them. The practical experience gained in his uncles' water-powered mill, and in a succession of railway construction jobs in Canada, had given Holt a good understanding of basic engineering principles. On the strength of that practical knowledge he had established a claim that he had studied engineering at Trinity College, Dublin. This was not the case, but his abilities were impressive, and in the 1880s and 1890s he worked as a successful contractor on the CPR main line and several branch lines.

In the early 1890s Holt moved to Montreal and became involved in the Montreal Gas Company and the Royal Electric Company, which manufactured electrical generators and appliances. Royal Electric supplied the equipment for the electrification of the Montreal Tramways and for Quebec's first hydroelectric generating plant. In return for this work the directors of Royal Electric obtained share holdings in the tramway and generating companies.

There were sharp conflicts of interest between Montreal Gas, which supplied fuel for the early coal-fired electric generators, and the new companies generating hydroelectric power. These difficulties were overcome in 1901 when Montreal Gas, Royal Electric, and the Chambly Manufacturing Company were merged to form the Montreal Light, Heat and Power Company. The Chambly Manufacturing Company was the first firm in Quebec to generate hydroelectric power for general distribution. Montreal Power took over contracts of its predecessor companies for the supply of gas and electricity to the city of Montreal and gained an effective monopoly in the distribution of gas and electricity in the city. It also established good relations with key politicians in the city and at Quebec City.

After 1901 there were several attempts by rival interests to break Montreal Power's distribution monopoly, but all of them failed. Rivals either were forced into bankruptcy or were amalgamated or bought out by the Montreal Power interests. In their dealings with consumers who demanded lower rates the Montreal Power owners tended to adopt harsh tactics. Such activities did not enhance Montreal Power's popularity in the city. There was a widely held hope that the Beauharnois company would provide effective competition once it completed the first phase of its construction program.

The fact that Herbert Holt was also president of the Royal Bank of Canada and of Canada's largest pulp and paper company and a director of many other large corporations made him a formidable foe. His penchant for secrecy and nasty surprises for those who crossed him added an air of sinister mystery. He was generally thought to be one of Canada's most successful and hated businessmen. Several of the speakers at the Beauharnois ceremony made oblique references to the tough and austere man ensconced in a spacious but almost completely undecorated office in the Power Building in Montreal.

Sweezey, McDougald, Haydon, Raymond, Henry, King, Holt, and after 1935 Bennett were the names that would dominate the history of the Beauharnois companies. On 12 October 1929 those promoting and working for the company put on an impressive and flashy show for the more than 2,000 guests. The company officials mingled freely with local politicians, community leaders, workers, and citizens. The mayors of the towns of Beauharnois and Valleyfield at the two ends of the project had a part in the ceremonies. An atmosphere of great optimism and good will prevailed, helped substantially by the fact that the company had made a sizeable financial donation to the local Beauharnois College to refurbish its main administration building and assembly hall. A sumptuous banquet in that same assembly hall later in the evening marked the conclusion of the happy event. Other local benefactions by the company were gratefully acknowledged. The Beauharnois promoters gave every indication that they would be exemplary corporate citizens and that many local needs might be met through their generosity and enterprise.

The Beauharnois promoters also demonstrated great public relations skills with the press. Reporters from all the major Montreal, Ottawa, Toronto, Quebec City, and New York newspapers received special invitations. At least three cars of 'newspaper boys' were part of the official motorcade from Valleyfield to Beauharnois. Sweezey, when planning the ceremonies, was concerned about whether they could be kept in order, but a stop for beer at the construction company head office was mandatory. Later the journalistic 'hoi polloi' (Sweezey's words) was furnished with generous quantities of whiskey and carefully prepared press reports of the entire event. Any reporter who succumbed to the temptations laid out would still have excellent copy to send back to his eager editor. And if the reports in the various newspapers were curiously similar, and enthusiastic about the daring promoters and their great project, the interests of progress, development, and private enterprise would be served.[35]

Another important public relations success was the company's use of the coat of arms of Governor Charles, Marquis de Beauharnois, after whom the district and the company were named. Beauharnois had been governor of New France from 1725 to 1746. He had been granted a large seigneury on the south side of the St Lawrence River adjacent to the rapids. The salient features of his family coat of arms were already incorporated into the crests of both McGill and Queen's universities. The Beauharnois companies also obtained authorization to use the old Beauharnois symbols. The most distinguishing feature on the coat of arms were three martlets, mysterious and exotic birds which had no beaks and no feet. They allegedly lived only on air and ambrosia – the food of the gods. As a company brochure explained, 'the martlets originated in the times of the Crusades. Often knights came back from their travels with skins of oriental birds. These skins, of course, had neither beaks nor feet, and when included on a shield implied that the owner had been overseas.'[36] The three martlets across the top of the company's emblem together with the heavy red line across the centre, were copied directly from the coat of arms, but in the bottom portion a high-tension insulator was pictured to signify electric power. This emblem with its associations served, according to company publicity, 'not only as a commercial mark, but recalls to the inward eye those memories of courts, pomps, ceremonies, and crusades which all formed part in the long chain of cause and effect leading to the present development of the St. Lawrence.'[37]

The official blessing of the canal construction site at Valleyfield and the ceremonies marking the beginning of construction of the new powerhouse at Beauharnois on 12 October 1929 were romantic, colourful, flamboyant, and exciting, but behind those events lay years of exploration, study, planning, negotiation, lobbying, and much hard work. Many organizational, political, economic, legal, and technical problems had already been overcome. Many other obstacles remained. But Robert Oliver Sweezey and his associates were men of quick, aggressive, and imaginative action. They were confident that all remaining difficulties would be resolved and that power would be delivered from the site within three years. It was the preparatory work, however, which ultimately determined the fate of the Beauharnois companies and their promoters. It is to that preparatory work that we must now devote our attention.

2

Success in Quebec

The ecclesiastical, political, and entrepreneurial enthusiasm and support evident in the ceremonies on 12 October 1929 were the product of years of study, planning, negotiation, and lobbying. That preparatory work can be divided rather neatly into four separate phases or aspects, even though, chronologically, there was considerable overlap.

The first phase involved the acquisition of the provincial charter of the Beauharnois Light, Heat and Power Company by R.O. Sweezey and his associates; the creation of the Marquette Investment Company, colloquially referred to as the first Beauharnois syndicate, and the subsequent passage, by the provincial government of Quebec, of a necessary amendment; and the granting of a provincial lease which allowed the company to divert 40,000 cubic feet of water per second.

The second phase involved the approval of a federal order in council which dealt with the navigational aspects of the project, and with ongoing dominion-provincial disputes regarding water rights in navigable streams. Major constitutional, political, and organizational problems had to be overcome before the necessary order in council could be approved. Once approved, there was another corporate reorganization resulting in the creation of the second Beauharnois Syndicate.

The third phase involved a further major reorganization of the company in the summer of 1929, resulting in the elimination of some of the early promoters and a friendly accommodation between the remaining Beauharnois promoters and Montreal Power.

The fourth phase involved the negotiation of critically important power contracts with the Ontario government's Hydro-Electric Power Commission.

Significant dates and events marking the completion of each of these four phases are as follows. On 23 June 1928 the Quebec government granted the Beauharnois Light, Heat and Power Company its lease to divert 40,000 cubic feet of water per second. The critically important federal order in council was approved on 8 March 1929. The breakup and reorganization of the Beauharnois syndicate, admitting the Montreal Power interests, occurred on 26 July 1929, and the power contract between the Beauharnois interests and the Hydro-Electric Power Commission of Ontario was signed on 28 October 1929. A basis of agreement, however, had been reached late in July of that year. All four phases were essentially completed before the official start of construction on 12 October 1929, and each phase will form the subject of a separate chapter.

Robert Oliver Sweezey, as already indicated, first became enthusiastic about the power prospects in the Soulanges Section in 1913 while working for the Royal Securities Corporation. His 1913 report has apparently not survived, but the conditions and opportunities on which he reported are documented in considerable detail elsewhere.[1] It was well known in engineering circles that a major development harnessing the entire flow of the river over the full eighty-three-foot drop was technologically feasible. The obstacles to such a development were competitive, political, and financial and were rooted in the early history of hydroelectric developments in Quebec.

The first important fact that anyone contemplating the development of a major new power project in the Soulanges Section had to consider was the strongly entrenched position of Montreal Power. This company had gained an exclusive franchise for the lighting of the streets in Montreal, which it expanded into an effective monopoly over the distribution of electricity in the city generally. When faced with competitive threats, Montreal Power had placed whatever obstacles it could in the way of potential rivals. If that tactic failed, as it had on at least two previous occasions, Montreal Power was able to buy out its competitors.

Montreal Power earned substantial profits, but its business strategy was widely regarded as unduly cautious and defensive. Most of the profits came from the distribution of electricity on the Island of Montreal, and the Montreal Power managers were not interested in developing more power than they could profitably sell. They feared that new developments might create a surplus of power which would depress prices. One author described Montreal Power's policies thus:

'Technological unconcern and acute concern for profits made for passivity. Although it was situated within a few miles of the largest power resources in the province, the Montreal Power never made a move entirely on its own initiative to develop them or to extend its influence outside of Montreal. It was satisfied to act as lord of its domain, a policy which required only defense of that domain.'[2]

Robert Sweezey had a similar assessment of Montreal Power's attempts to manage and limit available supplies of electricity. He complained that 'Our hydro-electric power interests in Canada have been since their inception quite blind or indifferent to the immense possibilities of the application of cheap power in the manufacturing of products requiring large quantities of hydro-electric energy and of developing foreign markets for such products.'[3] Sweezey wanted to develop and sell electricity 'at prices substantially below those prevailing anywhere else in the United States or Canada.'[4]

The prospect of abundant cheap power was, of course, appealing to most Canadians other than those associated with Montreal Power. Inexpensive electricity might very well attract many new industries. But without access to the large and lucrative Montreal market, the short-term prospects for any new development not associated with Montreal Power were discouraging.

A second complicating factor was that four small powerhouses had been built in the Soulanges Section before 1913. Several other companies also had charter rights in the area but had not yet built anything. Any large new development would affect the rights and interests of these companies. One of them, the Cedars Rapids Manufacturing and Power Company, was owned by the Montreal Power interests. Two others, the Canadian Light and Power Company and the Provincial Light, Heat and Power Company, sold much of their electricity to Montreal Power under contract. The fourth was a hydroelectric plant built by the Montreal Cottons Company to provide power for its own textile mills. Herbert Holt, the president of Montreal Power, was also a director of Montreal Cottons.

These four plants together utilized only a fraction of the total power potential of that section of the river. None of them used more than a fraction of the total drop between the two 'lakes.' Any large new development, however, would have a direct effect on the operations of these four plants.[5]

Among the companies that held undeveloped water rights in the Soulanges Section, the Beauharnois Light, Heat and Power Company was most influential. It had been incorporated in 1902 but traced its claims back almost 200 years to the grant of a large seigneury in the area to the Marquis de Beauharnois in 1729 when Beauharnois was the governor of New France. Governor Beauharnois had built a small drainage canal from Lake St Francis to the St Louis River in order to drain some of the marshy lands of his seigneury. That small drainage canal was allegedly 'the beginning of the idea of diverting water from Lake St Francis to Lake St Louis through an artificial channel.'[6] After the British conquest this property, together with the right to divert water through the small canal, was given by the king of England to the Hon. George Ellice.[7] Several water-powered flour and lumber mills were established along this short canal in the ensuing years.

In the nineteenth century, as Canada struggled to improve navigation along the St Lawrence – Great Lakes waterway to meet the challenge and competition of the Erie Canal, a new canal with nine-foot-deep locks was built. This channel, later known as the old Beauharnois Canal, was constructed between 1842 and 1845. It bypassed all the rapids between Lake St Louis and Lake St Francis. Unfortunately the approach to the canal through Lake St Francis was shallow and did not permit the full utilization of the nine-foot-deep locks. Instead of dredging a deeper channel to the canal, engineers recommended that the two main outlet channels be blocked by means of long dikes, thus raising the water level of Lake St Francis by about two feet. This idea, when acted upon, however, flooded the existing developments along the old and small but well-used feeder and drainage canal built by Governor Beauharnois and then belonging to a descendant of the Hon. George Ellice. To stabilize and control water levels along the old channel, the Canadian government installed new headgates on the old drainage canal but then leased the headgates and accessories, together with the right to divert water through the canal, back to the Ellice family in return for a payment of $1 per year. The Ellices subsequently sold their interests and rights for £20 to Joseph Bartholomew Robert, a local mill owner, storekeeper, and politician.

Despite the dikes and other improvements, the entire Beauharnois Canal soon proved too small to accommodate the larger vessels that were coming into widespread use on the upper Great Lakes. As a result, the Canadian Board of Works was asked to recommend measures whereby the navigational facilities of the canal might be further improved. Engineering studies concluded that enlargement of the existing canal would prove very expensive, entail serious transportation disruptions during the period of construction, and do substantial damage to some of the developed properties. Construction of an entirely new canal along the northern side of the St Lawrence was recommended. This new canal, with locks that were 15 feet deep and 100 feet wide, was completed in 1899 and was named the Soulanges Canal.

Joseph Bartholomew Robert and his sons E.A. Robert and W.H. Robert tried to sell some of the water rights acquired from the Ellice family in 1901. They approached the Montreal Power interests immediately after that company was incorporated, but were unable to come to any agreement. The Robert family then organized their own company, the Beauharnois Light, Heat and Power Company.

The Roberts made a second determined attempt to develop the site after 1911 when they and their business associates wrested corporate control of the Montreal Street Railway from directors closely associated with Montreal Power. Immediately after 1911 the Montreal Street Railway obtained its electricity from generating companies hostile to Montreal Power, but the Roberts hoped eventually to utilize power developed at a new plant at Beauharnois. Towards that end they prepared a careful application for authority to divert 40,000 cubic feet of water per second. These plans of the Robert family, clearly enunciated in letters from W.H. Robert to F.D. Monk, minister of public works, attracted the attention of other developers, including the Royal Securities Corporation, for whom Sweezey then prepared his report on the site in 1913.

The Beauharnois Light, Heat and Power Company was granted its authority to divert 40,000 cubic feet of water per second, but wartime and market exigencies prevented construction. The 1911–16 plans, moreover, envisioned only a relatively small project which would market its power to the Montreal Street Railway, to any local industries that might be attracted to the area, and to Montreal users that could be reached despite Montreal Power's exclusive rights to erect poles and power lines in most Montreal streets.

The Roberts lost control of the Montreal Street Railway in 1918, but they never completely gave up their ambition to develop the Beauharnois water power site. In 1921 they found another ambitious businessman eager to enter into a partnership with them. This prospective new partner was Narcisse Cantin. Cantin was an unusual promoter. Born in the French parish of St Pierre aux Bouleaux in Huron County, Ontario, he had spent his youth in Buffalo, New York, where he became a salesman and promoter. He dreamed of some day developing a deep waterway and navigation system and of electrical power development from the Great Lakes to the Atlantic. Originally Cantin wanted to develop his deep waterway from Georgian Bay. He founded a new settlement, St Joseph, on the shores of Georgian Bay at the western terminus of his proposed deep waterway canal. He was able to raise enough money to erect several impressive buildings and to incorporate, in 1902, the St Joseph Land Improvement and Manufacturing Company. But at that point the project lapsed, and the buildings erected at the turn of the century were torn down in the 1920s.

The failure of the St Joseph colony did not end Cantin's interest in the development of a deep waterway. He was instrumental in the incorporation of the Great Lakes and Atlantic Canal and Power Company in 1914. This company was to develop the proposed navigation and power project between Georgian Bay and the Atlantic Ocean. Later, a new holding company, the Transportation and Power Corporation, was formed. It acquired all the shares of the Great Lakes and Atlantic Canal and Power Company and of other Cantin-controlled companies.[8]

Immediately after the war the Roberts renewed their search for partners who would help them develop the Beauharnois site. In 1919 they engaged the services of the Hon. Achille Bergeron, the local Liberal MLA and brother of the federal member of parliament for the district, to find a buyer and developer. Bergeron's efforts led to the signing, on 4 November 1921, of a twelve-month option to purchase a part interest and to develop the water rights held by the Roberts. This option was signed by Narcisse Cantin. The option itself cost $10,000 and required a full payment of $500,000 before the end of October 1922. The agreement was drawn up imprecisely, however, and Cantin later alleged that he was not required to pay the $500,000 but had only to give a written undertaking before the end of October 1922 that he would eventually pay that sum.

Cantin did not make the $500,000 payment. Consequently, in November 1922, W.H. Robert advised him that the option was cancelled and the $10,000 was forfeited. Cantin and his associates refused to accept the withdrawal or cancellation of the option and sued the Roberts for non-performance of the terms of the 1921 option agreement. Cantin also redoubled his efforts to raise funds and prepare appropriate engineering plans for the project.

These efforts brought Cantin to R.O. Sweezey's office, since he was aware of Sweezey's 1913 report. Cantin offered, and Sweezey accepted, an appointment as chief engineer of the Transportation and Power Corporation. Sweezey began his work for Cantin on 4 April 1925. Sweezey accepted this appointment because he was assured that Cantin held a valid option to the Beauharnois water rights, and that he, Sweezey, would be invited to become an active partner in any future Beauharnois development. He was enthusiastic about the potential of a major power development at Beauharnois, but he soon became utterly disillusioned and disgusted with Cantin and his associates. After examining the terms of the 4 November 1921 option, Sweezey concluded that the option had in fact expired and that Cantin had no water rights at all in the Soulanges Section. Worse, he believed that there was no significant financial or technical substance in the Cantin group. He later testified:

I discovered that Mr. Cantin and his company did not in any way own control in this company [the Beauharnois Light, Heat and Power Company]; that they had had an option at one time, but the option was expired ... Mr. Cantin continued to visit my office from time to time, and rather persistently, always with the desire to sell me stock ... at one time he had an idea that the way to settle this problem [lack of funds] was to issue a bond issue of a million dollars on the property, get Newman Sweezey and Company to buy the bonds with which he was to pay off the Roberts. I did not see the force of this argument, because that left Newman Sweezey to hold the bonds and nothing to pay the interest on the bonds.[9]

In the meantime, in his legal battles with the Robert family Cantin fared badly. Although he had won in the Court of King's Bench, the case was twice appealed, and the Roberts 'won the second and third rounds in court.' Cantin still had the right, which he eventually exercised, to appeal to the Supreme Court of Canada. Nevertheless, after Cantin's second court defeat, Sweezey decided that the Transportation and Power Corporation had no viable future. He resigned his position as chief engineer in December 1926. Cantin refused to accept Sweezey's resignation.

The resignation was hastened by the fact that he had opened private discussions with W.H. Robert with a view to purchasing the Robert water rights on his own, rather than on the Cantin company account. Sweezey was convinced that a major power development at Beauharnois would prove immensely profitable, but he had also concluded that the Cantin companies were not appropriate instruments to develop that site. Thus he resigned and immediately opened his own negotiations with the Roberts, which resulted in an agreement signed on 3 February 1927. To seal the transaction Sweezey had to pay $100,000 immediately, and the Roberts were also promised a variety of cash and stock options if and when the project went forward.

Sweezey's defection and immediate application of the information he had gained during the twenty months that he had been an employee of the Transportation and Power Corporation to acquire control of the Beauharnois company for himself absolutely infuriated Cantin and his associates. Cantin claimed he had never accepted Sweezey's resignation and regarded his action as one of base treachery. He demanded that all the shares of the Beauharnois company purchased by Sweezey be turned over to the Transportation and Power Corporation. Sweezey, of course, insisted that he had acted on his own, and he refused to have anything further to do with Cantin and his associates. He had made a bitter enemy. He had also paid a high financial price for control of a company which would encounter serious difficulties if the proposed construction proceeded. He later described his mood on the evening of 3 February 1927.

I wrote out the cheque, but somehow could not drive myself to pen the signature. I sat for half an hour, with the feeling that it was a sheer waste of money; that the job of getting a Bill through the Legislature was beyond my scope.

Then I decided to settle the question with a flip of a coin. I pulled a quarter out of my pocket, but realizing it was a damn-fool way to decide a business proposition, recklessly dashed off the signature and told my secretary to get it mailed before I changed my mind.[10]

A range of daunting problems and difficulties faced Sweezey on the morning of 4 February 1927. One of the first and most important was to put together an adequate financial syndicate which could carry the project through its developmental stage. The initial $100,000 payment had been made by Sweezey personally. His search for financial associates began only after he had control of the Beauharnois Light, Heat and Power Company.

The available documentation does not provide a precise date on which the first Beauharnois financial syndicate was legally established. The arrangements were apparently quite informal, but at some time during the summer of 1927 it was decided that a syndicate with 4,000 part-interests or shares should be established. Of those shares 600 were immediately issued to Sweezey in return for his interest and investment in the Beauharnois Light, Heat and Power Company. The Robert family, under the terms of its agreement with Sweezey, was given 500 shares. The investment firms of Newman, Sweezey and Company and the Dominion Securities Corporation each agreed to take 250 shares, paying $30 in cash for each. The remaining shares were to be sold to syndicate members as the planning and other preparatory work proceeded.[11] Sweezey later explained that the investment firms were brought in 'not so much from the point of view of their work in building up the basis of the thing as for their ability to assist me in financing. The financing is always a factor comparatively easy provided the legal and political difficulties and the difficulties provided by my opponents were overcome.'[12]

This syndicate and its successor, had one unusual feature. All syndicate assets were transferred to and held by a separate corporation – the Marquette Investment Corporation. Sweezey explained the nature and purpose of this corporation thus:

> It would be customary in organizing a syndicate or a group of men conducting a partnership operation to lodge in one of their number or with a trust company or in some other fixed place the custody of the assets of the partnership or of the syndicate. In this particular case we might have vested the title to our assets in an individual or in one of the incorporated trust companies or in some other ongoing organization, but we preferred, because of the particular nature of our business to incorporate and create for the sole purpose of acting as the depository agent or trustee of the syndicate the Marquette Investment Corporation which was incorporated under the Companies Act of the Province of Quebec.'[13]

That was the official and perhaps also the most important reason for the arrangement with the Marquette Investment Corporation. A company memo, however, also states that this was a means whereby the syndicate hoped to avoid a situation whereby taxes on windfall profits would be payable '(a) by the company itself; and (b) the shareholders upon any distribution of these profits by way of dividends or upon any general distribution of the assets of the Company.'[14] The Marquette Investment Corporation simply held the assets and would make no taxable profits. For the sake of clarity, future references in this book will refer to the first and second Beauharnois syndicates, rather than to the Marquette Investment Corporation, which had custody of the assets of those two syndicates.

As already indicated, 2,600 of the 4,000 shares in the first Beauharnois syndicate were distributed when the syndicate was organized. The remaining shares were sold, at prices between $30 and $50 per share, as more money was needed. Sweezey, for example, increased his holdings to 800 shares. When the 4,000 shares were sold, the syndicate increased the number to 5,000. A total of $261,000 in cash was raised from the sale of shares of the first Beauharnois syndicate. This amount did not include the shares issued directly to Sweezey and Robert at the time the syndicate was organized.

These shares were not widely distributed. Only selected investors were approached and offered a participation. The first was Frank P. Jones, a native of Brockville, Ontario. Born in 1879, Jones had risen to become assistant to the president and then general manager of the Dominion Iron and Steel Company. In the course of his work he had met and impressed Max Aitkin. When Aitkin put together his great cement merger in 1908, Jones was invited to become general manager and later president of the Canada Cement Company.

Under Jones's management Canada Cement had become an exceptionally successful and profitable company. That success attracted the attention of Herbert Holt and J.H. Gundy. These two masterminded a number of corporate reorganizations and mergers in the late 1920s. In 1927 they made an offer for the shares of Canada Cement which allegedly left Jones with a personal profit of $47 million.[15] It was indicative of the euphoric atmosphere in the Canadian business community that Holt and Gundy reorganized Canada Cement and reportedly made as much on that reorganization as Jones had made in almost twenty years of work for the company. Holt and Gundy's profits, however, were mostly on paper. Jones got cash and blue-chip securities. The size of the profits made in these transactions was probably exaggerated in the business press. Nevertheless, in 1928 Frank Jones was a man who had substantial sums available for investment.

Sweezey and Jones had worked for Max Aitkin at the same time and knew each other well; Sweezey persuaded Jones to put up $30,000 in return for which Jones received 800 shares in the first Beauharnois syndicate. Jones immediately became one of five official syndicate managers, and on 27 September 1928 he was named president of the Beauharnois Light, Heat and Power Company. It was expected, of course, that Jones would provide much additional capital once construction began. He gave the project financial and managerial credibility.

R.O. Sweezey was happy to have Jones's financial support, but he knew that political help and influence would also be necessary. When first developing his plans to take over the Robert interests he wrote to a business associate that 'we must enlist with our syndicate two or three individuals, who in addition to providing some cash as their fair share, can assist us in getting our rights extended or enlarged so as to develop the entire available flow of the St Lawrence at this point. As the whole situation is entirely within the Province of Quebec, our influence has to be exerted only in Canadian political circles – that is at Ottawa and at Quebec.'[16] The influence Sweezey had immediately in mind when he wrote this particular letter involved the brother of the recipient. J. Aldric Raymond was the manager of the Queen's and Windsor hotels in Montreal and dabbled in various business ventures. His brother Donat, however, was a person of considerable influence. He was a key Liberal organizer and fund-raiser in Quebec. According to his own testimony later, Donat Raymond was invited to subscribe 800 shares in the first Beauharnois syndicate, at a cost of $30,000. He said he agreed to invest the money mainly because he had great confidence in the business acumen of Frank P. Jones.[17] Raymond insisted, however, that the shares not be placed in his name but held in trust for him by the Crédit Général du Canada. When asked later why he did not want the shares placed in his own name the senator explained: 'Because I have adopted the principle that I do not want to put my name to any new venture. I am willing to gamble my money, but I do not want my friends to gamble with my name, and for that reason I always do subscribe through a trust company or a broker's name in all new ventures.'[18] That may have been one reason for Raymond's action. It was also helpful when lobbying politically for the project if the senator could be seen more or less as an independent supporter rather than an interested party. He soon put pressure on Premier Taschereau and Prime Minister Mackenzie King to pass necessary legislative amendments and orders in council. The prime minister was given to understand that Raymond was 'not personally interested,' but soon realized that this was not the case.

Raymond's services as a political lobbyist were urgently needed in both Quebec and Ottawa, but it was to Quebec that the company first turned its attention. It needed a relatively minor but nevertheless critically important amendment to the provincial charter and water lease of the Beauharnois Light, Heat and Power Company.

All the early plans of the Beauharnois company had called for construction of a small hydroelectric project utilizing only 40,000 cubic feet of water per second through a small new canal. When Sweezey gained control of the company, he too thought of an initial development plan which would utilize only 40,000 cubic feet per second. But if an entirely new canal had to be built, why not build it in such a way that, when demand increased, the project could be enlarged until the entire flow of the river could be diverted through the company's canal and powerhouse? The original charter had given the company authority to build its canal from Lake St Francis to the St Louis River. Such a canal, however, could not easily be enlarged later. Instead, Sweezey now wanted to build the canal from Lake St Francis to Lake St Louis itself, a plan that would require that the words 'St Louis River' in the company's charter be changed to 'Lake St Louis.' 'In doing so,' Sweezey explained later, 'we were able to alter the direction of the canal so that the powerhouse end of it would be on Lake St Louis where we could build a decent powerhouse.'[19]

This amendment might seem minor, but without it the Beauharnois company could not proceed. Those opposed to the project decided to exert their influence in Quebec City to prevent passage of the amendment. It was well known that Premier Taschereau and many members of his government feared that a large new power canal might also become part of a widely discussed St Lawrence deep waterway. Such a development would divert trade and commerce from Montreal to points further upstream. In addition, it was pointed out that there was actually a surplus of power in Quebec but a serious shortage in Ontario. Beauharnois was located very near the Ontario border and would probably export some of its power to that province, or perhaps even to industries in New York State, thus fostering further industrial development in Ontario and New York rather than in Quebec.[20] These were powerful arguments against which the Beauharnois promoters could offer only a rather vaguely documented promise that they would provide power at lower rates and enter into vigorous competition with the monopolistic power interests in Montreal. In 1927 that was not enough, and the Quebec legislature refused the requested amendment. Sweezey later described the situation in the Quebec legislature when his company first sought its amendment. 'The session had been on for some time when we appeared there, and when we asked for an amendment to our charter we were opposed by a very powerful body of legal talent, and we didn't get a chance ... They were representing powerful financial interests and power companies.'[21]

The failure to have the charter amended in 1927 did not prove a permanent set-back, but it indicated that there would be powerful and effective opposition, and that the company would need 'individuals who can assist us in getting our rights extended.'[22] Senator Donat Raymond and a little later Sir Clifford Sifton and Senators Wilfrid Laurier McDougald and Andrew Haydon proved to be such individuals. But in Quebec City Sweezey himself also established close and amicable relations with Premier Taschereau.

The situation in 1927 was also influenced by the fact that Premier Taschereau called a provincial election for 6 May 1927. He did not wish to take controversial initiatives just before the election. Prospects for favourable consideration of the Beauharnois application were better after the election. It seems probable, in the light of the revelations of campaign contributions by the Beauharnois promoters to Ontario and federal election campaigns, that similar contributions were made in Quebec. But no direct evidence of such contributions has yet appeared. What can be documented is the fact that discussions between Sweezey and Taschereau after the election were amiable and productive.

Premier Taschereau's attitude towards the Beauharnois proposal was ambiguous throughout. He feared any possible links between that project and the deep seaway proposals and also opposed exports of electricity from Quebec. But he supported the development of more power as a means of attracting new industries to Quebec and of undermining the monopoly enjoyed by Montreal Power in the distribution of electricity in the Montreal area.

Sweezey and Raymond developed persuasive arguments that their project and the proposed deep waterway should be regarded as separate matters. Support for them need not include support for the deep waterway. But their most effective points concerned the low cost of development at Beauharnois, resulting in lower prices for power. The Beauharnois promoters assured Taschereau that their project would lead to extensive new industrial development. As a result, the Quebec premier decided to support the requested amendment. He explained his position thus: 'May I explain my support and endorsement of this Company's [Beauharnois Light, Heat and Power Company] project as primarily due to the fact that I am satisfied that the Company will produce and sell power materially cheaper than it is now available in the Province of Quebec. I anticipate this will result in the establishment of new industries with consequent further prosperity to the country.'[23]

The popular press further elaborated in rather exaggerated and sensational articles on the prospective competitive struggle between Montreal Power and the new Beauharnois company. The popular talk of hydroelectric competition grew so intense that it sent tremors through St James Street, and Montreal Power found it appropriate to issue announcements designed to steady the nerves of skittish investors.

> We do not see any danger of Montreal Light, Heat and Power being forced to make a downward move in their charges for energy. As a matter of fact, the company has made regular reductions in both gas and electricity rates from time to time, while, on the subject of disparity between rates in Montreal and Toronto, the claim is made by Montreal Power and has never been successfully refuted that, in the ultimate, Montreal users of electricity are actually paying less for their power than Toronto users. In the light of the past record of Montreal Power, we strongly believe in saying, which has become more or less a market axiom, that Power is always a buy.[24]

Once the premier of Quebec was persuaded that the Beauharnois amendment should be passed, matters proceeded smoothly. Passage of the amendment was further expedited when the Beauharnois company paid off some long-outstanding obligations. The company, originally incorporated in 1902, had never paid any provincial taxes, and a substantial sum was owing. The provincial government made it clear that those taxes must be paid before the amendment could be granted. Consequently, the Beauharnois company hurriedly negotiated an appropriate loan from the Marquette Investment Corporation, and the taxes were paid in full.[25] With these matters attended to, the Beauharnois amendment passed on a vote of fifty-one to ten in the Legislative Assembly, and unanimously in the Legislative Council 'after a bitter fight.'[26]

Once the amendment to the company's charter was passed, there remained the relatively simple matter of amending the company's provincial water lease, allowing the company to divert 40,000 cubic feet per second of water through the proposed canal and powerhouse. The changes were approved on 23 June 1928. The Beauharnois promoters had scored an impressive political victory in Quebec City and removed an important obstacle, despite the determined opposition of the Montreal Power interests.

The negotiation of this lease, while a significant victory for the Beauharnois promoters, also required substantial new expenditures. The provincial taxes had to be paid, and one of the conditions of the provincial lease required payment of a $500,000 performance bond or deposit which would be forfeit if the company failed to develop the project as promised. If the project went ahead, the payment of royalties, set at $1 per year per horsepower generated, would be taken out of the money thus deposited.

The members of the first Beauharnois syndicate did not have sums of this magnitude on hand. Their assets might eventually be valuable if necessary authorizations were also obtained from the federal government, but that was still an uncertain prospect in June 1928 when the $500,000 had to be deposited in Quebec. A loan for that amount was successfully negotiated with the Bank of Montreal, but the syndicate members had not only to pledge the credit of the syndicate but also to give their own personal guarantees in order to obtain this loan.[27]

The requirement of $500,000 for the Quebec deposit, as well as the projected costs of further planning and development, made it necessary to raise more money. Unfortunately the first syndicate agreement proved an impediment to the acquisition of substantial additional funds. The Robert family, fearful of having their shares in the first Beauharnois syndicate watered down by the indiscriminate issuance of more and more shares, had insisted that a limit of 5,000 shares be clearly set for that syndicate.[28] All those 5,000 shares had been sold or issued. Now additional funds and a new arrangement were needed. The passage of the amendment to their charter and the granting of the Quebec water lease had also substantially increased the value of the syndicate's assets. A reorganization therefore seemed opportune, and was consummated on 4 April 1928.

A new syndicate with 30,000 shares was created.[29] The holders of the 5,000 shares in the first syndicate were entitled to exchange those shares, on a one-for-two basis, for shares in the second syndicate. Most of the members of the first syndicate had obtained their shares for $30 each. Their cost for the first 10,000 shares in the second syndicate was therefore $15 for each share.[30]

After issuing themselves the 10,000 shares in the new syndicate, in return for their 5,000 shares in the first syndicate, the syndicate members established a price of $100 for each of the remaining 20,000 shares of the second syndicate. They immediately subscribed 10,000 of those shares, paying $1 million in cash. The immediate objective was simply to raise the $1 million, half of which would be used for the

Quebec deposit and the other half of which would pay for the organizational, promotional, and technical work required to secure federal approval for their plans.

The reorganization provided the funds needed immediately and still left 10,000 shares which could be sold when more money or other services were required. The promoters were now ready to go to Ottawa to seek federal approval for their plans.

3

Political intrigue in Ottawa

The amendment of the charter of the Beauharnois Light, Heat and Power Company by the Quebec government was an important achievement. But it was only the first of many obstacles to be overcome by the Beauharnois promoters. The next and far more difficult task was to obtain federal approval of the project. Such authorization of construction was necessary because of the federal government's jurisdiction over navigation on Canadian navigable rivers and streams.

The Beauharnois promoters knew from the beginning that it would be difficult to get the necessary federal approval. Strong opposition to their proposal could be expected from several important sources. Sweezey and his associates believed that they could successfully counter any criticisms that might be raised. Their most important concern was to ensure that they would be allowed to make their presentations and that the appropriate politicians and bureaucrats would listen. In Quebec City Senator Donat Raymond had been helpful, and R.O. Sweezey was personally on friendly terms with the premier and several other cabinet ministers. But in Ottawa the Beauharnois promoters still had to establish such relationships. Sweezey later claimed that he went to Ottawa with great apprehension. 'I knew absolutely nothing about the ramifications and doings in Ottawa, or politics or politicians,' he modestly told inquiring parliamentarians in 1931.[1]

In order to correct this serious deficiency Sweezey made inquiries to determine who might 'advise me on how to get along without doing something that might be foolish.'[2] He was advised to consult with members of the Sifton family, who knew a great deal about politics in Ottawa. Specifically, Winfield Sifton, son of Sir Clifford Sifton, was recommended, partly because Sweezey and the younger Sifton already knew one another. Both had spent several years in the employ of that master entrepreneurial hustler Max Aitkin. Winfield Sifton, in fact, had worked for a time in the department of the Royal Securities Corporation of which Sweezey had been the chief, but Sifton was a lawyer, whereas Sweezey was an engineer.

There were several other compelling reasons why it seemed useful to bring the Siftons into the Beauharnois circle of friends. Sir Clifford Sifton and his sons had spent many years valiantly but unsuccessfully promoting another canal and power project – the Montreal, Ottawa and Georgian Bay Canal and Power Company. This ambitious project called for the construction of deep waterway canals and huge new hydroelectric generating plants along a route from Georgian Bay via the Ottawa River system to Montreal.[3] The Siftons were associated with British interests in the promotion of this project, but Ontario's hostility to private development of hydroelectric resources on the Ottawa River and the personal unpopularity of the Siftons in Quebec had prevented progress on the Georgian Bay project. It was generally agreed, moreover, that the market for additional electricity was insufficient to support two or more projects simultaneously. It would be either Georgian Bay, Beauharnois, or a development in the International Section of the St Lawrence. The prospects for the Sifton-supported Georgian Bay development were discouraging in 1927. It was a good time for Sweezey to approach Winfield Sifton and invite him to throw in his lot with the Beauharnois promoters.

A second important consideration for the Beauharnois promoters when they approached the Siftons was the fact that Sir Clifford Sifton, Winfield Sifton's father, was a member of the influential National Advisory Committee which advised the federal government on all future deep waterway developments. It would obviously be useful to have the Siftons as friends, and Sweezey approached Winfield in June 1927, immediately after the first Beauharnois application for a charter amendment had been refused by the Quebec legislature.[4]

Winfield Sifton proved receptive to Sweezey's overtures, and a fairly simple agreement was negotiated between the two men. Sifton agreed to do whatever he could to ensure that the plans of the Beauharnois company were approved and construction was authorized by the federal government. In return, Sweezey agreed to pay Sifton's expenses as these were incurred and $50,000 in cash if and when the Beauharnois plans were approved and construction was authorized by federal order in council. If the Beauharnois plans were not approved, Sifton would have only his expenses paid. The matter was formalized in an exchange of letters between the two men, and Winfield Sifton, with assistance from his father and brothers, began to lobby and work in Ottawa for the Beauharnois company. Sweezey explained his relationship with the Siftons thus: 'I knew very little about who was who in Ottawa. I did not know whom to approach, and Sifton with his experience was able to operate to advantage in that respect. His first duty was to figure out the number of obstacles in our way and from time to time we came to the conclusion that they were insurmountable, and kept at them until we wore some of them down.'[5]

The Siftons did not personally become members of either the first or second Beauharnois syndicates. Winfield Sifton ultimately collected $31,409.47 in expenses and expected to collect the $50,000 when the Beauharnois plans were approved. Unfortunately he died in 1928 before the Beauharnois plans were approved, and the payment or non-payment of the $50,000 subsequently became the subject of a bitter, but for the historian highly informative, lawsuit. In their lawsuit Winfield Sifton's heirs claimed that he 'worked incessantly on the scheme from the time of his employment early in September of 1927 until his death on 13th June 1928. By that time everything he was to do had been done.'[6]

Thus, beginning during the late summer of 1927 with the Siftons as his guide, Robert Oliver Sweezey began to explore the mysteries and challenges of the smoke-filled back rooms of Ottawa politics. They soon discovered a number of serious obstacles to their project and together devised the means to remove or wear them down. They worked on many of those problems simultaneously over the period of eighteen months from September 1927 until the crucial federal order in council was approved on 8 March 1929. It is possible, however, to identify a number of specific obstacles, each of which requires some explanation, with regard to both the nature of the difficulty and the manner in which it was resolved.

The first formidable obstacle identified by Winfield Sifton was the strong opposition in Quebec generally, but particularly in Montreal, to any proposal for a canal that might become a part of a deep waterway from Montreal to the Great Lakes. Such a development threatened to divert traffic from Montreal to ports further inland. The Siftons thought the difficulties they had encountered in the promotion of their Georgian Bay project were largely attributable to opposition in Montreal. The logical focus for such opposition was the Montreal Harbours Board. The chairman of that board, Senator Wilfrid McDougald, as explained in chapter 1, had a dubious business reputation but was a friend and occasional dinner guest of Prime Minister Mackenzie King. Sifton and Sweezey thought McDougald might be a person who could garner Quebec, and particularly Montreal, support for their project. They discussed the matter at length and agreed 'that it might be a good thing to get Senator McDougald in.'[7]

Sifton approached the senator but came back with the official reply that 'the Senator could not become interested, that there was some obstacle, and that he was on a committee that had to do with the St. Lawrence, and he did not advise me to pursue the thing further.'[8] The committee in question was the National Advisory Committee – the same one on which Sir Clifford Sifton served. Senator McDougald's official response was proper, but he followed it up with another which directly contradicted his official refusal to become involved. Sweezey explained that 'he [Winfield Sifton] told me, however, that he would like me to put 800 shares [of the first Beauharnois Syndicate] in the name of Clare Moyer ... I did not know whether those were for Mr. Sifton or for somebody else, and he was very vague about it.'[9] Clare Moyer was an Ottawa barrister who had served as Mackenzie King's private secretary until September 1927. He left that position when Sifton became associated with the Beauharnois project and worked closely with Sifton on behalf of the Beauharnois promoters. The 800 shares in the first Beauharnois syndicate placed in Moyer's name were held for, and subsequently transferred to, Senator McDougald, who paid $30,000 in cash for them.[10]

The legal work involved in the transfer of these shares was handled by Clare Moyer. Most of Senator McDougald's legal affairs, however, were handled by the Ottawa legal firm in which Senator Andrew Haydon was a senior partner. After McDougald joined the Beauharnois syndicate, much of that company's legal work was also directed to Haydon's law firm. Thereafter both senators lobbied effectively on behalf of the Beauharnois syndicate.

That legal connection was further strengthened in June 1928 immediately after Winfield Sifton's death. The necessary federal order in council had not yet been approved. Sweezey thought that Sifton's death relieved him of his obligation to pay Sifton the $50,000 contingent on the approval of the order in council. Sweezey therefore offered Andrew Haydon the $50,000 contract previously held by

Winfield Sifton, again payable only if the federal order in council was approved.

The Beauharnois promoters and their political friends and hirelings quickly realized that the prime minister himself would be the key to their success or failure. But Mackenzie King was convinced that any future St Lawrence or other deep waterway proposals were politically dangerous. In these matters he believed that 'we cannot move too carefully.' He was determined to exercise 'great care and no haste, but sure and certain steps all the way,' and he believed that the issue, if mishandled, could lead to the defeat of his government. He particularly emphasized 'the importance of keeping in mind political as well as economical considerations.'[11] The prime minister did not want to be rushed into any decision on the matter and was quite prepared to refer controversial aspects to the courts or to special technical or advisory committees for lengthy study and report so that all ramifications of the project could be evaluated. Since he believed the Americans had a strong interest in any new deep waterway scheme, Mackenzie King also hoped that he might be able to exploit the situation to obtain other largely unrelated concessions. Specifically, he wanted American tariff concessions which might meet the demands of the Progressives in parliament. The prime minister's entire approach to the issue was cautious, slow, methodical, and completely political. The Beauharnois promoters, on the other hand, were men in a hurry who wanted to get on with their project as soon as possible.

Mackenzie King was particularly concerned about two aspects of any proposal for power and navigational developments on the St Lawrence. The first concerned federal-provincial relations. The federal government was responsible for all matters pertaining to navigation on Canadian rivers and streams. It had the right and the duty to review and, if appropriate, approve any and all plans that might affect navigation. Ontario and Quebec insisted, however, that that was the limit of federal jurisdiction. All water in navigable streams that was not needed for navigational purposes, and the riverbed itself, were, in the provincial view, lands and natural resources belonging to the provinces. The federal government, however, contended that water power leases adjacent to, or a part of, the canal system had historically and properly been granted by the federal government and that the lands on which the canals were built were also federal property.

There had been intermittent discussions and negotiations between the federal and provincial governments, but the question of ownership of the water rights in navigable streams had not been resolved. Consequently, when the Beauharnois promoters outlined their proposal, the federal cabinet decided to refer the matter to the courts. That, of course, was a lengthy process, particularly if the matter was appealed to the Judicial Committee of the Imperial Privy Council. King was not prepared to act until this legal situation was clarified. He was, however, at least partly overtaken by events in Quebec. The Beauharnois company, as already indicated, applied for and obtained from the provincial government a lease authorizing the diversion of 40,000 cubic feet of water per second. The federal government did not challenge or disallow the provincial action, but the promoters and federal and provincial politicians agreed that the $500,000 deposited by the Beauharnois company would be transferred to the federal government if the courts found the water belonged to the federal government.

Sweezey was convinced that the entire constitutional dispute could be sidestepped by the federal and Quebec governments. His company's plans could be approved before the courts rendered their decision, since the Beauharnois company would pay for the water it used. If necessary the money could be paid into an escrow fund, awaiting the appropriate constitutional decision from the courts. The merits of their proposal were not at issue – rather, which government would receive the royalties for the water used. The matter did not seem so simple to the prime minister, but political pressure and direct provincial action in granting the lease had seemingly forced the issue. King nevertheless hoped a legal decision would be available before the federal government made any commitments to Beauharnois.

The implications of the Beauharnois project for any future St Lawrence deep waterway were even more problematic for the prime minister. The initial plans of the Beauharnois promoters called only for the diversion of 40,000 cubic feet per second, but their long-term plans called for the diversion of the entire flow of the St Lawrence. In order to leave open the option of the full development, the proposed Beauharnois power canal had to be built to specifications that would also make possible its use as a link in any future deep waterway. But the necessary diplomatic, political, technolgical, and financial arrangements for the construction of the deep waterway had not yet been completed. How then could the federal government approve the plans of the Beauharnois Light, Heat and Power Company to build a huge new power canal and generating facility that could not be separated from the proposed navigational improvements?

The discussions and consultations about the proposed deep waterway had been going on for many years. In 1920 the possibility of building a new seaway had been referred by the Canadian and American governments to the International Joint Commission for detailed study and report. This commission recommended, in December 1921, that Canada and the United States enter into an agreement providing for the dredging of the St Lawrence waterway between Montreal and Lake Ontario, to a depth of twenty-five feet. The commission also recommended that further and more detailed engineering studies be completed before the work was started. A Joint Board of Engineers, with three American and three Canadian members, was established to prepare more detailed plans, reports, and recommendations. In addition, the Canadian government established a National Advisory Committee to inform the federal government about various political aspects of the question. As already noted, Sir Clifford Sifton and Senator Wilfrid Laurier McDougald were members of this committee.

The Joint Board of Engineers presented its report on the cost, engineering feasibility, and power possibilities of the proposed deep waterway in November 1926, a mere two months before Robert Sweezey acquired control of the Beauharnois Light, Heat and Power Company. The board projected a total construction cost for the entire St Lawrence deep waterway of between $620 and $650 million, and a potential development of 5 million horsepower of electricity. The Soulanges Section would make up approximately 40 per cent of the total development.

The report of the Joint Board of Engineers was immediately referred to the National Advisory Committee. That committee raised several objections to the engineering proposals but recommended that there be further negotiations with the Americans, leading to the signing of an appropriate treaty.[12] It was readily conceded, particularly in view of Quebec's objections, that the deep waterway proposal was politically sensitive and would require exceptionally careful handling. In a general review of the debates in Canadian newspapers and magazines on the deep waterway proposals *Maclean's* stated: 'It seems to be pretty generally conceded that before any agreement concerning so vast an undertaking is entered into with the United States, every angle of the situation must be carefully canvassed and considered.'[13]

R.O. Sweezey and his associates could not wait until all these difficult questions were resolved. And they did not think a decision on their project need be delayed. This issue, like the constitutional problem, could be sidestepped. The Beauharnois proposals in this regard could probably best be summarized by paraphrasing a well-known utterance of the prime minister – a deep waterway if necessary, but not necessarily a deep waterway. Initially the Beauharnois company would divert only 40,000 cubic feet of water per second, which would not disrupt continuing operations on the Soulanges Canal. The Beauharnois proposal could therefore be viewed and approved as a power project pure and simple. But if, at some future date, a decision was made to develop the deep waterway, the new Beauharnois Canal, built to appropriate specifications, would be available free of charge. The federal government need only install appropriate headgates and locks, and the deep waterway would be a reality between Lake St Francis and Lake St Louis. An obviously attractive feature of this scheme was the fact that the federal government would save an estimated $16 million in the construction of a new navigational canal if and when the decision was made to proceed with the deep waterway. A decision on the waterway, the promoters argued, could and should be treated separately from the power considerations.

These arguments in favour of a speedy approval of the Beauharnois proposals, while leaving the federal-provincial and deep waterway implications unresolved, were strenuously advanced by Senators McDougald and Haydon in a series of formal and social meetings with the prime minister in December 1927 and January 1928. A diary entry on 3 January 1928 indicates that the two senator-lobbyists had achieved substantial success. The prime minister, on that day, noted that McDougald and Haydon had 'presented to me what seems to be a perfectly complete plan for St. Lawrence development, without cost to the country, & helping to meet a very difficult situation both locally & internationally. I had both to lunch with me at Laurier House.'[14] The senators may have been persuasive, but numerous other diary entries throughout 1928 show clearly that the prime minister continued to worry about the constitutional and navigational questions. There were further lengthy delays, even though friends of the Beauharnois promoters had the ear of the prime minister throughout that year.

Mackenzie King's attitude may also have been influenced by another consideration. His close friend, Peter C. Larkin, had established a special trust fund to defray the cost of refurbishing Laurier

House, which was King's personal residence, and to give the prime minister financial security and independence. The funds raised by Larkin were deposited to a special account in King's name with the Old Colony Trust in Boston. Wilfrid Laurier McDougald contributed $10,000 to that fund on 29 December 1927,[15] precisely when he and Senator Haydon were lobbying intensively with the prime minister, and only three weeks before the Beauharnois company submitted its official proposals to the federal government. King personally reviewed the Old Colony Trust account on 8 January 1928, noting with pleasure that: 'The fund was started September 1925 with $25,000 deposited by Mr. L[arkin], he had it up to 75,000 by Sept 1926 now it has reached $177,500.'[16]

It was Larkin's practice to give the prime minister the names of those who had contributed to the fund. It is not entirely clear whether Mackenzie King knew of the $10,000 contribution by McDougald in January 1928, but he certainly came to know about it and about a further $15,000 contribution made by the senator in October 1928.[17] This awareness is clearly indicated by a later diary entry. 'This morning I received from Mr. Larkin a letter giving me a statement of the monies he has raised as a fund for me ... I should have preferred not knowing by whom the contributions had been made, & that the names should have been solely in Mr. Larkin's keeping. However, one cannot look a gift horse too closely in the mouth ... It may after all be the way of rich men in matters of the kind; be all for the best.'[18]

It is clear that by January 1928 Sifton, McDougald, and Haydon had prepared the prime minister and others in Ottawa for the Beauharnois application which was officially filed on 17 January 1928. Behind that application, however, there was a great deal of technical and engineering work. R.O. Sweezey himself was a very capable engineer, but a massive project of this kind required an enormous amount of professional and technical work. In that regard Sweezey encountered serious difficulties. He later claimed that the rival power companies had hired away all the most able engineers in Canada, in part to deprive his company of the required technical expertise. The local situation was sufficiently serious that the Beauharnois promoters felt they had no alternative but to go to New York and there engage the services of the large consulting engineering firm of William States Lee. Lee was closely associated with the Duke interests of North Carolina and had built a large and innovative powerhouse for J.B. Duke and some of his Canadian associates on the Saguenay River. Sweezey explained the situation thus. 'I thought the power companies were in a position that they could prevent any engineer working for us. That is how, for instance, we had to get Mr. Lee, although an American citizen, who had done some big works in Canada. He was one of our good engineers.'[19] It was only with Lee's help that the Beauharnois promoters were able to file their official application and preliminary engineering plans in January 1928. Detailed and comprehensive engineering plans were not submitted until July of 1928, although the proposals were extensively studied and discussed throughout that year.

The Beauharnois application filed in January of 1928 sought federal authorization to develop the first stage of the huge canal and power project. It entailed the initial diversion of 40,000 cubic feet of water per second through a canal fifteen miles long, 3,000 feet wide at the top of the embankments, and with a twenty-seven foot deep ship channel; and the construction of a powerhouse capable of generating up to 500,000 horsepower per year. The application stated that the power canal to be built by the company would 'when completed ... conform to the navigation standards set out in paragraph 111 of the main report and paragraph 13 of Appendix C of the report made by the International Joint Board of Engineers, 1926-27.'[20] The total cost of all remedial works, power canal, and powerhouse in the first phase of development was estimated at $50 to $55 million, of which the canal and remedial works alone would cost an estimated $16 million.

The Beauharnois application, together with the report of the International Joint Board of Engineers, was immediately referred by the prime minister to the National Advisory Committee for discussion and advice. The members of this committee had been deliberately selected to represent various and diverse interests and viewpoints, and the Beauharnois application elicited a wide range of views and opinions. After one lengthy meeting King noted:

> It was amusing to note Dunning's attitude, full of suspicion, full of objections, without force some, others with force, but mostly it seemed to me begotten of the circumstances that he was not controlling the situation. On the other hand it was apparent the committee had a plan of their own in mind, which was probably shining through their report. The report was made to suit an ultimate plan, instead of presenting general situation & permitting plan to evolve ... Sifton is the dominating figure & mind, he has worked out matters. McDougald & Walter Foster are "interested' parties in what may ultimately transpire.[21]

It did not take long for King's cautious nature to reassert itself, and for him to conclude that 'we cannot move too carefully.'[22] This despite King's more optimistic note a few days earlier, just after he had seen McDougald and Haydon who had presented what had then seemed 'a perfectly complete plan for St. Lawrence development.'[23] All King's subsequent efforts throughout 1928 were to urge caution and delay. In May he noted that 'we are wise in going very slow, step by step.'[24] In July he thought 'delay ... was better than undue haste on our part,'[25] and at the end of the year he was still convinced that the 'matter of granting charter to Beauharnois Canal Co. could not be hurried unduly.'[26] King's position throughout that year was clearly enunciated when he wrote on 13 December 1928, 'I have come to the conclusion we must arrange for all steps to be taken pretty much simultaneously, viz Beauharnois Canal – along with deepening international channel, & that arranged with U.S. in form of an agreement which might prevent any raising of tariff on part of U.S. It is the largest proposition any Canadian government has been called upon to deal with.'[27]

The first substantive political decision regarding the Beauharnois application and the report of the International Joint Board of Engineers was a negative one. On 20 January the government decided to make no mention at all of the matter in the speech from the throne.[28] The next day the government gained more time by referring the matter of ownership of the water power rights on navigable streams to the Supreme Court of Canada.[29] These delays stimulated increased pressure from the Ottawa lobbyists, which eventually led the exasperated prime minister to note on 26 June that 'Dr. McD. came next, most intent on work going ahead on Beauharnois Canal, suspicious as usual of others, professing desirous of aid for party etc. I spoke to him about being careful to keep confidential any talks with me, & also to understand I had made no commitments whatever.'[30] Whether they liked it or not, the Beauharnois promoters had to reconcile themselves to the fact that the political processes in Ottawa took a great deal of time, even when they had influential persons such as the Siftons and Senators McDougald, Haydon, and Raymond doing what they could to expedite matters.

The most serious political problems and objections faced by the Beauharnois promoters in Ottawa were, nevertheless, addressed in the last months of 1927 and in the early months of 1928. The answers and solutions to those problems, as provided by the promoters and their political friends and lobbyists, were ultimately persuasive. The intrigue, lobbying, and propaganda throughout 1928 were intense, and journalists resorted to colourful language when describing the state of affairs in Ottawa.

For more than a year, Ottawa has been the cockpit of a battle, which for drama, for romance and stakes of millions, for the bitterness and character of its warfare, and for the picturesqueness of the contending personalities, has had no parallel in our time. Not since the spacious eighties when Donald Smith and his confederates made Ottawa their last desperate stand for the CPR, not since William Mackenzie and Donald Mann made lobbying an art, has this city, plagued by intrigue and lobbying and propaganda, had anything approaching it. All the agencies of political and economic warfare, all the tactics that highly-paid ingenuity could muster, have been marshalled into a mighty combat between power magnates, millionaires, high-powered lawyers, veteran lobbyists, cunning propagandists, everything and everybody in any way calculated to win the coveted prize.[31]

4

Bewildered bureaucrats and a divided cabinet

The Beauharnois promoters and their agents and friends in Ottawa were able to offer satisfactory ways and means of dealing with the constitutional dispute over ownership of the water in navigable rivers and streams, and with concerns about the long-term implications of their project for future navigational developments on the St Lawrence River. Once they submitted their official application to the cabinet, however, they also had to convince bureaucrats and engineers in the Departments of Public Works and Railways and Canals that their project was technically sound. The Department of Railways and Canals had to consider navigational matters, while the Department of Public Works dealt with all the technical and engineering aspects of the project. The departmental investigations and reports took a great deal of time and effort, and the promoters and lobbyists soon learned that there were some specific problems that had to be resolved before the bureaucrats would approve the project.

One of the first responsibilities of the civil servants was to check whether the Beauharnois application was in conflict with or impinged on the rights of other companies operating in the same area. They quickly found several other applications which had been filed at various times to develop some or all of the water powers in the Soulanges Section of the St Lawrence. Most of these prior applications were not regarded as serious obstacles in the way of approving the Beauharnois plans. Several were based on options never exercised and since expired. Others had been filed by individuals who lacked the means or the ability to proceed. There were, however, two prior applications that were regarded as serious obstacles. The first of these concerned the claims of R.O. Sweezey's erstwhile employer, Narcisse

Cantin, who was still fuming about Sweezey's actions. He filed a belligerent protest against the Beauharnois proposals, claiming that Sweezey had 'purchased for his own benefit that which he was entrusted to do for the Great Lakes and Atlantic Canada Power Company Ltd., and the Transportation and Power Corp. Ltd.'[1]

The bureaucrats and engineers of the Department of Public Works did not take this protest seriously. Narcisse Cantin had made himself a nuisance with his complaints and lacked the financial resources to develop the site. The department officials therefore readily accepted Sweezey's explanation that the Transportation and Power promoters had once had an option to purchase the Beauharnois company, but that option had expired before Sweezey had gained control of the company. An appeal by Cantin to the prime minister was also unsuccessful.

A second and much more controversial claim was entered by a company called the Sterling Industrial Corporation. This company had filed an official development application only a few days before the Beauharnois application. It sought authority to divert 30,000 cubic feet of water per second. The listed president of the Sterling Corporation was John P. Ebbs, a law partner of Senator Andrew Haydon and a lawyer for Senator McDougald. All the other listed directors and officers of the Sterling Corporation were secretaries and clerks in the Haydon and Ebbs law firm, but none of these was the real promoter of the scheme.

The Sterling Corporation was, in fact, the corporate instrument of Robert A.C. Henry, a former senior engineer with the Department of Railways and Canals. In 1928 Henry was the director of the Bureau of Economics of the Canadian National Railways. Henry had used information obtained in the performance of his official governmental duties and become interested in the power resources of the Soulanges Section 'as a hobby' in 1923.[2] He had hired a consulting engineer to examine the matter in greater detail. This task, however, involved greater expense than he could conveniently handle, and Henry persuaded Wilfrid Laurier McDougald, not yet a member of the Senate, to join him. Each man put up $10,000, which paid for a feasibility study and some legal costs. On the strength of the report submitted by their consulting engineer, Henry and McDougald incorporated the Sterling Industrial Corporation, and then, just before the Beauharnois application was filed, they submitted their own application.

The Sterling Industrial Corporation plans and financial arrangements had no more merit than those of other moribund companies, except for the fact that two very influential individuals were involved. McDougald and Henry had created in the Sterling Industrial Corporation a company with very few real assets but with a capacity to delay and obstruct approval of any rival plans, including those of the Beauharnois Light, Heat and Power Company. That capacity to delay and obstruct enabled McDougald and Henry to force, or blackmail, the Beauharnois promoters to give them a far greater participation in the Beauharnois project than they were entitled to on the basis of any investment in the Sterling Industrial Corporation. During the summer of 1928, several months after their official application, the Beauharnois Light, Heat and Power Company acquired the assets of the Sterling Industrial Corporation. McDougald and Henry each received 1,000 shares in the second Beauharnois syndicate in return for their Sterling shares.

Later, numerous searching questions were asked, regarding the assets of the Sterling Corporation. Sweezey candidly admitted that he had never seen the Sterling Corporation as anything more than a political and bureaucratic obstacle. He only dealt with it in order to remove that obstacle and to gain important political and bureaucratic influence and support. Later, under aggressive questioning, R.A.C. Henry conceded that the Sterling Corporation had no value, other than the potential to delay and probably to block rival applications.

Q. Am I right in this, Mr. Henry, that you having the knowledge you did have of the possiblities in this section, took the steps that you described of placing an application on record with the Dominion Government and at the time knowing that others were interested in the project as well? A. Oh, yes.
Q. And you did not propose to let anyone else go on and develop that without taking care of Henry and McDougald? A. Well, that is probably one way of putting it, Mr. Chairman.[3]

The agreement was finalized on 18 December 1928. Sweezey took the precaution, however, of insisting that the agreement be made conditional on the federal government's granting to Beauharnois the necessary authorization to proceed. If federal approval was granted, Henry and McDougald each would have 1,000 shares in the second Beauharnois syndicate in return for the assets of the Sterling Industrial Corporation in which each had invested only $10,000. This total was, of course, in addition to the 800 shares of the first syndicate, convertible into 1,600 shares of the second syndicate, which Senator

McDougald had purchased but which were held in trust for him by Clare Moyer.

This agreement with the Sterling Corporation removed an important obstacle within the bureaucracy of the Departments of Public Works and Railways and Canals. All the necessary plans, nevertheless, had to be prepared and filed. Appropriate remedial works had to be provided so the other four companies generating electricity in the Soulanges Section would not be adversely affected. Those four companies had direct or indirect links with Montreal Power and could therefore be counted on to raise objections whenever the opportunity presented itself.

The Beauharnois application and supporting documents were also referred to the Department of Justice, whose lawyers advised the government on the legal aspects and ramifications of the proposed construction plans. All three federal departments had their own experts who examined and then reported on the project. This process took a great deal of time. When considered in conjunction with the generally cautious and slow approach taken by the politicians, it is not surprising that all of 1928 was taken up in intensive but inconclusive bureaucratic wrangling, negotiation, and political lobbying in Ottawa.

Sweezey and his associates were impressed with the wealth, power, and influence that Montreal Power and its affiliated companies allegedly had with federal bureaucrats. Throughout 1928 Sweezey and Jones tried to placate the Montreal Power interests. They were absolutely determined to build their plant on their own terms and expected to reap substantial profits from it. But theirs would be a generating plant. Montreal Power was primarily a power distribution company. The Beauharnois promoters made it clear that they were willing to sell their power to anyone, including Montreal Power; they lacked the resources and had no intention of duplicating Montreal Power's urban distribution network.

Montreal Power was not interested in an accommodation with the Beauharnois promoters in 1928. If large profits were in prospect, either in generation or distribution, it naturally preferred those profits be earned by its own company, and Montreal Power was in a good position to pick up the pieces at very low cost if the Beauharnois application failed. So the company strenuously opposed that application in 1927 and 1928. The history of Montreal Power was instructive. Other prospective rivals of the company had also faced fierce opposition. When those rivals succeeded in spite of Montreal Power opposition, however, the latter company had either purchased the rival company on very attractive terms or agreed to buy power from those companies, thus safeguarding its distribution monopoly within the city.

The entire year of 1928 was spent in intensive lobbying, but there were repeated and frustrating delays. The *Financial Times* commented early in 1929 that 'when the Beauharnois promoters descended upon Ottawa with a corps of propagandists and high-powered lawyers, it looked as though their plan would promptly be approved. Unfortunately for them, the public evinced an interest in the matter. Newspapers began asking what the project involved, who were behind it, how it affected the St. Lawrence scheme as a whole.'[4] At times the Beauharnois promoters feared the governmental studies might continue forever, but by December of 1928 Senator Andrew Haydon learned that the major departmental engineering and feasibility studies were nearing completion and that the findings were encouraging. In order to expedite matters Haydon tried, and after several delays succeeded, in persuading the prime minister 'to sit down for a short time with McLachlan [chief engineer of the Department of Public Works] and Henry and listen to their outline of the Beauharnois Company's situation.' He was able to do so, however, only after almost twelve months of study, reporting, and delays.

When the private meeting was finally arranged, Haydon was particularly insistent that R.A.C. Henry be included. Haydon praised Henry as an engineer who was 'silent, capable, careful and absolutely straight.'[5] He did not inform the prime minister that Henry was also a major Beauharnois shareholder, thanks to the agreement between the Beauharnois company and the Sterling Industrial Corporation. The meeting of public works engineer McLachlan, R.A.C. Henry, Andrew Haydon, and the prime minister took place on 11 December 1928. When it ended, Mackenzie King was impressed with the need for action on what he referred to as "the largest proposition any Canadian government has been called upon to deal with.'[6] Two days later he raised the matter for discussion in cabinet. Other lengthy meetings with departmental officials and engineering experts followed, several of which were arranged by one of the three interested senators.[7]

In cabinet strong opposition to the Beauharnois proposal centred on J.C. Elliott, the minister of public works. Elliott was a lawyer from London, Ontario, who had served for a time in the Ontario legislature before being elected to the House of Commons in 1925. He was a director of the London Street Railway Company and of the Equity Insurance Company. According to his critics, Elliott was susceptible to considerable pressure from J.H. Gundy, who was Sir Herbert Holt's financial associate. Gundy was a generous contributor to the Liberal party. The Quebec Liberal fund-raiser, Senator Raymond, in a letter to the prime minister lobbying for the Beauharnois company, expressed the opinion that Elliott was very much under the influence of Gundy and described Gundy as 'Sir Herbert Holt's partner and financial servant.'[8]

Elliott's arguments made no reference whatever to the Montreal Power interests or to contributions Gundy had made to the Liberal party. Instead, he questioned whether a matter of this magnitude could properly be decided by order in council. He advocated a full debate in parliament, where he expected that the Beauharnois application would be strongly opposed by Ontario Conservatives and western Progressives. Such a debate was politically dangerous for the Beauharnois promoters. They urged that the federal cabinet approve the controversial order in council before parliament reconvened on 7 February 1929. Senator Donat Raymond specifically warned the prime minister, 'If the matter is not settled before the next session you will have a fierce lobby fight which will be very annoying, and to say the least, not alone to us but also to you, and may be most embarassing to the party, and there would be debates, where every question from public ownership down to Montreal lighting monopolies including St. Lawrence canals would be debated.'[9]

Elliott, a minister from Ontario where there were strong public ownership sentiments, had good political as well as personal reasons to demand a full parliamentary debate before the Beauharnois application was approved. According to the press, 'The argument of these Ministers is that the policy of granting power rights in a haphazard, hit-and-miss way, may result in more misses than hits; that it is not an adequate way of dealing with one of the nations greatest resources.'[10] Mackenzie King was not impressed with Elliott's arguments. He noted that 'his [Elliott's] grounds [in opposition to approval being granted without a full parliamentary debate] were not sound.'[11] King believed the cabinet had the authority to make a decision and was not obliged to refer it to parliament. The matter nevertheless continued to take up much time in cabinet throughout December, with King obviously leaning towards approval but still determined 'not to be hurried.'[12]

On 21 December 1928 J.H. Gundy of Toronto had lunch with the prime minister. Gundy did his best to persuade King not to approve the Beauharnois plans. He specifically told the prime minister that the Montreal Power interests had contributed to the federal Liberal party's election campaign in the last election and that 'there was no reason why they [the Liberals] shld not get all assistance needed from Holt group.' King regarded these arguments as 'an effort to have me feel party had been helped & wd be helped by Holt interests (tho Tory).' He was not impressed and thought he left Gundy 'with the impression the Beauharnois people might get their plans approved.'[13]

Additional evidence that the government was moving towards a decision had come on 17 December 1928, when the cabinet requested an opinion from the Department of Justice on constitutional questions. The legal reference to the courts to resolve the federal-provincial dispute about ownership of the water and riverbed in navigable streams was still before the Supreme Court. The question now to be answered was whether the government had jurisdiction to approve the Beauharnois plans before the court ruling was handed down. The Department of Justice had obviously anticipated this request and sent an affirmative reply four days later, clearing the way for federal action.

Christmas provided a brief but happy respite from the relentless pressure. In his diary entry for Christmas Day 1928 Mackenzie King noted that, 'I rec'd many beautiful gifts ... from Dr. McDougald a silver cigar & cigarette set (very handsome.)'[14] A short time later the prime minister went over his Old Colony Trust, Boston, account with P.C. Larkin and was very pleased to note it had risen to 'the magnificent sum of $225,000.'[15] He was, however, 'a little disturbed to find that Mr. Larkin at Christmastime while sending each contributor a gold guinea as a 'token' of this good deed, sent a letter as well giving to each the names of the other contributors to the fund. I felt the embarassment to which this may give rise.'[16]

Senator McDougald, as already indicated, had contributed $10,000 to that fund in 1927 and a further $15,000 in 1928. The prime minister's diary entry of 14 January 1929 makes it absolutely clear that he knew who the contributors were, but there is no evidence whatever that his decision on the Beauharnois application was directly influenced by McDougald's contributions to the Old Colony Trust funds. It is obvious, however, that all three senators closely associated with the Beauharnois project had the ear of the prime minister throughout the period when the matter was under active consideration by the government.

The situation for the prime minister and the Beauharnois promoters became more complicated on 13 January 1929. On that day Major Bell, the deputy minister of railways and canals, died. Charles Dunning, the minister, intended to bring forward important new railway legislation pertaining to the Canadian National Railways. He felt keenly the loss of Bell and his expert knowledge. Dunning was eager to find a replacement who was thoroughly acquainted with the railway situation and could provide advice and technical information to the minister as the important and controversial legislation made its way through parliament. There was no one in the department, in Dunning's opinion, who possessed the required expertise. As a result, at Major Bell's funeral, Dunning approached R.A.C. Henry and offered him the deputy ministership. Henry was at that time the director of the Economic Bureau of Canadian National Railways and widely regarded as one of the best-informed men on the Canadian railway situation.

Henry expressed reluctance, in part because of his involvement in the Sterling and Beauharnois projects. Dunning became more insistent, and the prime minister also wrote, urging Henry to accept the deputy ministership, at least for the duration of the parliamentary session. Henry explained the situation thus.

> Sir Henry [Thornton, president of Canadian National Railways] called me in and he told me that Mr. Dunning was insisting upon my taking the position because it was approaching the session, and he knew of nobody else in Canada who had the knowledge of the railway situation – and particularly the Canadian National Railways – that I had. There was a heavy railway program going through and he thought I ought to consider accepting it at least for the session.[17]

Henry accepted and was officially appointed deputy minister of railways and canals on 14 February 1929. He later falsely insisted that, as an interested party in the Beauharnois project, he did not take part in the final departmental discussions and reports that led to the order in council approving the application of the Beauharnois company. In fact, as will be shown below, Henry's participation in such discussions was carefully arranged by Senator Andrew Haydon.

It is true, however, that the Department of Railways and Canals dealt with only some of the navigational aspects of the proposal, while the more important and detailed review of the numerous engineering aspects had to be approved by the Department of Public Works. The precise influence exerted by Henry is not clear. But the crucial order in council authorizing the Beauharnois project was approved only three weeks after R.A.C. Henry became deputy minister of the Department of Railways and Canals. Henry, moreover, held the position of deputy minister of railways and canals only from 14 February 1929 to 30 March 1929, a scant six weeks. Yet, even before he officially resigned as deputy minister, Henry began work in a new job and was officially appointed general manager and vice-president of the Beauharnois Light, Heat and Power Company on the day he resigned from the civil service. This curious set of circumstances later raised suspicions in the minds of those opposed to the Beauharnois proposal.

In the meantime, the debates in the cabinet and in the House of Commons became increasingly divisive. Public Works Minister Elliott's opposition was so determined that the cabinet decided, in January 1929, to hold public hearings, so that all the arguments for and against the project could be clearly stated and evaluated. The hearings took place in Elliott's office and began on 15 January 1929. They did not really help the government. As expected, three of the four other power companies already operating in the Soulanges Section opposed the Beauharnois application arguing, among other things, that their own works would be seriously damaged. Only the Montreal Cottons Company did not protest, choosing instead to seek an accommodation with the Beauharnois interests.

There was one important new development at the hearings in Elliott's office. The Cedars Rapids Manufacturing and Power Company, with the backing of Montreal Power, made a proposal for the development of a new power project which would also utilize the full flow and drop of the river. In almost all respects the proposal was identical to that of the Beauharnois company. But the Beauharnois proposal deviated in some relatively minor aspects from the recommendations of the Joint Board of Engineers, which had been established by the International Joint Commission. The proposal sponsored by Montreal Power promised to adhere strictly to all the recommendations of the Joint Board. Montreal Power spokesmen argued that even minor variations could lead to complications from the Americans. Their proposal entailed no such risk.

This new offer by the Montreal Power interests had to be taken seriously. It had the backing of the largest and most profitable power company in Canada and of one of Canada's largest banks, the Royal Bank of Canada, of which Sir Herbert Holt was also president. The offer was accompanied, moreover, by a vigorous newspaper campaign against the Beauharnois project. Senator Haydon attributed the increased hostility of the newspapers entirely to the influence of J.H. Gundy and the 'Holt interests' with which Gundy was closely associated. That interpretation, however, was an oversimplification.

A crucial factor in the increased newspaper hostility was the anger and frustration of the Siftons after Winfield Sifton's death. The Beauharnois promoters were unwilling to pay Winfield Sifton's estate the $50,000 promised if and when the required federal order in council was approved. They had instead made a new and separate arrangement to pay that $50,000 to Andrew Haydon.

A further very important concern which found strong emphasis in the newspapers was the advocacy of public rather than private ownership of Canadian hydroelectric resources. Such a policy was popular in the west, particularly among the Progressive and Labour members of parliament, and found expression in most of the western newspapers. Public ownership also had great appeal in Ontario and was advocated by several influential newspapers in that province.

The Montreal Power interests were, of course, no advocates of public ownership. But they were happy to see the opposition to the Beauharnois project growing. Their alternative proposal provided a convenient focus for some, but not all, who opposed the Beauharnois application, and it was the most spectacular development of the public hearings in January 1929. But several other interested parties also protested against the Beauharnois project. The Dominion Marine Association feared the destruction of the rapids which were described as 'one of the great scenic assets of Canada [which] belongs to all Canadians.' Engineers from the Department of Public Works worried that the diversion of water might impair 'the sanitary functions of the river ... the lessened flow may result in impure water with dirty bays and shores.' The Canada Steamship Lines filed a separate objection expressing concern that the diversion would so reduce the flow over the rapids that their passenger vessels, the *Rapids King* and the *Rapids Queen*, would no longer be able to traverse the rapids. Runs through those rapids had become a major and profitable tourist attraction. After the hearing, perhaps encouraged by their minister, Public Works officials prepared a detailed and well-documented report enumerating and explaining all the arguments against the Beauharnois proposals.[18]

The January hearing also attracted considerable public attention. The *Financial Times* reported: 'almost nation-wide protests against the Beauharnois scheme ... The press of nearly the entire country is opposed to the project. The latest to come out in opposition to it is the Manitoba Free Press, a newspaper whose opinion not only counts with the government, but which is even more potent with members from the West.'[19] The hearing and the public reaction, nevertheless, did little to help the government make up its mind. The press reported immediately after the hearing that 'The opposition to the company's project, represented by important public and private bodies, was unquestionably impressive; and on the day following the hearing Mr. Elliott, the Minister of Public Works, made it clear that the Cabinet does not intend to be rushed.'[20]

The rival lobbyists continued to pursue their objectives with such frenzied intensity that Mackenzie King was driven to complain bitterly in his diary entry of 25 January 1929:

I have had a very difficult day. All the forces for & against Beauharnois Power Scheme have been lobbying incessantly. I have kept them away but today they became insistent. Jones wrote me a long letter pressing the situation. It was followed by a letter from Aime Geoffrion, the attorney, with a draft order in Council. This seemed to me an outrageous procedure, and I said so in Cabinet this afternoon. I was determined to spike the guns of the lobbyists present and future, & gave all the Cabinet to understand that this procedure had exasperated me & that I did not intend to permit it. Billy Moore, too, turned up on appointment, apparently to talk of tariff, in reality to be an agent for Senator Raymond to have me see him. He sd Raymond was 'not interested' & also that he had seen the letter Raymond had sent me. I gave him to understand 'lobbyists' would defeat their own ends. I was much annoyed & an inner something asserts itself. I try to control myself, but it is difficult.[21]

King's anger about Aimé Geoffrion's letter reflects the tense situation, but King in fact seriously misread and misinterpreted that letter. Geoffrion had enclosed a copy of an earlier federal order in council which had authorized construction of the Cedars Rapids power plant and then suggested that a similar order in council might be approved for the Beauharnois application. Geoffrion did not submit a draft copy of the proposed Beauharnois order in council.[22]

The long letter from F.P. Jones focused specifically on the opposition organized by the Montreal Power interests. Jones suggested that his opponents had overcharged the people of Canada $30 million per year for hydroelectric power. He further alleged that he had been approached by the Montreal Power interests with an offer to withdraw their opposition to the Beauharnois application if they were given a one-third interest in the Beauharnois company and a contract to purchase up to 125,000 horsepower of Beauharnois power at $15 per horsepower. Jones alleged that the Montreal Power interests were 'extremely anxious to have their monopoly on the Island of Montreal and other districts continue.' He then sought to ingratiate himself with the prime minister, saying, 'I considered it a piece of impertinence that he [a representative of the Montreal Power interests], or anyone else should consider their opposition was sufficient to prevent your Government doing what they considered best in the interests of the country.'[23]

All this intense lobbying did more to confuse than to enlighten cabinet ministers. A financial reporter, perhaps recalling Billy Moore's former career as the Canadian Northern Railway's most successful lobbyist, commented that 'Power, indeed, has come to play the part in Ottawa that railways used to play in the prewar days of Mackenzie and Mann. It has produced so many and such contradictory demands, so much lobbying and propaganda, and is charged with so many economic and engineering perplexities, not to speak of political dangers, that the Cabinet, bewildered by it all, does not know what to do with it.'[24]

It also exhausted the prime minister's patience, and he took steps 'to ensure pressure against myself did not get too keen.'[25] A cabinet committee of five, which included spokesmen for the various factions, was named to draw up an appropriate order in council which would grant the Beauharnois application but also secure any and all federal interests and rights on the St Lawrence.

The appointment of this cabinet committee entailed further delay and meant that the Beauharnois application would not be approved before parliament reconvened on 7 February 1929. King thought this delay was necessary, even though he knew there would be 'a difficult situation in Parliament ... where we will have a stormy time as Consv. will oppose. Ont. members will not be favourable, & Labour & Progs. probably join with Conservatives in alleged saving of assets of Dominion.'[26] The prime minister and his cabinet still had not made a final decision on the Beauharnois application, but they were moving towards a decision favourable to the Beauharnois interests.

The situation was further eased on 5 February when the Supreme Court of Canada handed down its long-awaited and several times delayed decision regarding the conflicting federal and provincial jurisdiction over the water in navigable streams. Mackenzie King read the judgment eagerly and with great care but lamented, 'I ... could not make head or tail of it.' He also read Chief Justice Duff's opinion, from which he got the impression that 'it is a very intricate and complicated business. But it seems to me we have been very wise to await this judgement & that it has made easier if not imperative granting to the Beauharnois Power Co. approval of its plans.'[27] The Supreme Court had, in fact, avoided a direct decision on the jurisdictional dispute, but it had stated clearly that the federal government had the right and the power to approve the construction of projects on navigable streams, such as those proposed by the Beauharnois company.

King apparently made up his mind to approve the Beauharnois application after reading the court decision. On the next day, still apprehensive but also well prepared, the prime minister addressed his cabinet. For the first time he declared his unequivocal support for the Beauharnois project. After the cabinet meeting he gratefully noted in his diary that 'I prayed very hard for guidance & I believe I was helped & able to give colleagues a clear view of the whole situation.'[28]

King had prepared his cabinet well, but parliament reconvened on 7 February. A.A. Heaps, the Labour member of parliament from Winnipeg North immediately gave notice that he intended to present a motion requiring parliamentary approval before any hydroelectric development and canalization of the St Lawrence were approved by the cabinet. Heaps was so eager that he announced his intentions even before the address in reply to the speech from the throne could be delivered.[29]

The real fight in parliament began on 19 February when Tommy Church, a Toronto member of parliament, moved an amendment to the Navigable Waters Protection Act. The amendment required parliamentary approval before any further works on navigable streams could be approved.[30] There was little debate on Church's motion. King was disappointed when J.C. Elliott did not rise to defend the government position. He was particularly concerned that Church's motion would put the Liberals in the position 'of appearing to disapprove of [parliamentary] control,' and regretted that he had not entered the debate. 'What I felt most was that I had in my head & before me on paper a complete reply which I could have made & which I believe would have saved a division. I should have stepped into the breach & I could have scored brilliantly if I had, as it was all my followers were "let down" so to speak, really the whole party was put in a false light by the neglect.'[31]

The prime minister would get his chance to debate the Beauharnois application, even though the Liberal majority defeated Church's first motion. Following that defeat, the irrepressible Tommy Church moved, on 21 February, that the government enter into immediate negotiations with the United States for the construction of 'a great St Lawrence waterway' and that the construction and operation of the canals be 'a public undertaking itself and the power incident herein should be developed and generated at cost by the government for the people under public ownership and not alienated to private interests.'[32] In the ensuing debate the prime minister became the leading government spokesman. King's two diary entries for 25 and 27 of February indicate how he viewed the debate.

> At 3 reached the H. of C. by 3:30 Church had concluded his speech and I followed immediately. I was not in the least nervous but was sort of 'fussed' up to a certain point, not at all as clear as I should be. I covered a lot of ground and did not forget many points was a little confused in one or two places, and did not give to what I was saying a clear-cut definiteness I should have. I might have done much better & yet I might have done much worse.[33]
>
> ...
>
> With all my heart I thank God for the power given me to speak today in the House of Commons, for the first time since I have been a member I have spoken for the most part to my satisfaction.[34]

The debate on the motion by Tommy Church got mixed up with a second motion by J.S. Woodsworth, who was concerned about proposals that the federal government would transfer natural resources in the prairie provinces to provincial governments, who might, in turn, alienate those resources to private developers. Woodsworth did not want such transfers to take place until they were ratified by parliament.[35] King tried to deal with both matters in his speeches.

During the debate the special cabinet committee, and then the entire cabinet, worked on the specific wording of the order in council authorizing the Beauharnois project. On 2 March King was pleased to note that the order in council 'seems to be in excellent shape, or rather we seem to have brought everything to the converging point where it can be approved without possibility of political injury.'[36] The parliamentary debate concluded on 6 March, the government using its parliamentary majority to defeat the motions by Church, Heaps, and Woodsworth. King noted that this had been the longest debate in some years on a single subject, and that 'the way is now paved for issuing approval [for] the Beauharnois lease.'[37]

The critically important order in council, PC 422, was approved two days later. J.C. Elliott made the necessary statement in the House of Commons, and the prime minister expressed his obvious relief that the matter had at last been resolved. He confided to his diary that 'It is a relief to have it out of the way. I think we prepared the ground well.'[38]

In Senator McDougald's Westmount mansion the lights burned late, and expensive champagne from France flowed freely that Friday evening of 8 March 1929. The federal order in council had just made millionaires of most of the imbibers.

The value of the charter and other rights of the Beauharnois Light, Heat and Power Company had increased greatly. Those assets and rights could now be either developed or sold. The Beauharnois promoters had won a crucial battle in which they had been pitted directly against the entrenched Montreal Power interests. But there were already rumours on St James Street that Montreal Power had other schemes afoot to protect its distribution monopoly.

5

Sir Herbert Holt insinuates himself

Federal order in council No. 422 was passed on 8 March 1929. It gave general approval to 'the plans and site of the proposed works' of the Beauharnois Light, Heat and Power Company. Together with the company's amended Quebec provincial charter, it constituted one of the company's most important and valuable documents. The order in council did not grant unrestricted rights or concessions; included were twenty-eight conditions which the company had to meet. Most of these conditions were directly related to the requirements of navigation on the St Lawrence. The order in council specifically stated that only the company's general plans and site selections had been approved. Many more detailed and specific plans had to be prepared by the company and submitted to federal engineers for approval before construction could begin: 'the company shall not commence the construction of the works until detailed plans of construction and all necessary information respecting the said works have been submitted to and approved of by the Minister [of Public Works], provided that such plans and information shall be submitted within one year.'[1] The order anticipated that there would be continuous governmental review and approval by the public works minister and the engineers in his department of all the company's plans and activities. Thus, although the Montreal Power interests had lost an important battle, the war was by no means over.

The opening shot in the next skirmish between the rival power interests was fired within the month. On 27 March 1929 the Cedars Rapids Manufacturing and Power Company, a company generating power in the Soulanges Section of the St Lawrence and owned by Montreal Power, filed an official document expressing concern that 'there would be some adverse effect on the plant of the Cedars Rapids Manufacturing and Power Company,' if the Beauharnois company proceeded. The appropriate clauses in the order in council requiring that the Beauharnois company submit detailed plans to the government before commencing construction were cited. The Cedars Rapids officials then asked 'that before detailed plans are approved our [Cedars Rapids, and thus indirectly Montreal Power] Engineers should be afforded the opportunity of examining them, and in particular the plans of the remedial works, so that they can offer such suggestions to you as may seem advisable with a view to minimizing the adverse effects upon the plant of the Cedars Company in so far as it may be practical.'[2] The potential for mischief and interminable delays inherent in this request was obvious, and past history indicated that Montreal Power had considerable expertise in such delaying and harassing tactics.

The Beauharnois promoters also had to consider another problem. They intended to make extensive use of electrical power in their construction program. The most convenient plant to supply that power was Cedars Rapids, or one of the other local generating plants controlled by Montreal Power. Sweezey and Jones were never particularly interested in competing or fighting with the Montreal Power interests. They were determined to develop their own site, which they believed would prove very profitable. When opposed in this by Montreal Power they fought back vigorously. And when they discovered that the promise of rigorous competition and lower power rates helped to get necessary concessions in Quebec City and Ottawa, they were willing to play up the theme of competition. But when asked later about the competitive stance of his company, R.O. Sweezey offered a weak explanation, which stands in sharp contrast to F.P. Jones's claim that Montreal Power was annually overcharging its customers the colossal sum of $30 million: 'Well, there was a feeling at the time, perhaps, that there might be too much of a power monopoly. I did not know what the idea was; but we thought it would be a good thing for the province of Quebec to develop that water-power in proximity to Montreal.'[3]

Once the Quebec amendment and the federal order in council were safely in hand, the enthusiasm of the Beauharnois promoters for a competitive battle with Montreal Power quickly dissipated. As already indicated, the Montreal Power interests had suggested a possible basis of accommodation before the federal order in council was approved.

Beauharnois president, F.P. Jones, thought the essential feature of that proposal was that Montreal Power obtain a one-third interest in his company, in return for which Montreal Power would withdraw its opposition to the Beauharnois application.

A second condition set out by Montreal Power was of far greater importance. The Montreal Power representatives offered to purchase a large block of Beauharnois power for $15 per horsepower at the Beauharnois bus bar. They also offered to assist in Beauharnois financing, but only if the Beauharnois officials agreed 'not to sell power on the Island of Montreal and at certain other points.'[4] These Montreal Power overtures in January 1929 had been rejected.

Immediately after the issuance of the order in council, discussions between the Beauharnois and Montreal Power interests resumed. Lord Beaverbrook, who had close business and personal relations with the major participants in both companies, served as facilitator and intermediary in these discussions. Jones and Sweezey were his protegés,[5] but Beaverbrook was also a business associate of Sir Herbert Holt. Those contacts were greatly strengthened when Holt's second son, Andrew, became Beaverbrook's private secretary and business partner in several European and British motion picture ventures. These investments complemented the interests of Famous Players Theatres of Canada, of which Sir Herbert was one of the key promoters.[6]

It was Frank Jones who first contacted Beaverbrook to solicit his assistance in coming to an agreement with Sir Herbert Holt. Neither Jones nor Beaverbrook had much use for competition that threatened the profits of their companies, and Jones even seemed willing to sell the entire Beauharnois venture to Holt if the price was right. He had, after all, just sold Canada Cement at an enormous profit to a syndicate headed by Sir Herbert Holt and J.H. Gundy.

The basic facts, obvious to all the businessmen involved, were simple. Montreal Power was primarily a hydroelectric distribution company which generated some of the power it distributed but also purchased power from other companies. Beauharnois wanted to build a huge and exceptionally efficient and therefore very profitable generating plant. Promises had already been made to Quebec politicians that Beauharnois power would be sold for not more than $15 per horsepower delivered at Beauharnois. The interests of the two companies were not mutually exclusive. There really was no reason why Beauharnois could not become a profitable generating company while Montreal Power retained its profitable distribution monopoly on the Island of Montreal.

Passage of the federal order in council strengthened the Beauharnois company, but it still had to dispose of its power. R.O. Sweezey's optimisitic promises of vast new industrial developments immediately ajacent to the power plant would inevitably take time to materialize. A contract to sell a large block of power to Montreal Power therefore made good sense, and in May 1929 Sweezey announced that 'Our aims for the future ... do not include the adoption of those unfriendly tactics which can only result in injury to some of the existing power companies, injuries to Beauharnois, and last, but more important, ultimate poor service and higher rates to the consumer ... There is no reason why we will not sell power to the Montreal Light, Heat and Power at prices which they cannot afford to ignore.'[7] Informal discussions between the two companies had begun early in 1929, before the federal order in council was approved. But there had not been much progress then. Price was not a serious problem. It cost Montreal Power considerably more than $15 per hoursepower to generate their own power. Buying at that price from Beauharnois therefore made good sense. The major obstacle to any agreement was Montreal Power's insistence that the Beauharnois promoters agree not to sell power to anyone else within Montreal Power's distribution area on Montreal Island.[8]

No one ever expected negotiations with Montreal Power to be easy. They seemed necessary, but Sweezey in particular was desperately afraid that he and his company would somehow be swallowed up by the Montreal Power octopus. Montreal Power's negotiating tactics included great patience, coupled with relentless harassment and effective financial, legal, political, and technological pressure. Time often seemed to be on its side. Sooner or later something that could be exploited always seemed to turn up. Until then, Montreal Power could afford to wait.

In this case Montreal Power did not have to wait long. In July 1929 something did indeed turn up, which substantially altered the balance between the two companies. The two main promoters of Beauharnois, Robert O. Sweezey and Frank P. Jones, quarrelled and had a serious falling-out which led to the abrupt withdrawal of Jones from the venture. The immediate issue in dispute between the two men concerned the best means to finance Beauharnois construction costs. Those costs were expected to exceed $50 million for the first phase. Construction was expected to take three years. Jones thought all the financing for the first phase of construction should be arranged at once.

Sweezey disagreed. Most of the money was not needed immediately, so why should the company issue construction bonds and pay interest on them for three years before the last of the money was needed? It would be much less expensive, Sweezey reasoned, to raise funds as they were required.

Specifically, Frank Jones wanted the company to issue $50 million or $55 million worth of first-mortgage construction bonds to finance the project. Sweezey thought the company should first negotiate major contracts for the sale of power. The income to be earned from those contracts should then be pledged as security for special construction bonds issued by the company. These special bonds would be called collateral trust bonds. The security behind them would be the income to be earned under contracts by the company to sell electric power. Only when additional funds were needed should the company issue its first-mortgage bonds, which would then be secured by the physical assets of the company.

Sweezey's plan was unusual, but it had two important advantages. The company would save substantial interest charges during the period of construction, and it would issue its junior securities first, leaving all the physical assets of the company intact for later financing. The first-mortgage bonds, secured by the company's physical assets, would have priority over the bonds issued against the security of the power contracts. This procedure was expected to enhance the appeal of the first-mortgage bonds when they were offered for sale. This arrangement also proved very confusing to investors, however, since companies normally issued their senior securities first.

Jones and Sweezey were deeply concerned about the unstable state of the financial markets during the summer and fall of 1929. Both expected that there would be a substantial contraction. Sweezey argued, correctly, that this would lead to significantly lower interest rates, while Jones, also correctly, insisted that a general financial contraction would make it more difficult to raise additional money required in the future. Jones therefore favoured complete financing immediately, even if it increased interest costs.[9] Sweezey was convinced that first mortgage bonds secured by the unencumbered physical assets of the company would remain readily saleable even if the financial markets weakened substantially.

A further point of disagreement between the two men had to do with the underwriting arrangements for the bonds. Sweezey wanted his own firm of Newman, Sweezey and Company, and the Dominion Securities

Corporation, to handle the entire issue of his proposed $30 million collateral trust bonds. He was willing to sell all these bonds to the two securities companies, both of which had been members of his earliest Beauharnois syndicate, at a 10 per cent discount, or $27 million net. In addition, he proposed that the underwriters be given substantial stock bonuses which they could keep or pass on to clients who purchased the bonds.

Jones was convinced the Beauharnois company could realize a better price for the bonds and gain much wider support for the project if all interested underwriters were allowed to bid on the bonds – including rivals such as J.H. Gundy and Herbert Holt. The proposed deal with Newman, Sweezey and Company, and Dominion Securities was not, Jones insisted, in the best interests of the Beauharnois company. There were also rumours, however, that if the underwriting arrangements, including the stock bonuses, were sold publicly, the Montreal Power interests would buy in, at least to the extent that one or more of their nominees could be placed on Beauharnois's board of directors. They would then have direct knowledge of that company's secrets and working problems. There were, in fact, rumours on the street that Jones's objections were nothing more than an attempt to turn over complete control to Montreal Power.[10]

A special general meeting of the Beauharnois company shareholders was called for 27 July 1929 to approve the financial arrangements, as proposed by Sweezey and his associates, who had the support of the majority of the company's directors. Prior to that meeting Jones, still the president of the company, and those who agreed with him wrote a letter to all the shareholders, urging the defeat of the financial proposals. A bitter proxy fight at the shareholders' meeting seemed likely.[11]

It did not come to that. The Jones letter did not bring in enough proxies to defeat Sweezey and his associates. Instead, Sweezey and Senator W.L. McDougald offered to buy out Jones and those associated with him. Jones later testified that he had personally invested a total of $190,000 and, together with the other directors, assumed a $100,000 contingent liability for his shares in the second Beauharnois syndicate. In July Sweezey and McDougald offered Jones and his associates a total of $3,795,000 in cash and bonds. Approximately $950,000 went directly to Jones, who thus made a net profit of approximately $750,000 out of his rather brief association with the Beauharnois syndicate.[12] He and his associates wanted the entire sum in cash. Sweezey, McDougald, and those connected with them did not have that much cash. But there was a ready source from which the needed funds could be obtained – at a price, of course. That source was Montreal Power, which had a substantial, profitable, and diversified investment portfolio.

Sweezey and his partners needed large sums of money quickly to buy out Jones and his associates. And they needed a firm contract to sell their power if Sweezey's proposed financing scheme was to succeed. Montreal Power had the money and a market for additional electricity. The time had come for Sweezey, McDougald, and associates to enter 'into an agreement to sell them 150,000 horse power and [to] bury the hatchet between one another about the end of July or the beginning of August.'[13] The resulting arrangements were rather tough and remained secret for several months. Montreal Power took over the shares formerly held by Jones and his associates at the same price Sweezey had agreed to pay to Jones. Montreal Power also agreed to a contract to take 150,000 horsepower per year from Beauharnois at a price not higher than $15 per horsepower delivered at Beauharnois. In addition, Montreal Power agreed to supply Beauharnois with power from its Cedars Rapids plant during construction, albeit at a price considerably higher than the $15 per horsepower. In return Beauharnois had to agree that it would sell no power within Montreal Power's distribution area, except to Montreal Power.[14]

These arrangements protected Montreal Power's distribution monopoly and provided it with needed additional power. It also gave Montreal Power representatives access to information on the internal working and operations of the Beauharnois company. Donat Raymond was correct when he informed the prime minister that 'Sir Herbert Holt does not lose any time fighting for vengeance or to help political parties once he has been beaten.'[15] Holt and Montreal Power had lost a battle when order in council 422 was passed in March of 1929. Within four months they had taken effective measures to ensure that the Beauharnois company would not threaten their distribution monopoly on the Island of Montreal.

It was nevertheless unfortunate that no one bothered to inform the Quebec premier of the new arrangements. Taschereau had based his support of the Beauharnois proposals on the promise of competition. The premier's biographer has suggested that Taschereau, who served on numerous corporate boards of directors, was only 'lightly duped' when the Beauharnois promoters failed to inform him that Sir Herbert Holt had secretly 'insinuated himself into the Beauharnois organization.'[16] Anyone familiar with the ways of big business and reading the financial papers during the summer of 1929 must have known that some arrangement between the Beauharnois and Montreal Power companies was being negotiated.

The agreement between the two power companies did not involve a change of control over the Beauharnois company. That remained firmly in the hands of R.O. Sweezey and his associates. An arrangement between the two companies was necessary and beneficial to both, but it did not consititute a complete amalgamation. Nor was there any real trust or good will between Sweezey and Holt. The former remained deeply suspicious. He had to do business with Montreal Power, but he was determined to take all possible precautions to ensure that the Montreal Power tycoons would not deprive him of the profits resulting from his promotion of the Beauharnois project.

Montreal Power never sought or demanded trust or affection. The important thing for the company was that the agreement provided it with cheap power and safeguarded its Montreal distribution monopoly. If Sweezey succeeded in building and operating the Beauharnois power plant, he would reap substantial profits. If, on the other hand, he and his associates got into any serious difficulty, Montreal Power was in a strong position not only to protect itself in any Beauharnois reorganization, but to participate directly and perhaps to dictate the terms of subsequent reorganizations. Montreal Power had at least a foot in Beauharnois's door. For the time being, however, Sweezey was in control and would make the major decisions.

The Beauharnois directors elected Sweezey president at the same meeting at which they accepted the resignation of Frank P. Jones. Immediately after his election Sweezey sought to counter various rumours circulating on the street, by stating publicly that he, not Montreal Power, controlled the Beauharnois project. He issued the following, partially correct, statement.

> There is to be no change in the already well-defined policies of the company. The interest in the undertaking held formerly by Mr. Frank P. Jones has been acquired by W.L. McDougald and myself. The policies which we shall pursue will assure the maintenance of the identity of the company, and will preclude the possibility of any change in the control of the undertaking; and will permit, insofar as possible, the ownership of the company to remain in the hands of those responsible for its initiation.[17]

In the midst of these stresses and strains the Beauharnois promoters were also able to complete another happier arrangement. They recognized that their project might damage the small generating plant of the Montreal Cottons Company. This company had located its major new mill near Valleyfield where it generated the necessary electricity. Its interests, however, were in textiles, not in electricity. The accommodation with Montreal Power made possible a new arrangement between Beauharnois and Montreal Cottons, since Herbert Holt was an influential director of Montreal Cottons.

The Montreal Cottons Company had the right to divert up to 13,000 cubic feet of water per second, but its generating facilities made inefficient use of the water. As a result, a contract between the Beauharnois Light, Heat and Power Company and the Montreal Cottons Company was negotiated. Under the terms of this contract Montreal Cottons subleased to the Beauharnois company its right to divert 13,000 cubic feet of water per second. Added to its own right to divert 40,000 cubic feet of water per second, the Montreal Cottons arrangement thus gave the Beauharnois company the use of 53,000 cubic feet of water per second. In return for this concession the Beauharnois company agreed to provide Montreal Cottons, free of charge, with the electricity it needed to operate its mill near Valleyfield.[18] This arrangement had to be approved by officials in the Department of Railways and Canals, but the Beauharnois promoters encountered little opposition in that regard. Montreal Power lobbyists were no longer opposing Beauharnois's plans.

With these arrangements completed, R.O. Sweezey and those associated with him were ready to commence construction. But they were also determined to reorganize the Beauharnois Light, Heat and Power Company in such a way that their control over the venture would be safeguarded. In addition, they could now begin the difficult task of raising the finances required to build the canal and powerhouse.

Preliminary construction work had in fact begun on the Beauharnois work site several days before the fight between Sweezey and Jones was resolved. The engineering work on the site was entrusted to the American engineering consulting firm of William States Lee of New York City and Charlotte, North Carolina.[19] Lee already had experience with large hydroelectric developments in Canada, having done the engineering work for the huge power project at Isle Maligne for the Duke and Price interests.[20]

The chief engineer directly in charge of the construction work and the man who wrote regular reports and memoranda on the progress of all aspects of construction was F.H. Cothran, another American associated with the W.S. Lee Engineering Corporation. Cothran's first 'Memorandum of Operations' was, coincidentally, dated 26 July 1929, which was the same day on which Sweezey bought out the Jones interests in the company. Cothran had arrived on the site several days earlier and had begun some of the surveying, the drilling of test holes, and the construction of the work camps.[21] This preliminary work on the site thus began almost three months before the official opening of construction on 12 October 1929, discussed in chapter 1. Beauharnois was, in fact, always further advanced in its engineering and construction work than it was in some of its other arrangements. Engineering and construction work, however, could not proceed very far unless the other essential arrangements were completed. Illustrative of that fact was the necessity of financing all survey and construction work from mid-July until the end of the year through short-term bank loans.

The arrangement with Montreal Power assured the Beauharnois company of income from the sale of 150,000 horsepower of electricity per year. That figure could be used as a basis for some of the financing along the lines proposed by Sweezey. But the Montreal Power contract alone was not large enough to meet operating costs and fixed charges on the collateral trust bonds Sweezey wanted to issue. In its first phase of development the Beauharnois company intended to build a plant capable of generating up to 500,000 horsepower per year. At least one and perhaps several other large power contracts were needed if Sweezey's financing plans were to succeed.

6

Ontario Tories make a deal

Passage of the coveted federal order in council in March of 1929, the fight with Frank Jones, the accommodation with Montreal Power, and the unofficial commencement of preliminary construction work on site all signified that Sweezey and his associates in the Beauharnois Power Corporation had overcome the most serious obstacles in their path and that their project would proceed. There were, however, several important matters still to be looked after. Specifically, two interrelated matters had not been finalized.

The financial arrangements necessary to pay the enormous construction costs had not been made, and the creation of a new corporate structure to safeguard the Beauharnois promoters' interests while providing for participation by Montreal Power representatives still had to be completed. These necessary arrangements, however, could proceed only if another important contract to sell Beauharnois power was negotiated. It was to the negotiation of such a contract that Sweezey devoted a great deal of attention in 1929, particularly after the events of July.

Sweezey, as explained earlier, hoped and expected to issue and sell as quickly as possible $30 million worth of collateral trust bonds. The security for these bonds was to be the income the company would receive from contracts for the sale of power. A contract for 150,000 horsepower per year had been negotiated with Montreal Power, but contracts for the sale of at least 400,000 horsepower were needed to generate sufficient income to pay operating costs and the interest and sinking fund charges for $30 million worth of collateral trust bonds.

There was in 1929 a serious shortage of electric power in Ontario. Sweezey hoped and expected to negotiate a contract with Ontario

Hydro similar to that negotiated with Montreal Power. He had opened preliminary discussions in Toronto as early as 1926, before even acquiring the charter of the Beauharnois company and long before the Montreal Power deal was finalized. Serious bargaining began after the federal order in council was approved.

The Ontario Hydro negotiations proved difficult. Ontario with its need for additional power was determined to block any major new power development unless that development also helped meet the province's needs. The Ontario politicians wanted the next major power project to be developed in the international section of the St Lawrence, or on the Ottawa River. But joint development with New York State in the international section, or with Quebec on the Ottawa River, seemed impossible because of the Ontario Conservative government's strong commitment to public ownership of Hydro and the equally strong opposition to public ownership by Quebec Liberals and New York state politicians.

Quebec could not, however, take too narrow a view of the power situation. Premier Taschereau of Quebec was officially opposed to all power exports from Quebec. He saw the development of hydroelectric projects in Quebec as a means of attracting new industries to that province. If the power were exported, new industries and jobs would also be established outside the province. Taschereau hoped and expected that the Beauharnois development would create a power surplus in Quebec that would attract many new industries to the province.

The Beauharnois promoters therefore had to spend a great deal of time in 1928 and 1929 placating the Quebec politicians, while negotiating with politicians and Hydro officials in Toronto. In Quebec they simply argued that both financially and politically their project could not proceed unless some accommodation was reached with Ontario. New industrial developments would take time, while funds for construction had to be provided immediately. They pointed out that the Beauharnois project would generate enough cheap electricity to permit extensive industrial development in Quebec. But some power had to be sold to Ontario in order to finance construction and to meet political requirements in that province. Premier Taschereau eventually agreed that it was better to develop Beauharnois than one of the alternative sites, even if some of the power then had to be exported to Ontario. He continued to insist that none of the power generated at Beauharnois be exported to the United States.

In Ontario the Beauharnois promoters had to deal with the public ownership issue. They did so in a fairly simple and effective way, arguing that the hydroelectric industry is naturally divided into three separate though interrelated parts – the generation, transmission, and distribution of electricity. There was no reason why a particular company must control all three functions. Beauharnois would be a generating company. As such it could both attract new industries because of low electricity costs and sell surplus power to other distributing companies, including publicly owned systems.

Ontario Hydro had allegedly been established in the early 1900s to resolve difficulties and inequities in the distribution and transmission of power by Toronto- and Hamilton-based private interests. There was no reason, however, why Ontario Hydro could not fulfil its distribution mandate if it purchased some of its power from privately owned generating companies, particularly if it could do so at rates lower than what it would cost for Ontario Hydro to generate its own power. The Ontario Hydro monopoly in the distribution of power would not be affected if it bought power from Beauharnois.

The discussions with Ontario politicans were lengthy and difficult. An informal understanding was reached, however, before the federal order in council was passed in March of 1929. Premier Ferguson of Ontario had even been persuaded to write directly to Premier Taschereau of Quebec, indicating that 'Beauharnois would seem to me to be a very convenient and favorable point' to meet Ontario Hydro's anticipated power requirements.[1] A copy of this letter was sent to the prime minister as part of the campaign to secure passage of the required federal order in council.

Immediately after the passage of the order Beauharnois and Ontario Hydro engineers and technical experts began the difficult work of drafting plans and terms for a contract between the two companies. But there were continuing difficulties because many of the Ontario Hydro officials were committed to public ownership and opposed any and all dealings with privately owned companies.[2] A satisfactory contract was, however, a precondition for the issue of Beauharnois's collateral trust bonds.

Initially the technical discussions between the two companies were informal, but on 5 June 1929 the Beauharnois directors appointed Frank Jones and Robert Sweezey to enter into official negotiations with Ontario Hydro.[3] Later documents state that 'after much discussion at a number of conferences, during which the details of the proposed agreements were discussed with the Beauharnois interests' a tentative agreement was reached and its terms set out in a letter, dated 10 June 1929, from Ontario Hydro to the Beauharnois Light, Heat and Power Company.[4] This tentative agreement called for the delivery of 35,000 horsepower of Beauharnois power on 1 October 1932, rising to 75,000 horsepower a year later, 129,000 horsepower on 1 October 1934, 196,000 horsepower on 1 October 1935, and finally 250,000 h.p. on 1 October 1936 and each year thereafter. The price was to be $15 per horsepower with the Beauharnois company agreeing to construct a transmission line from its generating plant to the Quebec-Ontario boundary.

The upheaval in the internal affairs of the Beauharnois company leading to the resignation of Frank Jones in July of 1929 inevitably delayed the finalization of the contract with Ontario Hydro, which required the concurrence of the provincial government. Premier Ferguson and Robert Sweezey agreed that the terms of this proposed contract, as outlined in the Ontario Hydro letter, were satisfactory. The issue became politically sensitive in Ontario, however, and was further complicated by the fact that the Ferguson administration was seriously thinking of calling an early provincial election. Sensing that the prosperous economic conditions during the summer of 1929 might not last much longer, and eager to take advantage of confusion and disorganization among the provincial Liberals, Premier Ferguson took the plunge and dissolved the legislature on 16 September 1929, setting 30 October as the election date.[5] That, as it later turned out, was only one day before the worst day in the disastrous Wall Street crash in New York.[6]

It is always difficult to transact major government business in the midst of a corporate upheaval or an election campaign, and doubly so if the business to be transacted is controversial and involves large sums of money. Yet, the Beauharnois promoters absolutely had to have a contract for the sale of their power. Otherwise Sweezey's plans for the financing of the project had to be radically altered. If the contract were not signed before the provincial election and, heaven forbid, the Conservatives were to lose that election, Sweezey and his friends would be in serious trouble. The provincial Liberals had come out in opposition to the proposed contract.

In the meantime Beauharnois's construction expenses were mounting rapidly. A consortium of three banks – the Bank of Commerce, the Bank of Montreal, and the Royal Bank – had agreed, after the passage of the federal order in council and the accommodation with Montreal Power, to advance the required funds, provided the promoters gave their personal guarantees for the repayment of the funds thus advanced. If anything went seriously wrong with the financing arrangements, it would be possible for the banks, perhaps with encouragement from Montreal Power, to put on a squeeze which would force Sweezey and his associates to 'sell their assets for a song.'[7]

Throughout the provincial election campaign the negotiations between Beauharnois Light, Heat and Power, and Ontario Hydro proceeded at a snail's pace – until the last few days. In later testimony Senator Andrew Haydon, lawyer and political agent with very close connections to Beauharnois, testified that Premier Ferguson refused to allow any contract to be signed between Beauharnois and Ontario Hydro until he was paid $200,000.[8] In addition, John Aird, Jr, the son of Sir John Aird, the president and former general manager of the Bank of Commerce 'gave him [Sweezey] to understand it was essential or highly desireable that he make a large contribution to the Ontario Conservative party if the contract with the Hydro Commission was to go through.'[9]

John Aird, Jr, was known to be one of the key fund-raisers for the Ontario Conservative party and had already extracted a political contribution or levy of 50 cents per horsepower from other power companies that were negotiating to sell power to Ontario Hydro.[10] Sweezey was a director of at least one of those other companies and thus knew what was expected. According to later testimony by both Sweezey and H.B. Griffith, Beauharnois's secretary, Aird initially demanded a contribution of $1 per horsepower, or $250,000, in a meeting he had with Sweezey and Griffith in the Ritz Carlton Hotel in Montreal.[11] Some rather vigorous negotiations ensued, and it was eventually agreed that a contribution of 50 cents per horsepower, or $125,000, would be satisfactory. This sum was in addition to the $200,000 demanded by Ferguson. Both Sweezey and Griffith were absolutely convinced that the $125,000 levy was to be a contribution to the Ontario Conservative party election campaign. Sweezey later referred to it as a 'tax' but admitted it was not a tax authorized by any provincial statute.[12] Several persons later stated that they had heard Sweezey complain that 'Ferguson has just stuck me for $325,000.'[13]

Sweezey was neither surprised nor offended by these demands. He believed they were part of the cost of doing business with governments: 'I knew that all parties in all provinces, and the federal governments as well, look for contributions; I knew sooner or later we would get a request in some form from Ontario ... I was doing it as a form of habit, which unfortunately has developed in this country, in every province, and in every political party. I was the victim of a condition for which I was not responsible.'[14] Sweezey was nevertheless unhappy with the Ontario demands because they came at a particularly difficult time for him and his associates. Their company had begun construction, was borrowing very heavily, but was not yet able to do any of its planned long-term financing. The delays in arranging its finances in fact led to a very serious financial crisis on 13 October 1929, when the banks threatened to stop all further advances unless a more satisfactory arrangement was made quickly.[15] Any payment to the Ontario Tories in October 1929 had to come directly from the promoters. The Beauharnois company had no funds and had exhausted its credit at the banks.

Sweezey was astute enough to insist that no money would be paid to Aird and the Ontario Conservative party until the Ontario Hydro contract was safely signed, sealed, and delivered.[16] As a result, following the first meeting with Aird in Montreal, there were further meetings in late October, just before the provincial election, in a suite Sweezey and Griffith rented at the Royal York Hotel. There, on 28 October less than two days before the provincial election, the parties came to an agreement. A document outlining the terms was drawn up and then taken over to the Ontario Hydro offices where it was duly signed. It was later suggested that throughout these discussions 'Mr. John Aird Jr. was so closely in touch with you [Sweezey] that he was in your room at the hotel almost as soon as you and Griffith got back there from signing in the Hydro office.'[17] Forty-eight hours later Howard Ferguson and his Conservatives were re-elected with the largest majority in Ontario history. The smooth and well-financed election campaign earned the premier the dubious title of 'Boss Ferguson.' And Beauharnois had a contract to sell up to 250,000 horsepower of electricity to Ontario Hydro.

The agreement of 28 October 1929 between Beauharnois Light, Heat and Power and Ontario Hydro was legally binding and allowed the company to proceed with its financing plans. Many terms of the contract had been drawn up in great haste, however, and a number of important matters still had to be settled. There was particular trouble about the construction of the necessary eighteen-mile transmission line from the Beauharnois powerhouse to the Ontario-Quebec boundary.

The early proposals had provided that the Beauharnois company should build the transmission line to the border, but at some point Ontario Hydro officials insisted that it was their policy to own the entire transmission system. This approach, however, ran counter to policies of the provincial government of Quebec which, as a matter of principle, was opposed to the notion 'that the Ontario Government own anything in the Province of Quebec.'[18]

Aside from this constitutional impasse there was the further problem that Ontario Hydro used three-phase 20-cycle power, while Montreal Power and most of the other Quebec power companies used single-phase 60-cycle power. Beauharnois would have to generate both and was in fact planning two quite different generating systems to meet the requirements of its two dissimilar contracts. There was a fear at Ontario Hydro, however, that Beauharnois lacked adequate engineering expertise and experience to meet the requirements of its system. It wanted Ontario Hydro engineers to be involved, at Beauharnois's expense.

All these items entailed additional costs, and even after it was agreed that Beauharnois would own the transmission line which would be built under the supervision of Ontario Hydro engineers, there were disputes about who should pay for various costs. A total of $600,000 to $700,000 was involved, most if not all of which would be payable by Beauharnois if the terms of the agreement reached by the engineers of the two companies in early June of 1929 were interpreted in a rigorous manner. The terms of the agreement signed on 28 October 1929, were less precise and gave rise to further negotiations.[19] In the end a compromise was reached, under which Beauharnois was required to pay $400,000. Lawyers later suggested, but were prevented by the chairman of the inquiry commission from introducing any evidence to substantiate their claims, that the settlement at $200,000 less than required under the earlier agreement was made in order to permit a special payment which Sweezey allegedly made directly to Premier Ferguson.[20] The limited evidence presented later indicated that Sweezey had transferred bonds he owned, with a par value of $194,000, to Ferguson or one of his emissaries. With accrued interest the bonds were worth $200,000. That transaction apparently took place before the provincial election, while the additional $125,000 demanded by John Aird, Jr, was paid only after the election.

The final negotiations between the Beauharnois company and Ontario Hydro were successfully concluded on 29 November 1929, when an appropriate provincial order in council approved the signing of an operating contract between Ontario Hydro and the Beauharnois Light, Heat and Power company. The contract was signed the next day.[21] Within a day or two of the signing of this contract, Sweezey in Montreal received a telephone call from John Aird, Jr, demanding payment of the promised $125,000. Sweezey had steadfastly refused to pay until all details of the Ontario Hydro contract were settled in a satisfactory manner. Aird's approach, according to Sweezey, 'was one of persuasion, and not of a threat – or something between a threat and persuasion.'[22] Sweezey asked for time, but Aird was insistent. Sweezey described his situation thus:

> It was not the consideration so much as the fact that funds were not plentiful with us at the time. We were financing by taking money out of our own pockets and we had incurred expenses of about $6,000,000 on our construction. We started in August or July, and this was about the end of November, and all the money we were getting was coming in by bank loans with personal endorsations, and any money we gave out we liked to scrutinize very carefully, and we were not inclined to suggest payments of anything until we knew our project was ready to proceed without interruption and at that time we had a great deal of nervousness about being able to carry on.[23]

Sweezey was particularly concerned about the state of the financial markets in Toronto and New York following the catastrophic stock market crash. He later recalled that 'The financial crash, so-called, had occurred in October and November, and on the 13th of October we had the worst kind of financial disturbance, and then our contract [with Ontario Hydro] was signed, or agreed to about the end of November, and we were gravely in doubt of whether we could finance it until spring.'[24]

John Aird's demand for immediate payment of $125,000 during the first week of December was, therefore, only a small part of Robert Sweezey's worries: 'When he [John Aird, Jr] appeared, I believe I felt that we had been successful, and the thing would go ahead without trouble, and if he was satisfied with $125,000 I could act right away, but if he wanted more I would have to put him off.'[25] Aird was willing to take the $125,000, which was delivered to him in the form of Canadian victory bonds owned by Sweezey personally. Since these victory bonds did not quite come to the $125,000 total, Aird was also given a cheque in the amount of $857.84 to complete the transaction.

This cheque was simply made payable 'to bearer' and Aird immediately gave it 'to a friend of mine down there and he gave me his check.'[26] The friend was bank teller D.T. Main of the Bank of Commerce who cashed the cheque without any endorsement by Aird. John Aird, Jr, was, after all, the son of the bank's president. When asked later why this devious procedure was used, John Aird could think of no good reason other than 'Well, it was a very jolly time we were having afterwards.'[27] The bonds taken by Aird were apparently stuffed rather hurriedly and loosely into his vest pocket, prompting the Beauharnois officials to warn, in a somewhat jocular tone, that he had better take care to ensure that the bonds not be lost.[28]

Getting the Ontario Hydro contract signed had been absolutely necessary, but expensive. Since the negotiations coincided with a provincial election, the Beauharnois company was expected to make substantial contributions to the election campaign of the provincial Conservatives. Sweezey made the necessary promises but refused to pay Aird until he had in hand the provincial order in council approving the Ontario Hydro contract.

The date and circumstances of the payment of $200,000 to Premier Ferguson, or one of his emissaries, are much more difficult to establish, but Sweezey later took great care to point out that he had not paid any money before there was a contractual agreement. This fact, he believed, proved there had been no bribery. But he readily admitted that throughout the latter part of 1929 he had kept in close contact with the provincial politicians, and that he had taken particular care 'to keep Aird interested and hopeful.'[29]

Later federal and Ontario inquiry commissions refused to hear any evidence respecting the $200,000 payment Sweezey allegedly made to Premier Ferguson. A detailed examination of the financial statements of the various Beauharnois companies does not shed a great deal of additional light on the subject, other than that such a payment was made to a person or persons not further identified. Premier Ferguson, of course, later denied everything. In a carefully worded statement he insisted, 'I personally know nothing. I never heard from anybody directly or indirectly that Beauharnois, or anybody connected with it, ever made any contribution to any Conservative organization ... I never had anything to do with the arranging of finances for elections or anything of that sort.'[30]

Careful study of Ferguson's private papers does not reveal anything further about this alleged $200,000 payment. The papers do, however, flatly contradict Ferguson's claim that he never had anything to do with party or campaign finances. The payment made to John Aird was fully investigated later, but attempts by lawyers to introduce evidence regarding the payment to Ferguson were consistently ruled inadmissible.

Sweezey and his Beauharnois partners allegedly paid $325,000 for the contract with Ontario Hydro. Even at that price, they made a profitable bargain. The Ontario Hydro contract provided the Beauharnois company with assured annual payments of $3,750,000 from Ontario Hydro, after a five-year phase-in period. What was a paltry one-time 'tax' of $325,000 when compared with such numbers, especially if at least $200,000 in costs that should have been paid by Beauharnois would now be paid instead by Ontario Hydro? This, moreover, was only the first stage of a development that was expected, ultimately, to generate 2 million horsepower per year. At $15 per horsepower, the Beauharnois company would earn $30 million annually. Sweezey estimated that it would cost between $100 and $125 per horsepower to develop the first 500,000 horseower at Beauharnois, and only $65 per horsepower to develop the remaining 1.5 million horsepower. The potential profits if all this power could be sold at $15 per horse power were enormous. Without the Ontario Hydro contract, further development at Beauharnois would have been impossible in the last months of 1929.

7

A 'poison pill' and collateral trust bonds

The signing of the preliminary Ontario Hydro contract on 28 October 1929 made possible a long-delayed corporate reorganization and the issuance of the bonds to finance construction costs. That reorganization had obviously been worked out some time previously. It only awaited successful contract negotiations with Ontario Hydro and was officially approved three days after the signing of the preliminary Ontario Hydro contract at the end of October 1929. The bonds, although issued only in November, were officially dated 1 October 1929. The terms under which the bonds would be issued had been approved at the tumultuous shareholders' meeting of 26 July at which Frank Jones withdrew from the company.

The corporate reorganization, consummated on 31 October 1929, was fairly simple, with one unusual, innovative, and later troublesome feature. Like many other businessmen involved in a range of economic activities, the members of the second Beauharnois syndicate decided that it would be most appropriate if they created separate operating companies for the various aspects of their work and a central holding company which would own and control the subsidiary operating companies. Thus a new parent or holding company, the Beauharnois Power Corporation, was created. A federal charter for this new company was obtained quickly and without difficulty. The old Beauharnois Light, Heat and Power Company would continue to serve as the operating company for the hydroelectric generating works. A new provincially chartered company, the Beauharnois Construction Company, would be responsible, under contract with the Beauharnois Light, Heat and Power Company, for the construction of the canal and powerhouse. Any land needed for the project would be acquired, owned, and developed by another new company, the Beauharnois Land Company. Since construction plans called for a construction railway running the length of the proposed canal on both sides, another new company, the Beauharnois Railway Company, was incorporated, with responsibility for managing and owning the new railway. Yet another new company, the Beauharnois Transmission Company, was incorporated to build, own, and operate the transmission lines from the powerhouse to points where the power would be used or delivered to purchasers.

All the shares of the subsidiary companies were held by the Beauharnois Power Corporation Limited. Each of the subsidiary companies could acquire its own assets and incur its own liabilities, including the sale of its own bonds and debentures. Each subsidiary company could also enter contractual obligations in its own right. The division and assignment of various functions at Beauharnois to separate companies did not significantly affect the construction program or later operations. None of the subsidiary companies, except Beauharnois Light, Heat and Power, issued and sold its own bonds.

In the reorganization of 31 October 1929 the main focus of attention was the new federally chartered Beauharnois Power Corporation, which might well be described as the third Beauharnois syndicate. According to the by-laws of the Beauharnois Power Corporation, its capital stock consisted of five management preferred shares, 1,799,995 Class 'A' common shares, and 3,200,000 Class 'B' common shares, all without nominal value.[1]

The capital structure of the Beauharnois Power Corporation had one innovative and very unusual feature, which was specifically designed to thwart any hostile take-over of the company for the next ten years. Sweezey and his associates feared that Montreal Power would try to gain control of their company, and they devised a powerful 'poison pill' to hold the Montreal Power interests at bay. The 'poison pill' came in the form of the Beauharnois Power Corporation's five management preferred shares. These shares were indistinguishable from the company's class 'A' common shares in all but one important regard. The holders of the five management preferred shares had the exclusive right, for a period of ten years, to elect all the directors of the company. All five of the management preferred shares were held by Sweezey and his associates, who could not be forced against their will to give them up.[2] Even if Montreal Power acquired a majority of the company's shares, it would not be able to name any of the directors. The arrangement demonstrated the paranoia of the original Beauharnois promoters as they prepared to do business with Montreal Power.

Aside from the exclusive power vested in the holders of the five management shares to vote for the election of the company's directors, the capital structure of the new Beauharnois Power Corporation was similar to that of many other companies. The only notable distinction between the class 'A' common shares and the class 'B' common shares was that holders of the former could vote on matters other than the election of the directors. The class 'B' common shares were non-voting.

The way in which the promoters of the Beauharnois Power Corporation, all members of the second Beauharnois syndicate, allocated the shares of the company was probably also conventional, though very profitable and therefore the subject of much controversy later. In the language of the street, the promoters cut a melon when they organized and allocated the shares of the Beauharnois Power Corporation.

It was agreed that the Beauharnois Power Corporation would acquire all the holdings of members of the second Beauharnois syndicate for a cash price of $4,750,000, and to assume all liabilities and contingent obligations of the syndicate. In addition the Beauharnois Power Corporation would provide $10,000 to pay for the costs of winding up the syndicate. Members of the syndicate would then have the right to purchase up to 1 million class 'A' common shares at a price of $1 per share. Since the anticipated market value of the class 'A' shares was much higher, all members of the syndicate immediately exercised that option, the result being that the syndicate members were relieved of all their former obligations and liabilities, obtained 1 million class 'A' common shares of the Beauharnois Power Corporation and pocketed $3,750,000 in cash.[3]

The legal organization of the Beauharnois Power Corporation actually took place on 30 September 1929, a month before the Ontario Hydro contract was signed. That legal organization, however, was officially transacted by individuals who can only be described as proxies or 'dummy directors.' Each of five secretaries and clerks from the Ottawa law offices of Haydon and Ebbs officially held one management preferred share 'in trust.' At least one of these later said she was completely unaware that her name had been used in this way. It was a legal convenience, although these 'dummy directors' approved the company by-laws and the agreement to take over the assets and liabilities of the second Beauharnois syndicate.[4]

The first real directors were named on 5 November 1929 when Miss

M.H. Kelly, president, and Miss Lyla Brennan, secretary, resigned, and Robert Sweezey and Hugh B. Griffith were appointed to fill those two positions. This act was followed on 20 December 1929 by the election, by the holders of the management preferred shares, of the first full eleven-member slate of directors.[5] Robert Sweezey, W.L. McDougald, and Hugh B. Griffith were obvious candidates, as were A.F. White from Dominion Securities and J.P. Ebbs from the company's law firm. Lawyers G.H. Montgomery, Aimé Geoffrion, and J.P. Paradis, all of whom had been associated with the original promoters for many years, were also named directors.

The first full slate of directors of the Beauharnois Power Corporation also included three men who were prominently identified with the Montreal Power interests, and had until July of 1929 been bitter enemies of Sweezey's project. These three were J.H. Gundy, investment broker and partner with Sir Herbert Holt in numerous undertakings, Sévére Godin, Herbert Holt's former chauffeur, who had become a confidant and sometime partner of the Montreal Power president, and Morris W. Wilson, general manager of the Royal Bank of Canada, of which Sir Herbert Holt was president.

The composition of this new board of directors shows the significant changes that had occurred in the affairs of the Beauharnois syndicate. At the beginning of the year Frank P. Jones was president of the Beauharnois Light Heat and Power Company, with Vice-President Robert Sweezey wielding the real power in the company in which Senators Raymond, McDougald, and Haydon were also prominent. Then the promoters still spoke confidently of offering effective competition to the hostile Montreal Power interests.

By year's end Jones was gone, as was Donat Raymond, who had sided with Jones but who would later regret that action and reacquire an equivalent number of shares in the new company. Haydon and McDougald had supported Sweezey, who had become president and still exercised effective control. But they had been obliged to reach an accommodation with the Montreal Power interests. Montreal Power was still only a junior partner, protecting its distribution monopoly in Montreal, but Sweezey was convinced that its real objectives were sinister. He later told the parliamentary inquiry, 'I think what they [Montreal Power] were trying to do ultimately was to ... pick up our assets for a song. I think that was what was in the minds of those who were opposing us.'[6] Sweezey obviously did not trust the Montreal Power people and still boasted that if Montreal Power wanted to pick up the Beauharnois assets for a song 'they would have to get Caruso to sing that song.'[7]

The first major business to be transacted by the new Beauharnois Power Corporation after its formal organization was to approve the issue of $30 million thirty-year 6 per cent collateral trust sinking fund bonds. Proceeds from the sale of these bonds would provide the funds to repay the bank loans, pay the $4,750,000 due the syndicate members, defray construction costs, and meet other immediate financial requirements of the company.

The terms on which these collateral trust sinking fund bonds were to be issued had been discussed in detail at the meeting on 26 July 1929. The securities firms of Newman, Sweezey and Company and the Dominion Securities Corporation were willing to purchase the entire $30 million issue. Delays in the negotiations with Ontario Hydro and severe stock market problems during the last months of 1929 cast doubt on the ability of the securities companies to complete the transaction. But after the contract with Ontario Hydro was signed on 30 November 1929, the promoters and their financiers decided that, despite the depressed state of the financial markets, they should go ahead with their proposed new bond issue. The arrangements for the issue of the bonds were completed on 4 December 1929, although the bonds were officially dated 1 October 1929 to match the 1 October dates on which the power contracts with Ontario Hydro and Montreal Power were to be phased in. Interest and sinking fund payments on the bonds were carefully co-ordinated with the terms of those two power contracts.[8] The various legal and trust arrangments and documents under which these bonds would be handled or administered were not completed, however, until 17 December 1929.[9]

The entire bond issue of $30 million was immediately sold to the two securities firms, together with 750,000 class 'A' common shares, in accordance with the arrangement made immediately after the disagreement between Jones and Sweezey in July of 1929. The two securities companies paid $27 million net, in cash, for these bonds and stocks. This money was expected to meet the company's financial requirements until the end of 1930. The promoters planned that early in 1930 the subsidiary operating company, the Beauharnois Light, Heat and Power Company, would bring out a sufficiently large first mortgage bond issue to provide for all remaining construction costs in the first phase of the company's development.

Newman Sweezey and Company and the Dominion Securities

Corporation quickly obtained a participation by a number of other Canadian financial houses, including Wood Gundy and Co. This enlarged financial consortium then began to advertise the Beauharnois bonds in the business press.[10] The financiers had paid $27 million for bonds with a par value of $30 million and 750,000 class 'A' common shares. In December of 1929 they offered the bonds to the public at par, but as an inducement they also offered a bonus of five class 'A' common shares with the purchase of every $1,000 bond. These shares, however, would not be delivered to the purchaser of the bond until 1 October 1932, the date on which the Beauharnois Light, Heat and Power Company would begin its delivery of power to Ontario Hydro and Montreal Power. A further inducement to prospective purchasers of the bonds was the issue of a warrant that entitled the purchaser of each $1,000 bond to buy twenty class 'B' common shares at $35 per share. This option could be exercised at any time between 1 October 1932 and 1 October 1937.

Official company documents stated clearly that the security for these collateral trust bonds, issued by the parent Beauharnois Power Corporation, was the income to be obtained from the Beauharnois Light, Heat and Power Company's contracts with Ontario Hydro and Montreal Power. The documents also stated clearly that the subsidiary Beauharnois Light, Heat and Power Company still had the right to issue up to $50 million of first mortgage bonds, the security for those bonds being the powerhouse, canal, and other physical assets of the subsidiary company. Contrary to later claims by disgruntled investors, the documentation available at the time the bonds were issued clearly indicated that these were the junior securities of the company. The *Financial Times* advised its readers, long before any serious trouble developed, that

> Beauharnois Power bonds, being only a collateral trust issue, could not be classified as a high grade investment, but in the light of the company's prospects and the fact that the bulk of the initial production of 500,000 h.p. has already been contracted for at favourable rates, the security constitutes a somewhat attractive business man's investment, offering a healthy yield. At the present time there is very little equity behind the common stock, which cannot be classified as other than speculative, but the profit possiblities in the junior securities are very much greater than on the bonds.[11]

This cautious endorsement was not typical of the response of the business press to the new bond issue. In December, when the bonds were first offered to the public, the general reaction was enthusiastic. Typical of that reaction was the headline in the *Financial Times* on 6 December 1929 announcing that 'Big Beauharnois Issue has many bright features' and then going on to say that 'In the light of the fact that the corporation has already contracted for four-fifths of its initial development the yield of 6% is a generous one apart from the bonus of 5 shares of "A" stock which is given with each $1,000 bond and the purchase of warrants for 20 shares of Class "B."'[12]

The promoters of the Beauharnois Power Corporation had thus seemingly overcome the three remaining obstacles to immediate and speedy construction of their canal and powerhouse. The terms of the Ontario Hydro contract were agreed to on 28 October, and a comprehensive contract was signed a month later. The loosely organized second Beauharnois syndicate had sold all its assets to the reorganized Beauharnois Power Corporation and the $30 million (par value) collateral trust bonds had been issued and sold. The promoters had great confidence in their engineering plans and designs, and in the competence of their American contractors. The disruptions on the stock market had not prevented the sale of their junior securities at a good price. The onset of the depression promised to reduce both labour and material costs, while the income the company would earn from its power contracts with Montreal Power and Ontario Hydro was fixed. And the promoters had prescribed an effective 'poison pill' which would prevent Montreal Power or other predatory capitalists from taking over the Beauharnois company which was expected to earn large profits. Construction could now proceed at full speed, and well below projected costs.

8

Realizing the dream

The year 1930 was probably the busiest and happiest in Robert Oliver Sweezey's life. He was masterminding the administrative, financial, political, and technical aspects of an enormous construction program. The project he had dreamed about for years was becoming reality and would stand as a permanent tribute to his vision, energy, and talent. It was also an undertaking that promised fabulous financial returns and was expected to foster new industrial developments which would provide at least 2 million new jobs for Canadians, while also providing enough electrical energy to do menial tasks that would otherwise require the labour of an additional 4 million men.[1]

Workmen first moved onto the site of the Beauharnois Power Corporation in late July 1929 to do preliminary surveying, testing, and planning and to begin construction of the first of five large camps. Those camps would eventually accommodate the 2,500 workers, most of whom were expected to arrive in the spring and summer of 1930.[2] Other work in 1929 included the clearing of the area of the proposed works. The larger trees were cut down and the trunks sawed into rough lumber and sold. The Beauharnois promoters were not prepared to overlook opportunities to earn additional profits from various subsidiary operations connected with the larger construction program.

In order to understand the subsequent construction program it is necessary to outline in some detail the engineering plans and construction methods, and schedules of the company and its contractors. Those plans, methods and schedules were certainly daring and innovative. The most notable feature was the construction of a 15.5-mile-long power canal. This canal was to be 3,000 feet wide, with a 27-foot-deep ship channel. Initially the ship channel would be 300 feet in width, but that span would be increased to 600 feet when the entire flow of the river was diverted through the new canal. Water would move through the canal at a maximum velocity of 2.25 feet per second.

It was estimated that approximately 30 million cubic yards of earth, gravel, and rock would have to be excavated or moved to complete the canal, the powerhouse, the tailrace, various feeder canals, and the control and remedial works. For long distances the construction of the canal entailed not only excavation, but also the erection of massive dikes. At the Lake St Francis end the dikes were low but gradually increased to a maximum height of forty-five feet in the vicinity of the powerhouse forebay.[3]

In order to do the necessary excavating and dredging work the company used three types of earth- and rock-moving machines. At the upper end of the canal, near Valleyfield, Quebec, and subsequently along the length of most of the canal, the company put into service an enormous suction dredge – reportedly the largest of its kind in the world. This dredge, like most of the other excavating equipment, was assembled on site. It was equipped with a spiral cutter, seven feet in diameter, which could be raised or lowered and rotated to cut the appropriate channel at the correct depth and of appropriate width. This spiral cutter was powered by a 300 horsepower motor. The material dislodged by the spiral cutter, including rocks up to eighteen inches in diameter, was then pumped through a pipeline, twenty-six inches in diameter, to the top of the canal dike. The pump was powered by a 2,200 horsepower induction motor and moved a mixture consisting of about one-third solid materials and two-thirds water.

Before the dredge could begin its work, huge excavation shovels had to throw up three parallel dikes along both sides of the entire length of the new canal. The first two dikes on each side of the canal were raised to the level of the proposed dike when they were completed. The area between them created the first settling basin into which materials were pumped by the suction dredge. Ultimately this settling basin was to be filled entirely to form a wide, finished dike. Some 600 feet behind what would ultimately be the finished dike, a supplementary dike was built to create a second-stage settling basin which was filled with the overflow from the main settling basins.

This second settling basin, it was expected, would eventually form a raised area on which new industries using Beauharnois power could establish themselves. The Beauharnois promotors expected to sell that raised land behind the main dikes on both sides of their power canal at attractive prices. They had been successful in persuading the Quebec government to pass an expropriation bill which enabled them to acquire more than 36,000 acres adjacent to the canal. The Beauharnois Land Company held and proposed to develop much of this property for industrial use. A residential development was also anticipated, again on lands expropriated by the Beauharnois companies.[4]

The suction dredge had the capacity to move 1,100 cubic yards of solid material per hour and to advance up to 200 feet per day along the 300-foot-wide ship channel. Later, in one particularly good month, it reportedly moved 820,000 cubic yards of material. Operations, once the dredge was assembled, continued twenty-four hours a day. There were stops only for essential servicing and repairs, and on Sundays, during the spring, summer, and autumn months of operations. It was one of the marvels of the day to see the huge dredge, whose main booms stood as high as a five-storey building, moving relentlessly through the green and swampy countryside or across roads and railway tracks, cutting its canal channel and leaving in its wake an incredible mess of settling residue in what would be the main dikes, and in the 600-foot-wide settling basins on either side of the main dikes. The main canal, its dikes, and lateral settling basins were nearly a mile in width and initially had the appearance of an enormous and weeping open incision through the hitherto quiet and lush agricultural countryside.

The suction dredge, however, could pump its muddy mess only into settling basins already built by other excavation equipment. The main machines that built the dikes were a fleet of draglines and five huge tower excavators. The tower excavators were designed to move laterally on specially constructed tracks, the tail of the tower being some 800 feet from the middle of the canal. Each of the tower excavators was equipped with a ten-cubic-yard bucket with which soil, rocks, and debris were scooped up and placed in the canal embankments and dikes. Each of the tower excavators weighed 550 tons, with the bucket or dipper alone weighing 30 tons. The buckets had a sixty-five-foot lift and were similar to the excavating equipment developed for levee work on the lower Mississippi River.

Over the space of approximately one mile of the route of the canal there were large boulders and heavy clay which could not be handled by the suction dredge. Here two huge electric draglines were put to work to do the required excavation. The material thus excavated was used to rip rap, or establish a foundation of broken stone on, the inner sides of the canal.

At the eastern end of the project, at and below the site of the proposed powerhouse and tail race, there was solid rock. Large quantities of that rock had to be excavated, but there was an excellent base for the foundations of the new generating facilities. That was the location at which the governor-general fired the first blast on 12 October 1929. Many more dynamite blasts would be needed to dislodge large quantities of rock which were then excavated by a special electrical 'Marion shovel,' also assembled on site. This excavating machine had thirteen separate motors, each with its own special functions. The larger of these provided the power to lift and rotate a huge eight-cubic-yard shovel or bucket. Those who saw this machine at work later would marvel at how quickly and efficiently it could clear away the rubble created by successive dynamite blasts.

This equipment was powered by electricity generated at the Cedars Rapids plant, which the Beauharnois company obtained under a contract from Montreal Power. There were also a number of smaller draglines and excavating machines, some of which were gas powered and used for smaller and specialized tasks. The smaller excavating machines could also be moved if one of the larger machines failed at a critical point. It was the huge suction dredge, the tower excavators, and the specialized electric 'Marion shovel' at the powerhouse and tailrace sites, however, that attracted most attention from the professional engineers and numerous visitors who came to the site during the construction period.

The heavy excavating and dredging equipment reportedly cost the Beauharnois Company more than $4 million. Official estimates in 1929 placed the cost of the power canal alone at $16 million. The total cost of completing the first phase of construction to permit the generation of 500,000 horsepower was initially estimated at $50–$55 million, but that figure was increased in 1931 to $65 million or $130 per horsepower developed.[5]

Another very interesting aspect of the proposed Beauharnois construction program was the special construction railway which ran parallel to, or, more accurately, on top of the dikes on both sides of the canal for its entire length. More than forty miles of track were to be laid, on which ten locomotives, ten flat cars, and sixty dump cars, all standard gauge, moved equipment, supplies, cement, rocks, earth, and fill as needed. This use of a construction railway, operating with access to all the major work sites of the large and widely scattered project, had been developed by the engineers associated with William States

Lee. Lee had first made use of such a construction railway on another, very different hydroelectric construction project. When building the Isle Maligne power plant on the Saguenay River for the Duke and Price interests several years earlier, the engineers had been confronted with a serious problem of access to the main work sites.[6] The narrow canyons of the Saguenay made it difficult to get materials to the main work site. Those problems had been solved by the construction of a special temporary railway. The level and rather swampy site of the new Beauharnois canal and the rocky conditions at the powerhouse site were altogether different from the geographical conditions at Isle Maligne, but again a construction railway seemed to be the best way to solve the access problems.

Most of the Beauharnois Railway Company was built on top of the canal dikes, and one of its first major purposes was to build up the dikes. As more fill was added, the track was raised. Later the rocks needed to line or rip rap and stabilize the walls of the canal were hauled into place and dumped over the embankment by the construction railway.

The Beauharnois promoters also had to relocate three major railways – the Canadian National Railways, the New York Central Railroad, and the St Lawrence and Adirondack Railroad. They used the Beauharnois Railway to build the roadbed and to fill the large approaches to new bridges over which the relocated railways would cross the new power canal.

The Beauharnois company had come to an amicable agreement with the three railways, and the relocation plans were approved by the Department of Railways and Canals. But the relocation of these railways, first along temporary trestles which were subsequently filled in and graded, involved much work and was subject to all the usual inspections by engineers and officials of the Department of Railways and Canals. Engineers of the affected railways also kept a watchful eye on all the operations.

The Beauharnois Construction Company built a huge stone crusher and cement plant. Vast quantities of rock of all sizes were required for a wide range of construction purposes, and the main powerhouse and tailrace consumed astronomical quantities of cement. Using rock materials excavated at the powerhouse, tailrace, and remedial work sites at the lower end of the canal, the Beauharnois Construction Company crushed and prepared all the rock and sand it required. It also mixed its own cement on site.

The powerhouse itself had several important and rather unusual features. Some of these were made necessary by the fact that Montreal Power and Ontario Hydro had different equipment. At an early stage in its evolution Montreal Power had opted for a single-phase 25-cycle system, which was giving that company considerable trouble but had not yet been replaced. Ontario Hydro, on the other hand, had switched to three-phase 60-cycle power. Beauharnois Power had contracts with both these companies and devised its generating plant in such a way that both kinds of power could be generated, transformed, and transmitted efficiently.

The first phase of development for Beauharnois included the installation of a generating capacity of 500,000 horsepower. Ten generators, each with a 50,000 horsepower capacity were planned. Four of these were to be ready on 1 October 1932, when power deliveries to Ontario Hydro and Montreal Power were to begin. The others were to be completed and placed in operation as the power requirements of the company's contracts increased, until full operation of the 500,000 horsepower capacity was achieved on 1 October 1937. It was decided that units on one side of the powerhouse would generate the power required for Ontario Hydro, those on the other side would do so for Montreal Power. The appropriate one- or three-phase transformers had to be installed, but there would also be special 'disconnects' which would permit emergency taps from the other system. Between the two groups of 25-cycle and 60-cycle units there would be a sluiceway section in which smaller auxiliary units, capable of generating all the power needed to operate the powerhouse plant, would be installed. There was to be a single control room, on a floor one level below the generator floor – thus between the waterwheels and the generators.[7]

The engineering plans for the first phase of development, utilizing 53,000 cubic feet of water per second and generating 500,000 horsepower, were drawn with a view to future expansion. Indeed, in 1930, long before the first units were installed, the Beauharnois Power Corporation sought and obtained a supplementary lease from the Quebec government which authorized the diversion of 30,000 additional cubic feet of water per second. The promoters intended to apply for additional water diversion and development as the demand for power increased.

The Beauharnois construction plans were prepared in the New York City offices of the W.S. Lee Engineering Corporation, and the New Yorkers did their work very well indeed. Both R.O. Sweezey and R.A.C.

Henry were trained professional engineers. They were involved with the formulation of the general concepts and reviewed all plans drawn in New York. But Sweezey's primary responsibility after the commencement of construction was political and financial, while Henry was responsible for the local management of the company's affairs.

As indicated already, the first workmen moved onto the site during the last week in July 1929. They began work under the watchful eye of F.H. Cothran, a senior engineer with the W.S. Lee Engineering Corporation who was also appointed vice-president and general manager of the Beauharnois Construction Company. The first man hired by Cothran was a master mechanic named H.L. Bingley, who had served in a similar capacity with Cothran on the Isle Maligne job and subsequently at Arvida. The W.S. Lee engineers were not unfamiliar with Canadian hydroelectric construction projects.

Construction of the first workers' camp, including sleeping quarters and a cookery, was begun in late July, before the corporate reorganization and the sale of the company's collateral trust fund bonds. Cothran therefore 'hesitated to employ men with conditions unsettled as they have been. Also did not want to carry a heavy pay roll until necessary.'[8]

Early in August five draglines moved onto the site to begin 'stripping the surface of the ground at foundation of the dikes.'[9] Additional surveying and the digging of numerous test pits also proceeded apace. When the official celebrations marking the beginning of construction were held, the five draglines had already moved 296,447 cubic yards of material, and 104 test pits had been dug. Much of the locating and surveying work had been completed, and a small frame shack had been built and served as the on-site head office. Construction of the facilities to house the small number of workmen who were expected to remain on the site for the winter was nearing completion. It was only after reporting progress on this work, that Cothran briefly noted in his report of 14 October 1929 that official ceremonies marking the beginning of construction had taken place.[10]

The official opening, described briefly and factually by the engineers, but more colourfully portrayed by journalists who had been primed with appropriate press releases and copious quantities of liquid enlightenment, actually marked the end of most of the active work at Beauharnois for the 1929 season. Some blasting and clearing of rockwork at the feeder canal and powerhouse site would continue through the winter months, but the major concern during that period was to assemble and erect the suction dredge, the tower excavators, the special 'Marion shovel,' the rock-crushing and cement plant, and the facilities to accommodate up to 2,500 construction workers in 1930.

The small crew did its work well. Early in the spring of 1930 the huge suction dredge was ready to be tested. The winter had fortunately been mild, and on 31 March 1930 the pump on the dredge was started for the first time. It worked well as long as the discharge line was not connected, but when that line was attached, one of the joints in the line immediately failed. The line was repaired, and on 1 April the pump, with the discharge line attached, was started again. It ran for five minutes before another joint gave way. The remainder of the day had to be spent making the necessary repairs. When the pump was again started on 2 April, it ran for fifteen minutes before another joint in the discharge line gave way.

The next day a special ceremony was held. The new dredge was officially christened. It would bear the proud name 'R.O. Sweezey.' Unfortunately, the dredge was cantankerous that day, and the engineers reported: 'Pumped mud for 1 hour. Tuning up previous to christening of boat pipe line to cutter shaft being carried away. Same replaced with rubber hose. On starting up after christening ceremony bend astern of dredge was carried off the pontoon altogether. Same replaced by spare bend.'[11] These were normal testing and start-up problems. Eventually the entire system whereby the discharge pipes were attached to the dredge and then linked over distances of thousands of feet on floating pontoons, had to be redesigned and strengthened. Fundamentally, however, the system was sound. Within several weeks the temporary adjustments, which were later incorporated into the redesigned discharge system, permitted satisfactory operations.

A second problem with the dredge was not as easy to solve. Once the dredge got into material with larger stones, there were frequent references to rocks getting caught in the pump which could not handle stones larger than eighteen inches in width. The difficulty of dealing with the larger or awkwardly shaped stones that got caught in the pump was never resolved satisfactorily, but operators developed great skill in opening the line and removing the offending rock, often in as short a time as fifteen minutes.

The huge seven-foot spiral cutter was the subject of great concern before the dredge was placed in operation. But it performed well right from the beginning. The huge cutter blades had to be replaced periodically, and the machine required frequent and careful maintenance. In July 1930 work was going so well that the output of the dredge established a new world record.[12]

There was more trouble with the tower excavators. These huge machines were assembled while they lay horizontally on the ground. They were then raised, with some difficulty, by means of a crane into an upright position and appropriately positioned and fastened to the tracks on which they would operate. The first excavator was successfully raised and prepared for operation during the second week of April. Disaster struck, however, when the second tower was erected. The tower, while being lifted into position, dropped from a height of around forty-five feet when one of the back leg braces gave way. One workman was injured, but the damage to the machine was not serious.[13] The tower was repaired and raised two weeks later. The other two tower excavators were erected without incident.

Aside from the start-up difficulties with the suction dredge and the fall of the no. 2 tower excavator, the weekly memoranda of operations reported no unusual delays or problems. Detailed and extensive reports on the progress of the work were regularly made available to the press, and numerous newsmen, politicians, and industrialists visited the site to view the massive machinery in operation.

The work proceeded simultaneously on numerous sites. It is possible, however, to list the main construction sites and outline the progress on each in 1930. The suction dredge began its work at Valleyfield, and by late October, when operations ceased for the year and the huge machine was subjected to a complete overhaul, it had covered half the distance between Lake St Francis and Lake St Louis. Working twenty-four hours a day, stopping only for necessary maintenance and repairs, the machine moved relentlessly southeastward. It was the most impressive illustration of the mass production excavation methods adopted by the Beauharnois companies.

The tower excavators and draglines threw up dikes wherever they were needed along the entire length of the canal, but in many places they were not raised to the required height in 1930. Nor were they built to the required width.

At the powerhouse site proper, and in the tailrace, approximately 500,000 cubic yards of rock were excavated in 1930. Early in September work at the powerhouse site had progressed to the point where it was possible to begin the pouring of the massive cement foundation. Before operations closed for the season late in 1930, 40,000 cubic yards of cement had been poured, but it was estimated that the project would require a total of 350,000 cubic yards of cement. Both the rock-crushing and cement-mixing plants were completed by mid-summer and served without serious difficulty or interruptions. Also during the 1930 construction season, twenty-six miles of the new construction railway were completed, at least to the point where temporary track could be laid. During the year the company had 2,422 men on the payroll, and spent approximately $1 million per month on construction. This sum, happily, was less than had been estimated. The machines performed more efficiently than expected, and wage rates gradually fell as the depression deepened.[14] Construction was not interrupted by any labour disturbances. Given the desperate job conditions in Canada during this period, workers at Beauharnois had little inclination to make trouble, much less to go out on strike.

Put simply, about one-third of the earth and rock excavation required to finish the installation of the first 200,000 horsepower generating units was done in 1930. The pouring of the foundations was completed to the point where some of the steelwork could begin, and excavation of the main feeder canal, and of the tailrace, had been advanced significantly, although more than three-quarters of that work remained to be done. The entire project was slightly ahead of schedule and slightly below estimated costs.[15] In short, the year 1930 was a very good one for the promoters and builders of the Beauharnois Power Corporation.

9

Helping political friends

Construction progressed in a most satisfactory manner throughout 1930 on the Beauharnois canal and powerhouse. Financing, despite the disturbances on world money markets, created no immediate financial problems for the Beauharnois Power Corporation. The entire $30 million issue of 6 per cent collateral trust bonds had been sold to the investment corporations of Newman, Sweezey and Company, Dominion Securities Corporation, and their associates for $27 million in cash. Accumulated debts could thus be repaid, and construction costs and other financial requirements could be met at least until the end of 1930. It was recognized that in 1931, as construction continued, it would be necessary to issue new first-mortgage bonds. Since those mortgage bonds would have priority over the collateral trust bonds already issued and sold, there seemed no reason to be unduly concerned about future Beauharnois bond sales. Construction, financing, and engineering all were proceeding exceptionally well in 1930.

The greatest worries of the Beauharnois promoters concerned the failure of the federal Department of Public Works to approve the detailed and final construction plans for the first construction phase. Until such approval was granted, the Beauharnois company remained exceptionally vulnerable to political pressure and, during the federal election campaign of 1930, to virtual blackmail.

The problem with the company's final and detailed construction plans was fairly simple. The federal government had the right and the duty to review the company's detailed plans to safeguard future navigational requirements on the St Lawrence. But the government had no coherent long-term policy regarding navigation on the St Lawrence. In the negotiations leading up to the passage of PC 422 the

Beauharnois promoters had persuaded the politicians to avoid or side-step the troublesome question of future navigational improvements on the St Lawrence. But PC 422 still required that detailed plans be filed and that the federal government review and approve these in so far as they pertained to navigation. Therein lay the problem. How could the officials in the Department of Public Works review and approve, or disapprove, any detailed construction plans filed by the Beauharnois Power Corporation if they did not know what navigational developments there should be on the St Lawrence? Premiers Ferguson and Taschereau of Ontario and Quebec, respectively, still disagreed about the seaway, even though both agreed that the power development at Beauharnois should proceed.

Several tense meetings between the prime minister and the two provincial premiers were held in January and March 1930 to try to resolve the impasse about future navigational improvements on the St Lawrence. The tone of those negotiations is captured rather well in Mackenzie King's lengthy diary entry on 24 January 1930.

> Taschereau held out for our stating theirs were the proprietary rights. We contended we could not meet them on that score, but we might agree as a matter of policy to treat with the provinces as if they had right to the powers ... I emphasized necessity of our not being put in position of having sold the nation's birthright for a mess of pottage, in parting with rights to provinces to develop power on St. Lawrence, without our keeping power to pay for construction of canal. The fact that the power cannot be developed except on the terms we agree to is answer to that.[1]

Mackenzie King was at his obfuscatory worst in these tangled negotiations, which dragged on and on and eventually became the subject of a substantial exchange of official correspondence between the prime minister and the two premiers. Meanwhile, the federal bureaucrats refused to approve the final construction plans of the Beauharnois Power Corporation until the political and constitutional muddle in Ottawa, Toronto, and Quebec City was cleared up.

Closely related to the long-term plans of the Beauharnois company were the rights and interests of the other companies generating electricity in the Soulanges Section. Those companies were no longer opposed to the first Beauharnois construction phase, but there would have to be further negotiations before that initial development could be expanded. Engineers from the various companies operating in the

Soulanges Section were in fact appointed to discuss and negotiate, but after three years of meetings the general manager of the Beauharnois Power Corporation admitted that 'They have come to the first stage of development. They know what would satisfy the Montreal Light, Heat and Power Co., or rather the Cedars Rapids, but that has not been fitted into the navigation side of it yet.'[2]

The engineers and bureaucrats in the federal Department of Public Works discovered another problem. The Department of Railways and Canals owned some of the remedial works that would be disrupted by the Beauharnois construction program. Specifically, Railways and Canals owned a remedial dike at Hungry Bay, and Public Works officials learned that 'it was necessary to cut into Hungry Bay Dyke by doing dredging out into the lake to a certain extent to let the water come in.'[3] The Public Works officials thought that such interference necessitated referral of the Beauharnois plans to the Department of Railways and Canals before they were approved. Officials at Railways and Canals, however, were as uncertain as those at Public Works about the long-term navigational requirements on the St Lawrence. Confused and suspicious bureaucrats are not easily persuaded to make important decisions.

The Beauharnois officials also contributed to the delays in the filing and approval of detailed and comprehensive construction plans. They knew that they would be expected to adhere closely to their plans, once those plans were officially filed and approved. It would be difficult to make even minor changes later. Yet, every large project undergoes numerous minor changes and adjustments. Sweezey and Henry thought the important consideration was that all proper standards, safeguards, and technical conditions were met, not that a specific plan had been followed in every detail.

The result was disarmingly simple but politically dangerous. No detailed, official, and final construction plans for the Beauharnois project were filed prior to construction. The general and preliminary plans appended to PC 422 were, of course, on file. Engineers from the departments of Public Works and Railways and Canals were provided with detailed construction information and invited to visit the site to inspect and make recommendations about the work. They could assure themselves that all was being done according to established rules and standards. The departmental engineers prepared detailed reports on all aspects of the work, even though final plans for the entire project had not been approved.[4]

Officials of the Department of Public Works and of the Beauharnois offered an ingenious excuse or explanation for the lack of approved detailed construction plans. They insisted that, owing to a legal technicality, there was no need in 1929 or 1930 to submit or approve of the detailed plans required under the terms of PC 422. What the Beauharnois company was building were not 'works' within the narrow technical definition of that term in the Navigable Waters Protection Act on which PC 422 was based. A 'work' according to this definition was anything 'built or placed in, upon, over, under, through or across any navigable water.'[5] The deputy minister of public works later insisted that 'the work which is proceeding now is entirely on the company's private property, and is not in any way connected with the St. Lawrence at all.'[6] A Beauharnois lawyer explained what he understood to be the deputy minister's official position.

Now it is quite true that the Governor in Council will have to approve of the plans of the proposed canal before it can be used as a navigable stream. There is no question about that, and we will have to get that approval; but at the same time the works, and the only works that the Governor in Council can deal with under chapter 140 are the works which are proposed to interfere, under section 4, with navigable streams, and that has not been attempted, nothing has been done in regard to that. We take our chances on having the Governor in Council approve of what we propose to substitute for the St. Lawerence River at that time. But at the same time, what we are doing is on our own property.[7]

It was a legalistic and bureaucratic argument to justify or excuse the unwillingness or inability of the department and the cabinet to approve detailed construction plans of the Beauharnois company. Beauharnois engineers tried to file and gain official approval for their detailed plans in July of 1929 and again in August of 1930, but the federal bureaucrats refused to co-operate. When pressed hard on the matter, the deputy minister of public works delayed matters further by referring the matter to the Department of Justice for a legal opinion. The deputy minister of public works was a cautious and politically sensitive individual who was unwilling to make any decision that was not, in the words of a later witness, 'corroborated ... rip-rapped ... and double-soled.'[8]

The failure to have their detailed plans approved left the Beauharnois companies vulnerable. The construction project on which they were engaged would be completely useless unless, at some point, water from the St Lawrence were channelled through the new canal. Such a diversion of course, would affect navigation, and required federal approval. There was a possibility that, after the entire project was completed, federal bureaucrats and politicians could decide that the construction plans were not satisfactory and refuse to permit the required diversion of water. There was no doubt, moreover, that the deputy minister would follow the wishes of his political masters in the matter. What might happen if a new government, more sympathetic to the Montreal Power interests, won the next election?

The Beauharnois promoters took a colossal calculated risk when they began construction without prior approval of their plans. They could not afford to wait while Ottawa settled its serious attack of political and constitutional constipation. But the promoters had to keep their political fences carefully mended. The task of building close political friendships and currying favour with influential politicians was left primarily to Sweezey and the three Liberal senators. Senators Haydon and McDougald played a particularly important role in befriending and exercising influence with Prime Minister King. Senator Raymond was influential with the Quebec wing of the federal Liberal party and also had a good deal of influence with the provincial Liberals in Quebec.

The King diaries contain numerous references to visits, meetings, and conferences with both McDougald and Haydon and to a variety of personal gifts and mementoes which they gave the prime minister. This relationship was further strengthened in April of 1930 when both senators accompanied Mackenzie King and others on a vacation to Bermuda. The spring parliamentary session of 1930 had been difficult and frustrating for King, as he and his ministers groped for solutions to the problems of a severely depressed economy. And adding to the worries of everyday political adminstration, there was the fact that the last federal election had been held in 1926 and another would have to be called either late in 1930 or some time in 1931. The prospects for substantial economic improvement in 1931 were not encouraging, and King was thinking of calling an election in 1930. But the end of the parliamentary session in April 1930 provided an opportunity for a short holiday and respite.

There was later considerable controversy about who asked whom to go to Bermuda. King's recollection was that he had decided to go and then had invited a number of friends and associates, including Senators Haydon and McDougald. Shortly before going to Bermuda, however,

King had called in Senators Haydon and Raymond to talk over party finances and to ask them to work together as treasurers for the coming federal election campaign.[9]

The prime ministerial party left Halifax on the evening of 14 April 1930 and arrived at Hamilton, Bermuda, on 16 April at 10:30 a.m. The Hamilton *Royal Gazette and Colonist Daily* described the arrival thus:

> We understand that his visit is to be a private one, but His Worship the Mayor, the Hon. S. S. Spurling and the Hon. J. P. Hand will be on the dock at 10:30 a.m. to greet the distinguished visitors. We venture the suggestion that flags should be flown on his arrival. Bermuda will offer him a cordial welcome and trust that his visit in search of 'a breath of fresh air' which is how he described his objective in coming, will be eminently successful.[10]

Although the trip was officially a private one, Mackenzie King and Senators Haydon and McDougald did pay a visit to the House of Assembly. They were entertained at tea by the speaker of the house, and later they were official guests at Government House. The visit continued until 21 April 1930, and, judging from the lengthy farewell speech King delivered just prior to his departure, it had been 'such a wonderful holiday.'[11] From Bermuda King and several other members of the group, including Senators Haydon and McDougald, travelled to New York.

King and the senators stayed at the Bermudiana Hotel – the largest and most luxurious of the Hamilton hotels, renowned for its spacious and beautiful grounds and gardens. Senator McDougald left a day before the others but rejoined the group in New York. Before leaving the Bermudiana, however, the good senator paid the bill for the entire party. That prompted the following note in King's diary. 'Dr. McDougald left this morning. Before he went he settled the bill for us at the hotel $400 in round figures ... It was mighty generous of McDougald. All he seems to seek in return is recognition & friendship which he craves.'[12] The Senator's generosity did not end in Bermuda. Several days later the prime minister could confide to his diary:

> We reached New York at 4:30 and were at the Ritz-Carleton by 5. On the way I called at the Harvard Club and received the letters which had been sent on. Dr. McDougald had arranged for a suite of rooms for Haydon & myself, another palatial apartment with an Adams drawing-room etc. It was a joy to sit there and read over the personal mail, letters from Joan, Lord Dawson, from Jennie &

Sir John Aird & others ... After luncheon with Dr. & Mrs. McDougald & Haydon at the Ritz I went out again.[13]

It was a successful holiday. After spending more than a week in luxurious hotels and in the company of wealthy individuals, the prime minister could reflect on the experience in his unique and sanctimonious manner.

The trip to Bermuda would have been more enjoyable had work been completed first – still more enjoyable had I held throughout to all lenten resolutions, touched no wine, not sat up late at night & read only books of an inspirational character. The life of the Countess of Warwick & Byron have been worthwhile in what they revealed of the conditions of English society, but they have been disillusioning. I have come to have a stronger antipathy to all that pertains to aristocracy & privilege. How wise the pioneers of the U.S. constitution were to do away with all titles. Now as to myself, I have been eating too much, drinking not to excess, very little in fact, but on the holiday better to have drunk nothing at all, not exercising enough & letting my thoughts wander too much. I have let myself get out of hand in the matter of play & self indulgence in one form or another. My power is a spiritual one. I must get back to that at all costs and with God's wish I shall.[14]

In short, the prime minister had a more enjoyable time on his holiday than he normally allowed himself. The trip would come to haunt him in short order, however, because, one month after his return to Ottawa, charges were made in the House of Commons alleging wrongdoing in the relationships between the government and the Beauharnois promoters.

On 7 April 1930 E.J. Garland, the Progressive member of parliament from Bow River, Alberta, had placed on the order paper a seemingly innocuous request for a return of various Beauharnois documents. This was followed, on 22 May 1930, by 'a motion for adjournment to discuss a matter of public importance.' This motion and a subsequent speech criticizing the Beauharnois arrangements, was made by Robert Gardiner, the Progressive member of parliament from Acadia, Alberta.[15]

King's reaction to these first suggestions regarding possible irregularities at Beauharnois was surprising, particularly when it is taken into account that he had just spent a holiday with, and enjoyed the hospitality of, two senators closely linked to the Beauharnois project. King evidently believed the Beauharnois promoters had somehow provided the information on which Garland and Gardiner based their charges. He noted in his diary on 28 May 1930: 'The men dealing with B[eauharnois] are about as stupid a lot from a political and equally business point of view as I have ever seen. They should be silent until at least parliament is over.'[16] Two days after this irritated diary entry parliament was dissolved and a general federal election was called for 28 July 1930. The prime minister was optimistic and pompous as he prepared for the election.

> I go into this election with the belief that God is on my side, that I am being guided in order to fulfil a destiny, the instrument of other lives to work out God's purpose as they have sought to effect in dealings with His people & to pass on to others a greater faith ... I wrote to Sir Arthur Currie, thanking him for a fine letter expressing appreciation of what has done for the soldiers, to Dr. McDougald for gold engraved tray presented to me for opening Montreal Harbour Bridge.[17]

The election call found the Beauharnois company in a most awkward position. It had been a tremendous struggle to get the Liberal government to approve PC 422. The entire project had been the subject of fierce debates, with opposition coming from many different quarters. Sir Herbert Holt, Beauharnois's former formidable opponent, was a Conservative. The attitude of the Conservative party towards the Beauharnois project had never been clearly defined. There was some hope that former Conservative opposition had been at least partially mollified by the strong support the company had given, or at least thought it had given, to the Ontario Conservatives in their election in 1929. With both Ontario and Quebec in support of the project it was hardly likely that the Conservatives, if elected, would try to shut down the project, but there was still the worrisome fact that the company's final plans had not been approved. Modifications might be demanded to suit the demands and prejudices of friends and supporters of the Conservative party.

Robert Sweezey expected that his friends and associates, Senators Raymond and Haydon, who were also the official co-treasurers of the federal Liberal party, would approach him for substantial campaign contributions. And the Liberal bagmen did not disappoint. Several days after the election was called first one, and then the other, called on the Beauharnois president and were given substantial sums of money. Sweezey later testified that while he dealt with the two men separately, it became obvious to him that each was aware of the other's activities, and Sweezey decided that the precise division of funds between the Quebec and federal wings of the Liberal party could be left for them to settle. 'Contributions were made to both parties in Quebec [the federal and the provincial Liberal parties]. I am unable to state how much went to Quebec [the provincial Liberal party] because in delivering securities to Senator Raymond and Senator Haydon we expressed the hope that some of those would be for the Province of Quebec, but we have no knowledge of how much went to the Province of Quebec.'[18]

The sums given to Senators Raymond and Haydon by Robert Sweezey were impressive. By his own calculations and those of the secretary of the Beauharnois Power Corporation, Sweezey paid the two Liberal senators approximately $700,000. Of this amount Sweezey insisted that $600,000 came from his own personal funds, while $100,000 came directly from the Beauharnois Power Corporation. Later evidence, however, showed that the Sweezey contributions were made after Sweezey sold some personal assets, at considerable personal profits, to the Beauharnois Power Corporation, using those profits to make his election campaign contributions. When asked later why he had made such a substantial contribution Sweezey simply replied: 'Gratefulness was always regarded as an important factor in dealing with democratic governments.'[19]

In addition to these large gifts to the federal and Quebec Liberals, Sweezey also made a number of smaller personal donations of between $1,000 and $25,000 to both Conservative and Liberal candidates who were thought to be friendly to the Beauharnois company. The Quebec Conservative party also received $20,000. Sweezey, like many other large corporate donors, did not contribute to only one political party. During the 1930 federal election campaign he met at least once, and probably several times, with General A.D. McRae, the Conservative party campaign manager and fund-raiser. Sweezey and McRae came to an agreement that the Beauharnois promoter should contribute $200,000 to the federal Conservative party election campaign. General McRae, however, never came around to collect his $200,000. Sweezey later claimed he never knew exactly why the federal Conservatives had not taken his money. When it was later suggested 'that Mr. Bennett [the Conservative leader] would not accept it,' Sweezey merely replied, 'I do not know that, but I presume that may be so.'[20] Others were inclined to see the influence of Sir Herbert Holt behind this turn of events, since it was widely rumoured that General McRae had obtained a large contribution from the Montreal Power and Royal Bank president, the understanding being that the Conservative party would not establish stronger links with the Beauharnois interests.[21]

The substantial election campaign contributions by R.O. Sweezey were consistent with the Beauharnois president's general approach to politics and public relations. He had built up the entire project by applying financial grease in many strategic places. But for the Liberal party of Canada contributions of this magnitude were unprecedented. The political scientist who has examined Liberal party organization and finances in greatest detail offers the following conclusions about Sweezey's donations in 1930.

> The approximately $700,000 collected from this single source was more than the total amount which the party would be able to collect from all its sources on Bay Street in each of two subsequent elections, and in the light of Haydon's previously quoted remarks to King there is little reason to believe that the party had ever uncovered such a bonanza before. But like the magic wishes of the fairy tales which somehow always rebound on their wealth-struck recipients, this remarkable Aladdin's Lamp proved to be doubly deceptive: the election was lost in any event and, in its aftermath, Beauharnois re-emerged as the ugliest scandal ever to involve the national Liberal party, leaving in the public mind an exaggerated idea of the largesse lavished by business on political parties and on the Liberal party in particular.[21]

The affairs of the Beauharnois Power Corporation were not an issue in the 1930 election campaign, and the contributions made by Sweezey were not made public until a year later. Prime Minister Mackenzie King blamed the defeat of his party in the election on the problems and inadequacies of party and political organization. There is a good deal of evidence to support King's complaint that party organization was indeed weak. Campaign funds were not a problem, however, thanks to R.O. Sweezey. But campaign funds alone cannot win elections for governments that have lost touch with the electorate. In 1930 Canada was in the grip of the worst depression in the country's history, and the King government seemed to be unwilling or unable to deal with the economic problems. When Conservative Premier Howard Ferguson of Ontario requested federal assistance to combat unemployment, the prime minister, regarding the request as a piece of political opportunism, replied that 'I would not give them a five-cent piece.'[23] That speech, when contrasted with Opposition Leader R.B. Bennett's promise of immediate and vigorous action, contributed to the decisive defeat of the Liberals.

The election of the Conservatives was obviously not good news for R.O. Sweezey and the Beauharnois Power Corporation. In the week immediately following the election, as the Liberals cleared up unfinished business and prepared to hand over the reins of government to the Conservatives, the Beauharnois Power Corporation tried, for the third time, to file detailed construction plans to meet the requirements of PC 422. J.C. Elliott, the outgoing minister of public works, had received private financial support from Sweezey in addition to the contributions he had made to the national party, but neither Elliott nor the Liberal party demonstrated enough gratitude to approve the Beauharnois plans before leaving office. The Beauharnois promoters, their construction plans in a bureaucratic and political mess, now had to face the suspicious and sometimes hostile Conservatives.

10

The revenge of a thwarted rival

In gaining control of the Beauharnois Light, Heat and Power Company, Robert O. Sweezey had made a bitter and implacable enemy. That enemy was Narcisse Cantin, who held the positions of president and principal promoter of the Great Lakes and Atlantic Canal and Power Company and later of the Transportation and Power Corporation. (Sweezey's work for the Cantin companies in 1925 and 1926 has already been discussed in some detail in chapter 2.) Judging from the record of his other business ventures and the evidence given in the various legal cases he initiated and in the several governmental inquiries into the Beauharnois companies, Narcisse Cantin was a visionary who lacked the necessary business, legal, and financial acumen and resources to make his companies successful. He was not, however, a man bereft of all ability or honour. He understood the potential of the Beauharnois project and became paranoid about Sweezey's alleged treachery. He believed he had been robbed of the fruit of his developmental ideas. A biographical sketch of Cantin rather accurately describes the situation. 'Narcisse Cantin, dreamer and promoter of great navigation and waterway projects, was robbed of his dream by Robert O. Sweezey who, as an Engineer and Financier, had the technical expertise to recognize the potential of the Beauharnois site and the shrewdness to step in and intercept a rich deal that was being fumbled by less able hands.'[1]

Cantin and his associates took two actions to counter Sweezey's 'treachery.' First, they prepared and then filed with the Department of Public Works their own engineering and developmental plans for the Beauharnois site.[2] These plans, based largely on engineering work and drawings prepared by R.O. Sweezey when he was Cantin's employee, were submitted before new plans could be prepared and filed by the Sweezey-controlled Beauharnois Light Heat and Power Company. Cantin and his associates therefore argued that their plans had priority and should have been dealt with before any new plans by any other company were considered or approved. The Department of Public Works, however, never even bothered officially to acknowledge receipt of the Transportation and Power Corporation plans, much less to file or approve them. The Cantin group lacked the necessary financial resources and political influence to get anywhere in official Ottawa. They might be a nuisance or an obstacle for others, but they were not a serious contender to develop the Beauharnois site.

The Transportation and Power Corporation also entered a $10 million damage suit against R.O. Sweezey. This legal suit was largely the idea and project of an ambitious young Toronto lawyer named Frank Regan. Later evidence suggests that the suit was intended as harassment. It was a nuisance and an obstacle to speedy approval of the plans submitted by the Beauharnois company. Cantin wanted to force Sweezey and his new associates to make a proper settlement with his companies. The *Financial Post* later published an article which stated bluntly that Cantin's lawyer, Frank Regan, wanted $500,000 from Sweezey to drop the case.[3] 'If Mr. Sweezey had decided to respond to a demand for a half million dollars insistently made upon him by a rival in the power field it is doubtful if the story of Beauharnois ever would have come to the committee presided over by Hon. Wesley Gordon ... Sweezey, who had one set of rules for senators and political parties, who had been 'taken' for large gifts without murmur, would not cross the palm of an ancient enemy.'[4]

Cantin and Regan were determined either to become full partners in the Beauharnois project or to extract a $500,000 cash settlement from the Beauharnois promoters.[5] Sweezey, however, spurned all overtures and threats by Cantin and his associates, whom he held in utter contempt. As a result, Cantin's legal proceedings continued. When legal harassment did not achieve the intended result, Frank Regan explored other ways and means to exert increased pressure and thus to force Sweezey to come to an accommodation with the Cantin interests.

Regan's and Cantin's strategy in their $10 lawsuit against Sweezey was fairly simple. They wanted to show that Sweezey had obtained information and prepared plans for the development of the proposed power site while still Cantin's employee. In order to demonstrate this point they naturally called for copies of all the official plans submitted by the Beauharnois promoters. At first Sweezey refused to provide the information, but in March of 1930 the presiding judge issued a subpoena requiring Sweezey both to testify and to submit relevant plans and documents.

It was at the preliminary hearings in March of 1930 that Regan and Cantin first discovered that the detailed Beauharnois construction plans, as required by PC 422, had never been officially approved. In addition, they also obtained a great deal of interesting and confidential information about the history and financial reorganizations of the Beauharnois companies. That made it clear that the promoters had already made substantial profits, and that some financial payments were, at best, questionable. When Cantin and Regan discovered this potentially embarrassing information, they first tried to use it to force Sweezey to accept their terms. Sweezey refused even to meet with them. At that point Frank Regan thought the pressure might be further increased if some of the more damaging information were discreetly released to opposition politicians. Cantin was reluctant to do this[6] but was eventually persuaded by Regan to make some of the information available to the Conservatives.

Regan's first contacts with the Conservatives were not encouraging. They correctly surmised that this was, at least in part, an attempt to exert pressure to force Sweezey to make a settlement with the Cantin interests. The Conservatives were also reluctant to become involved in a process that might eventually reveal a great deal about unsavoury business practices and about the financial relations between businessmen and politicians.

Two Progressive members of parliament from Alberta, both of whom had a strong bias against business and a record of consistent advocacy of public development of Canada's natural resources, showed a keen interest, however, when Regan approached them with some of his information. The two were Robert Gardiner of Acadia and E.J. Garland of Bow River. On the basis of information he had received from Regan, Garland moved, on 7 April 1930, for a tabling in the House of Commons of 'all letters, telegrams and other correspondence and documents passing between any department of the government and the Beauharnois Power Corporation Limited ... [and] the Beauharnois Light, Heat and Power Company.'[7] There was nothing unusual about requests of this kind. They were typical of many 'fishing expeditions' by opposition members who hoped to find some information embarrassing to the government. Certainly no one on the government side was particularly alarmed when this first request was made. It is also clear that in April of 1930 Regan and Garland themselves still had only incomplete information.

In May of 1930, however, as Cantin's lawsuit against Sweezey progressed, Regan got more definite information. Specifically, he obtained details of the financial arrangements when the second Beauharnois syndicate exchanged its assets for cash and shares in the newly incorporated Beauharnois Power Corporation Limited. The profits of the promotors, particularly those of Frank P. Jones when he sold his interest, and of R.O. Sweezey when the company was reorganized, seemed to be unusually large. Taking an entirely fanciful view of the value of the Beauharnois shares, Regan projected that the promoters stood to make a profit of $104,850,000. Regan further pointed out that while Beauharnois had authority to divert only 40,000 cubic feet of water per second, the construction and development plans of the company included the ultimate diversion of the entire flow of the St Lawrence. In support of this allegation he cited statements filed in lieu of a prospectus when the Beauharnois Power Corporation issued and marketed its $30 million 6 per cent collateral trust bonds. That statement included the following:

> the Company's proposed development, in the opinion of its engineers, is the most efficient method of utilizing the entire drop in this section of the River. In view of the above, provision is made in the plans and considerable work is now being done with a view to installing further units if additional water becomes available. After the completion of the present 500,000 horse power installation it is estimated that further units can be installed at an average cost of less that $65 per horse power.[8]

The gist of Regan's early charges against Beauharnois were fourfold. First, the plans of the Beauharnois company did not follow precisely the plans recommended by the Joint Board of Engineers. Second, the Beauharnois promoters had made grossly excessive profits when the Beauharnois Power Corporation was organized. Third, the promoters, although they had not filed the required detailed construction plans, were in fact planning to take over the entire flow of the St Lawrence, either in an illegal fashion or on the basis of some secret arrangement with the government. And fourth, if they had no secret agreement with the government, the statement filed in lieu of prospectus constituted a fraud, since it held out the possibility of additional water diversions for which the Beauharnois promoters had no legal authorization.

Regan sent copies of his new information to Gardiner, Garland, and R.B. Bennett, the leader of the official opposition, on 15 May 1930.[9] The two Progressives, ever suspicious of big business and the alienation of the country's natural resources for the enrichment of capitalists at the expense of ordinary Canadians, were eager to raise the matter immediately in parliament. This was in spite of the fact that the end of the session was at hand and prorogation and a general election were expected. Thus, on 22 May 1930 Robert Gardiner notified R.B. Bennett and Public Works Minister J.C. Elliott that he intended to move adjournment of the House to consider a matter of public importance. He enclosed a memo outlining Regan's charges, together with a copy of the statement the Beauharnois Power Corporation had filed when its bonds were issued.[10] Later that same day Gardiner and Garland each utilized the forty minutes available to him to read into the parliamentary record the information they had obtained from Regan, with suitable embellishments and outbursts of righteous indignation about the nefarious ways of big business.[11]

The response of other parliamentarians on 22 May was measured and low key. The minister of public works pointed out that the water rights had been granted by the province of Quebec, not the federal government, and complaints about excessive profits should be forwarded to Quebec City. The deviations from the plans recommended by the Joint Board of Engineers were described as fairly minor, and all had been approved by the Canadian National Advisory Committee. And the company was following the general plans which were a part of PC 422, and its work was being monitored by government engineers. All the federal government needed to do, and had done, was to ensure that the diversion of 40,000 cubic feet of water per second would not adversely affect navigation. There was no further understanding or promise about future diversions, and the internal financial arrangements of the company were not known to the minister.

R.B. Bennett made a brief and cautious statement. He made a particular effort to emphasize that entrepreneurs enter into various ventures for the purpose of making money, which was proper and honourable. He was willing, however, to support the request for an inquiry to determine if there were irregularities in the relations between the Beauharnois companies and the government.

Several Ontario members felt obliged to add relatively brief statements about the glories of public ownership of hydroelectric resources in Ontario. The irrepressible Tommy Church from Toronto Northwest even went so far as to assert that 'The Conservative party is the only public ownership party in Canada today.'[12] That was too much for the venerable J.S. Woodsworth, who took the opportunity to subject the House to a short sermon on this most recent contest between good and evil. Quoting from an American writer he alleged:

Chemists in the past have been working for years and years ... to devise a method by which they could make gold, synthetic gold. These power trust officials have beaten the chemists to it. They have made hundreds of millions of gold out of water – nothing but water. It does not even need to be clean water; it is usually muddy dirty water, but they are making gold out of water daily, and the consumers of light and power, the little fellow who reads his newspaper by electric light, the woman who uses electricity to wash clothes, the bit manufacturer who consumes hundreds of thousands of horsepower in making things that the American people use, the miner who operates the coal mines – all of them are contributing their part to the great operation of the power trust of converting water into pure, yellow gold; and we sit idly by.[13]

Prime Minister Mackenzie King did not participate in the debate, save for one or two interjections. It was left to the solicitor-general and unofficial guardian of Quebec provincial rights in Ottawa, the Hon. Lucien Cannon, to reiterate that the water power belonged to Quebec, and the federal parliament should stay away from provincial matters. Within a day this little debate was over, with time to spare for the parliamentarians to turn their attention to a discussion of egg-grading regulations. At the end of the day Mackenzie King could write rather complacently in his diary: 'In H. of C. the day was taken up with an effort on part of progressive party & Bennett to arouse suspicion over Beauharnois, as a grafting proposition for which Govt was responsible. I have a contempt for part progressives play & hypocrisy of men like Bennett and Ryckman etc. Cannon got quite the best of the situation in replying tonight. We got on well with ways and means after.'[14]

The bombshell Regan and the Progressives had tossed into parliament had not exploded as they had hoped it would. It had hissed and sputtered briefly and then seemed to go out. But Regan was not through yet. He prepared a second memorandum for Gardiner and Garland, this time specifically pointing out and emphasizing that under the provisions of PC 422 detailed plans must be filed before commencement of construction on the 'works.' No such plans had been filed to supplement those filed prior to the passage of PC 422.

The contents of Regan's second memo were read into the parliamentary record on 28 May 1930, and on 29 May Gardiner specifically asked whether 'the plans in connection with the Beauharnois Light Heat and Power Company have been approved.' Public Works Minister Elliott replied simply stating that plans of the company had been approved.[15] Nothing further was done about the matter that day, and the next day Mackenzie King called the general election and prorogued parliament.

Frank Regan hoped and expected that the affairs of the Beauharnois Power Corporation would become a major election issue. Gardiner and Garland, however, had to concentrate their attention and efforts on pressing western agricultural issues and problems created by the severely depressed economic conditions. Denunciations of the machinations of big business were not new to the farmers of Alberta. They were already fully convinced that greedy eastern businessmen were largely to blame for all the problems of prairie agriculture. That is why they elected men like Gardiner and Garland. They were not satisfied if their elected representatives merely told them what was wrong. The farmers wanted their members to do something about it.

Regan tried to persuade the Conservatives to take up the matter, but R.B. Bennett did not find time even to meet with him. Regan then appealed to General A.D. McRae, the Conservative campaign organizer. On 10 July 1930 he wrote to McRae: 'It is a tragedy that the Conservative party does not take this matter up and make it an issue. No matter what may be said later on, nor no matter what the connection of the party is with the promoters, the people are beginning to wonder why the Conservative party is keeping silent. It is idle to argue tariff when the people are being robbed of their birthright and not a word raised in protest.'[16] The crusty old Tory general was not interested, informing Regan rather bluntly that

> I have made it clear to you and to hundreds of others that I was not disposed to press any scandal in this election or, in fact, any issue which would lead away from the main issues of the campaign, i.e. our present, unfortunate economic situation. You, of course, have a personal interest in this matter. The Canadian people, however, except those in Ontario, are not greatly concerned. Mr. Bennett, as you know, is clearly on record. I do not believe it is desireable to go further in this matter at this time as it would only detract from the main issues.[17]

Regan was not easily put off. He continued his efforts to have General McRae do something, but both McRae and Bennett would have nothing further to do with Beauharnois matters. The reasons for this refusal by the Conservative leaders to take up the Beauharnois matter during the 1930 election campaign are not entirely clear. In his evidence before the 1931 parliamentary inquiry R.O. Sweezey stated that he had come to an understanding with General McRae which included a $200,000 election campaign contribution. But McRae, according to Sweezey, had never come to collect the money. It is not clear whether either Bennett or McRae investigated Frank Regan's charges during the election campaign and then decided it was best not to take Sweezey's money. What is clear is that both Bennett and McRae were bombarded by Regan with letters and documents alleging serious irregularities in the affairs of the Beauharnois Power Corporation. And they declined to collect a $200,000 campaign contribution that had been promised by Sweezey.

Circumstantial evidence suggests that, at some point during the campaign, R.B. Bennett arrived at the conclusion that there was some substance in Regan's charges. General McRae was advised not to take Sweezey's money, and the Ontario Conservatives were warned that there might be further investigations. If the Ontario Tories had any skeletons in the closet they were given ample time to bury them before any federal investigation began. Immediately after the election Frank Regan again contacted Bennett, asking for an interview to press his complaints and charges against the Beauharnois promoters and the now-defeated federal Liberals. Bennett continued to put him off, until Regan was able to enlist the support of the Ontario attorney-general, the Hon. W.H. Price, who was a strong advocate of public ownership of power.

Both Gardiner and Garland were re-elected and returned to Ottawa eager to investigate the affairs of the Beauharnois companies in more detail. The resulting inquiry in 1931 revealed one of Canada's most serious political scandals.

11

The scandal revealed

The Beauharnois promoters were disappointed with the outcome of the 1930 federal election. They had offered campaign funds to the Conservatives, but their donation had not been accepted. In the parliamentary debate before the election R.B. Bennett had promised, albeit without evident enthusiasm, a judicial inquiry into the affairs of the Beauharnois companies. The election campaign, however, had shown that the new prime minister was more interested in ways and means of dealing with the problems of the economic depression than in an inquiry into the affairs of big business. After the election, neither the prime minister nor General McRae seemed willing to deal with the Beauharnois problems in ways the determined Frank Regan thought appropriate.

Regan's failure to persuade the Conservatives to make Beauharnois an election issue led him to search for other means to exert pressure. Thus, on 19 June 1930 he had a lengthy interview with Colonel W.H. Price, the attorney-general of Ontario, who, coincidentally, was also a strong supporter of public ownership of hydroelectric power. The main point Regan wanted to impress on Price was that the advertisements and statements made to promote the sale of the Beauharnois 6 per cent collateral trust bonds were misleading and fraudulent. Specifically, the reference in the prospectus to long-term expansion plans to divert the entire flow of the St Lawrence was, according to Regan, without justification. He also insisted that purchasers of the bonds were being misled regarding the security of the bonds, since it was not clearly stated that these would be the company's junior securities.

The interview with Price was sufficiently encouraging that Regan, at Price's suggestion, prepared a lengthy and detailed memorandum in which he discussed and documented his charges against the Beauharnois promoters. He concluded his diatribe by alleging 'That the promoters of this scheme are guilty of breach both of the letter and the spirit of the Security Frauds Prevention Act and its amendments' and demanding 'criminal prosecution of the men who were guilty of issuing this Prospectus.'[1]

Price promised to investigate the matter but did almost nothing for several months. Consequently, in October of 1930, Regan resorted to threats. 'In the event of your Department refusing to take action in this matter,' he wrote the attorney-general, 'I desire to advise you that certain people, for whom I am acting, are prepared to go before a Magistrate and lay the proper charges against those responsible for the sale of these bonds under the circumstances which I explained to you in my letter.'[2] Price replied that he had referred the matter to Colonel Denison, the Ontario registrar of joint stock companies but had not yet received a detailed report on the Beauharnois bonds.[3] This information merely enlarged the scope of Frank Regan's determined efforts. He immediately sent a blunt letter to Colonel Denison, in which he stated, 'A fraud of the very worst kind, in my opinion, is being perpetrated on the people of Ontario by the Company and it seems to me that something ought to be done and done without delay.'[4] Denison responded by inviting Regan to an interview on 27 October 1930. Regan thus forced the Ontario government to review in some detail the affairs of the Beauharnois companies and to consider appropriate action.

The investigations in Toronto, however, were soon overtaken and then co-ordinated with developments and investigations in Ottawa. R.B. Bennett and his Conservatives now formed the government. Both Robert Gardiner and E.J. Garland had been re-elected, and the ever-vigilant Frank Regan immediately noted that Sweezey was beginning to court those now in power. He informed Gardiner and Garland that 'R.O. Sweezey bought out The National Press a year or two ago, and during the last campaign it was most loud and vociferous in its support of Mackenzie King. Immediately after the elections, however, when King was defeated, Sweezey turns around and supports Bennett.'[5] Regan also warned that the Conservative organizer in Manitoba 'has gone over in support of Sweezey, and of course Sweezey in turn will support him or perhaps, in other words, put him on his payroll. This, of course, is all in anticipation of what might transpire in the house next season in respect of Beauharnois, Sweezey making as many allies as possible in the meantime.'[6] Regan further told Garland that this same Manitoba Conservative organizer was now trying to influence and silence Gardiner. An intermediary named Wilfrid Campbell, who had been re-elected Progressive member for the Mackenzie constituency in Saskatchewan and was thus a member of Gardiner's own loosely organized parliamentary caucus, had been recruited for the purpose. Gardiner himself had informed Regan of the overtures by Campbell.

I received a very cordial invitation through him [Wilfrid Campbell] to visit the works of the Beauharnois project with all our expenses paid. This invitation was to have been tendered to us through Mr. Campbell and through an intermediary between Mr. Campbell and Mr. Sweezey. It is just possible that this means may be used for the purpose of heading off any investigation of importance by the Federal Government.

I understand that Mr. Campbell is rather partial to the present Conservative Government and in view of the statement made by Mr. Bennett during the debate on this question in the House, it is just possible that such methods may be used for the purpose of permitting Mr. Bennett to get from under his promise of a judicial investigation. I am not sure on this point but that is what it indicates to me. We refused this invitation more particularly when generous expenses were to be allowed for our time and trouble.[7]

Regan was delighted. He wrote Gardiner that he had been told by someone who was

extremely close to the powers that be in the Beauharnois crowd [that] ... Mr. Campbell was approached by the Beauharnois crowd and advised them that he would be able to arrange with you not to bring the Beauharnois question up at the next session of the House of Commons, or in other words that he would see that you did nothing in the matter ... This man offered to bet me anything in the world that the matter would never be mentioned in the next session – not even by any of the Progressives ... I am delighted to learn that you refused to accept the invitation. It shows, at least, that there are some honest men in the world.[8]

Having opened up a new front in Ontario and stabilized the offensive in the House of Commons, Regan made a determined attempt to have the matter raised in the Senate as well. Several of the Beauharnois promoters were Liberal senators. Senator Charles Murphy, a Liberal but also a bitter enemy of Mackenzie King, was approached. Murphy, however, declined to take any action:

It seems to me that private and personal initiative in regard to an investigation of the Beauharnois matter is not called for, in view of the fact that Premier Bennett stated in the House of Commons and elsewhere, that he would have the whole matter investigated if he attained power. He has attained power, and it is now for those who are interested in having an investigation to see that he carries out his specific public promises. Personally I can appreciate the difficulties that are confronting him if the rumours be true that there are several Conservatives identified with the project as well as Liberals. If this report be well founded, it merely indicates that what is usually done in such cases was also done in the case of Beauharnois, and that politicians of both parties have come together so as to make sure that their respective parties will not interfere with their game of loot.[9]

In 1931 the focus of action for Beauharnois would be in Ottawa, where R.B. Bennett had promised a judicial inquiry. Immediately after the federal election and on the suggestion of the Ontario Attorney General, Bennett asked the departments of Public Works and Justice for confidential reports on the matter.[10] Those reports were prepared while Bennett was in England for the imperial conference and awaited him on his return. They were detailed, factual, and bureaucratic reports which dealt at length with the constitutional problems, with the several plans that had been filed, and with the fact that the detailed plans called for in PC 422 had not been filed.

While Bennett was still in England, Frank Regan, Robert Gardiner, E.J. Garland, and several legal advisers prepared their next assault on Beauharnois and on the former Liberal government which had passed PC 422. For more than two months this small group was busily at work in the Chateau Laurier preparing memoranda, questions, and speeches on or about Beauharnois. This work led initially to a series of questions raised by Gardiner in the House of Commons. At first there were only six queries, and several of those were later withdrawn while others were added, until two separate returns for five and fourteen questions, respectively, were requested.[11] Most of these queries were not answered immediately, and the case prepared by the small group working in the Chateau Laurier did not depend on the answers. Almost all the information used by this group was provided by Frank Regan and Narcisse Cantin. It was based on evidence given by Sweezey and others in the legal suit between Cantin and Sweezey. Regan's approach in that suit is well illustrated in some of the instructions he gave Cantin: 'It will be necessary for us to make Sweezey tell what he has been doing day by day from the time that he first came into contact with you over this transaction, and that covers a period of two years. You, I think, told me yourself when I was in Montreal that you had prepared some 4,000 questions to be asked.'[12]

One of the ironies of the situation was that Prime Minister Bennett had also established his Ottawa place of residence in the Chateau Laurier which, even in calm and normal times, carries a heavy volume of political traffic. Newsmen reported that Frank Regan was so paranoid that someone might be eavesdropping or spying on his little group that Hudson's Bay Company blankets were hung over the doors to prevent anyone who might be so inclined from spying through the keyhole. Elaborate rituals and passwords were initiated to ensure that 'the enemy' would not discover the identity of key informants who might then be silenced through bribery.[13]

Robert Gardiner and E.J. Garland launched their major attack in the House of Commons on 19 May 1931. They moved an adjournment to debate a matter of urgent importance and carried the House on a division. They then went over much of the information they had first introduced and read into the parliamentary record almost exactly one year earlier. The main thrust of their attack, however, had changed. They now challenged the legality of PC 422. That order in council had been approved under the general powers given the cabinet by the Navigable Waters Protection Act. Gardiner and Garland argued that the act did not give such power to the cabinet and that authority to divert water from navigable streams must have parliamentary rather than merely cabinet approval. If that was the case, they argued, 'the whole basis upon which the Beauharnois development is now being proceeded with is illegal, that it has no foundation or authority in any statute whatsoever, and that the government had no jurisdiction for passing the order in council.'[14] There were also references to the enormous and improper profits of the promoters, and to the fact that the promoters were proceeding without having their detailed plans approved by the minister of public works as required by PC 422.

Robert Gardiner, in his speech, referred directly to the legal suit between Cantin and Sweezey, and alleged that there had been improper judicial interference in that case. Specifically, he alleged that Chief Justice Greenshields of Montreal, whose close relatives in the Greenshields' investment and securities firm had substantial interests in the Beauharnois promotion, had improperly withdrawn Justice Patterson from Cantin's case against Sweezey and substituted

Justice Boyer. It was Justice Boyer who had decided the case against Cantin.

It was not clear whether Gardiner really intended to attack the judiciary. His entire speech had been prepared beforehand, almost certainly by Regan, and Gardiner was accused by other members of the House of simply reading what had been written for him.[15] Whatever Gardiner's intent, Prime Minister Bennett immediately rose to defend the impartiality of the judiciary. He also made it clear that in view of Gardiner's attack it was no longer appropriate to refer Beauharnois matters to a judicial inquiry. He was willing, however, to have the matter referred either to the Standing Committee on Banking and Commerce or to a special select committee to be appointed. He further offered that Gardiner could suggest appropriate terms of reference which must, however, avoid matters under provincial jurisdiction.[16]

In his speech Gardiner referred with particular vehemence to the fact that early in 1931 the Beauharnois Light, Heat and Power Company had applied to and received from the Quebec government authorization to divert an additional 30,000 cubic feet per second of water – this despite the fact that PC 422 allowed for the diversion of only 40,000 cubic feet per second. This, he insisted, was proof positive that the Beauharnois promoters intended to divert the flow of the entire St Lawrence. Such proof, however, was hardly needed. Sweezey had always said that the company would eventually harness the entire river. He readily admitted that, like the slaughterhouse that uses everything except the squeal of a pig, Beauharnois intended to use all the Soulanges Section of the St Lawrence except the roar of the rapids. But this declaration infuriated those who argued that the nation's natural resources should not be alienated.

Some Ontario politicians also feared that increased development in the Soulanges Section would further delay publicly owned development of the hydroelectric potential in the international section of the St Lawrence.[17]

The debate on 19 May 1931 added little information to what had already been said a year earlier, but it led to immediate party consultations and to the official appointment on 10 June 1931 of a nine-member Special Select Committee with broad terms of reference. Five members of the Select Committee were Conservatives, three were Liberals, with Gardiner making the ninth member. The committee chose as its chairman W.A. Gordon, the minister of immigration and colonization who had been elected for the first time to Parliament less than a year earlier. Mackenzie King doubted that this Select Committee would accomplish a great deal, noting in his diary that

> the personnel on the Tory side indicates an intention on the part of the Gov't to put as M.P.s of their number those who are of the lowest class in the house, a group that can be depended upon for dirty work of any kind, unscrupulous, & capable of being 'controlled'. They will doubtless find the canal people have exceeded their authority in construction & blame us for not having plans approved, but I question if they will go far in other directions.[18]

The Select Committee began its historic sessions on 15 June 1931 and immediately prepared what were officially referred to as its first and its second reports. The first report simply requested permission to print the minutes and proceedings of the evidence taken. The second report requested permission to employ counsel, while a third report, dated 29 June 1931, sought permission to employ a secretary.[19] In addition to these administrative matters the committee also made arrangements to subpoena various witnesses.

The substantive hearings began on 23 June 1931 when the committee, with the guidance of members of the Privy Council Office, reviewed the various orders in council, particulary PC 422, pertaining to Beauharnois. This, in the words of one reporter, made for 'unexciting reading.'[20] Interest increased slightly when the committee moved on to question the deputy minister and several senior engineers from the Department of Public Works. Great masses of plans and engineering reports were identified, discussed, and filed. The committee quickly established that the detailed plans required under PC 422 had not been filed or approved. The Public Works officials, however, were extremely defensive, testy, evasive, and unco-operative. Committee members did not appreciate this bureaucratic hedging. The basic explanation of why detailed plans had not been filed was, however, provided.

On the next day there was a brief airing of the relations between Sweezey and the Cantin companies, including evidence by J.N. Cantin, son of the promoter of the Transportation and Power Company. More important and much more interesting was an investigation of the finances of the Beauharnois companies, including Gardiner's charge that the promoters stood to make a profit of up to $104 million. The early evidence on that issue was unimpressive, however, leading one news reporter to write that 'on finance Mr.

Gardiner may be no more expert than were Farmer financiers in the government a while back.'[21]

All told, the first week of hearings was rather dull, and the *Financial Times* expressed the view that 'the impression is growing that the Beauharnois power inquiry will end just about where it began.'[22] There was nothing in the early evidence to cause that paper to drop its support of Beauharnois. An editorial on 26 June 1931 argued that 'The successful carrying out of the Beauharnois scheme, as with so many other great projects which have marked the development of Canada's resources, will be another triumph for modern finance and engineering.'[23]

On 1 July, after a week of hearings, the entire committee adjourned to make an official visit to the construction site. Beauharnois officials were by this time well versed in the entertaining of visiting dignitaries. Construction on the entire project was again in full progress, with more than 2,500 men busily at work when everywhere else in the country unemployment was the dominant issue of the day. The promise of numerous new industries, which were expected to establish themselves along the canal, gave hope of further help for the unemployed. For the visit of the parliamentary party a locomotive and several flatcars of the Beauharnois Railway Company were equipped with chairs and the entire party was given a free ride for the length of the canal. Those with a desire to do so were allowed to ascend the heights to sit in the operator's seat of one of the tower excavators. The huge spiral cutter of the R.O. Sweezey suction dredge was raised and those wishing a memento of the occasion were photographed standing before the seven-foot-high monster spiral cutter. The various impressive statistics of the proposed new generators were available for those with an appetite for such things, while more refreshing chilled liquids were provided for the thirsty. The large press party had ready access to free and well-cooled beer, and, lest some indulge too freely and encounter difficulty in writing up the story, assorted written pieces suitable for publication in the nation's daily press had been prepared. The Beauharnois promoters could certainly put on an impressive show – the more appealing in 1931 because their project seemed to offer one of the few opportunities of dealing with the disastrous unemployment situation in the country. Dominion Day 1931 was, unfortunately, a very hot day, and some of the railway flatcars were not equipped with canopies, leading one disgruntled journalist to write: 'Human sacrifices, sizzling on the brazen altars of Beauharnois, or statesmen patriots frying to make a Canadian holiday, the Beauharnois Committee of the

House of Commons slowly fried its way down the dry ditch on Dominion Day.'[24] In the very next paragraph, however, this writer, perhaps refreshed with a long cool one, conceded:

> They said it was 104 down Beauharnois way – but don't believe it. It was a bright sunny July day, and the whole trip a jolly picnic ... The committee rode the canal from end to end, on flat cars, lunched like Chateau Laurier customers at the company's mess at Melocheville, motored back to Valleyfield and slowly completed their self-cooked burnt offering on one of Sir Henry Thornton's [President of Canadian National Railways] trains back to Ottawa. What they saw of the job impressed them.[25]

Sweezey met the committee on the job site and proudly spoke of his company's excellent labour relations, no doubt for the particular benefit of Robert Gardiner. 'We have no labour troubles,' Sweezey boasted and then showed the committee members the company's camps which were described later in the newspapers as 'models of outdoor comfort, and the food excellent.'[26] In general, Sweezey, the dreamer, promoter, and engineer, was enthusiasm and confidence personified – a man who was masterminding one of the largest and most important construction projects in his country's history and was very eager to talk to anyone about it.

The entire first week of July was exceptionally hot and humid, greatly affecting the mood and pace of the hearings of the parliamentary committee. The *Telegram* reporter offered a colourful description of the committee's discomfiture. 'With Col. T. Herbert Lennox and Hon. Geo. B. Jones, C.L. Dorion and Sam Jacobs all molten to the point of invisibility and Gen Fiset vigorously fanning himself into the same blissful state, the Beauharnois Investigation Committee staggered through to a humid conclusion of the first fortnight of their labours when the chimes struck half-past five Friday.'[27]

It was all rather dull until the third week, but events became decidedly livelier after that. R.A.C. Henry and Frank P. Jones, two men who had already made millions from their association with Beauharnois, took the witness stand. They radiated an air of confidence and success, answering in 'crisp dried answers and genial well-what-about-it manner of the men who do things by the millions.' Their demeanour contrasted sharply with 'the tight-lipped reticences or generally defensive answers of some of the Government secondaries with whom these big businessmen are constantly in conflict, or should one say, in contact.'[28] Both men gave straightforward answers, Jones readily admitting that his investment of $190,000 had increased in value to $790,000 sixteen months later. The profit levels, he suggested for Gardiner's particular benefit, were similar to those earned by farmer co-operative grain and elevator companies.[29] Henry readily admitted that final plans had not yet been submitted and that the Beauharnois company hoped eventually to divert the entire flow of the St Lawrence. He promised that they would seek proper authorization before exceeding their allotted water rights.

This testimony was followed by a lengthy, detailed, and decidedly tedious examination of Hugh B. Griffith, the secretary of the Beauharnois Power Corporation. Griffith had brought with him and was asked to explain in detail the minute books and financial records of the first two Beauharnois syndicates and then of the Beauharnois Power Corporation. Unquestionably the most interesting aspect of Griffith's testimony pertained to the Sterling Industrial Corporation and of Senator McDougald's and R.A.C. Henry's use of that corporation to obtain a major participation in the second Beauharnois syndicate. No one could ascertain that the Sterling Industrial Corporation was of any value, except that it was seen as a nuisance or an obstacle that had to be removed. This new testimony surprised and worried Mackenzie King, who noted in his diary on 10 July 1931:

> I confess I am amazed at some of the things that are being disclosed of which I have known nothing, e.g. his [Senator McDougald's] association with Henry since 1922, the formation of the Sterling Corporation & sale of their rights to Beauharnois about 1926, at a sum which netted large profits to McDougald ... it would seem that McDougald had tried to leave impression that his friendship with me gave him an influence at Ottawa that he did not possess. I had not known of Henry's ... association with McDougald when appt'd Deputy Minister. My having made the apptmt & also Moyer a previous secretary being retained by McDougald makes a sort of grouping all of which has the appearance to an evil mind of design.[30]

The revelations regarding the Sterling Industrial Corporation provided an opportunity for friends of Narcisse Cantin to ask why Cantin's Transportation and Power Corporation, which had also filed plans before Beauharnois, had not been given equal consideration with the Sterling Industrial Corporation. The explanation was that Cantin's company had only an expired option and lacked funding and business acumen. Still, these revelations concerning the Sterling Industrial Corporation documented improper actions by a senator and a one-time civil servant, each of whom had used privileged information to his own advantage.

The Select Committee decided, in part because of the revelations of Senator McDougald's involvement in the Sterling Industrial Corporation, that all three of the senators who were known to be involved in the Beauharnois project be called to testify. Since the investigating committee was a special committee of the House of Commons, a special motion had to be passed in the House of Commons requesting that the Senate give leave to the three senators to attend and give evidence. This permission was readily granted by the Senate, and the three senators were duly called by the committee.[31]

Senator Raymond immediately expressed eagerness to tell his side of the story, but on the witness stand he could recall almost nothing that did not deal in one way or another with Quebec politics. He had never clearly separated his provincial and federal political fund-raising activities. And the parliamentary committee had no jurisdiction to ask any questions dealing directly or indirectly with Quebec provincial affairs. So Senator Raymond simply told the committee of his personal involvement in the Beauharnois project, most of which was apparent from the company's records.

Senator Haydon had suffered a serious heart attack. The precarious state of his health did not allow him to give evidence before the parliamentary committee, although he did appear later before a Senate committee.

Senator McDougald, lacking any other plausible excuse, let it be known that he would refuse to give any evidence before a Commons committee. There was not, in his opinion, any means whereby such a committee could compel him to give evidence. This obstreperous response prompted Prime Minister Bennett to threaten that if McDougald could not be compelled to appear before the committee a royal commission would be appointed to investigate the Beauharnois affair and McDougald's part in it. There was no question about the powers of a royal commission to subpoena senators. This threat, and the advice of his lawyers, convinced Senator McDougald to adopt a more co-operative stance. In due course he told the investigating committee his version of the events in which he had participated.

The committee hearings, and damaging political information, created an atmosphere in which gossip and rumours of all kinds flourished. The flavour and tone can be deduced from the following letter received by the prime minister from a senior and respected businessman.

On the afternoon of 20th June 1929, I was sitting in the rotunda of the Chateau Laurier when from one of the elevators emerged Sweezey, Frank P. Jones, Walter Mitchell and a fourth man ... They had five huge black club bags evidently crammed with currency. The bags were filled so full that the impressions of the tightly bound hand bills showed throu. They were surprised to see me in the rotunda, but Mitchell, whom I have known intimately for many years smiled defiantly. He had previously boasted that he had 'fixed' both parties. He and his friends evidently had telephoned for taxis, but they had not arrived. So the bags remained on the floor of the rotunda in full view for several minutes. Soon the two taxis arrived, and the four men and five bags drove west, and turned down to the office of McGovern, Haydon & Ebbs. A friend who went to that office at my suggestion and who knows Haydon intimately told me later that a leading Ferguson Tory was there with a bunch of Federal Grits ... It would make too long a letter if I told you many others things I know in connection with Beauharnois.[32]

This information was almost certainly incorrect. The major transfer of funds from Beauharnois to political campaign funds did not take place in June of 1929. The Beauharnois promoters did not have that kind of money available in June, and when they did make political payments, they transferred Canadian victory or savings bonds registered in Sweezey's name, not cash. Sweezey retained a reliable record of such transactions.

There was, however, another nasty rumour circulating in Ottawa. On 13 July 1931 Secretary of State C.H. Cahan notified Prime Minister Bennett that a curious piece of evidence had turned up in the review of the financial records of Beauharnois. It was a bill submitted by Senator McDougald for expenses incurred 'for Hon. W.L. Mackenzie King and self' on a trip to Bermuda, and hotel expenses in New York in April 1930. The amount of the expenses thus claimed was $852.32. Cahan asked Prime Minister Bennett to 'please consider whether it should be put in evidence. I doubt the expediency of so doing.'[33]

The existence of the voucher also became known to other members of the Select Committee on 13 July, and a Liberal committee member immediately notified King who was utterly 'amazed at this document' and noted in his diary later that day: 'I felt incensed at McDougald. It looked as though he were trying to use me, have the co. feel he had influence with me.'[34] King discussed the matter with several trusted advisers and then spoke to both Bennett and Cahan, explaining that he had gone to Bermuda for a rest and some business and that, without his prior knowledge, Senator McDougald had paid a portion of his Bermuda hotel bill. He further asked that this piece of evidence be suppressed out of respect for the high office of prime minister which might be improperly tarnished in the minds of those who did not understand all the circumstances.[35] Bennett and Cahan were willing to suppress the voucher. Robert Gardiner was not, and it was later filed.

The review of Beauharnois financial records revealed other troublesome matters. Large payments to prominent lawyers with close political connections and substantial campaign contributions, particularly to Ontario Conservatives and to federal and Quebec Liberals, had been made. These discoveries left the members of the Select Committee in a difficult position. Quebec committee members, the lawyer representing the Quebec government, and, of course, Senator Raymond, made it absolutely clear that the parliamentary committee had no jurisdiction whatever to investigate matters internal to Quebec, including any Quebec election campaign contributions.

Many of the politicians feared that a detailed investigation of campaign contributions made by Beauharnois would be difficult to contain. The federal Conservatives seemed fairly safe, having refused Sweezey's money in 1930, but only if the investigation dealt only with Beauharnois campaign contributions, not with election funds generally. But the same could hardly be said for their Ontario or Quebec colleagues, and the federal Liberals, of course, were obviously vulnerable. Many of the politicians therefore thought these were matters best left unexamined. King, for example, noted in his diary on 13 July 1931: '[Cahan] then went on to tell me what the Committee (Cons) members knew of funds from Beauharnois to Lib, Cons. etc. I was amazed when he gave me the figs ... which included $150,000 to Conservatives in Ontario (which meant Ferguson). The sittings of the Committee bring out very much concerning fees to lawyers of all sorts & kinds of purposes.'[36]

There was particular concern among the Conservatives about revelations of large election contributions to the Ontario party in return for help in securing the Ontario Hydro contract for the Beauharnois company. The former premier, G. Howard Ferguson, under whose administration all this activity had taken place, had since resigned the premiership and been appointed to Canada House in London. He was contacted for advice and information on the matter. The *Toronto Telegram* described the tense situation thus:

> This whisper, coupled with other intimations, caused one or more sleepless nights in Ottawa. The outcome is said to have been another transoceanic call to the Hon. G. Howard Ferguson in London, and the emphatic information from that gentleman that the inquiry could go through to China and come back but it would fail to find spot, stain or blemish in the record both of his own dealings with Beauharnois and those of all associated with him while he was Prime Minister in Queen's Park, or at any other time ... It was so emphatic and convincing that Conservative circles accepted it as well worth the $25 per minute the ocean telephone costs.[37]

This happy news from London encouraged the Conservative committee members to open up more unsavoury matters, or at least those portions that did not intrude into Quebec matters. The Ontario government waived further objections, Howard Ferguson having authorized his fellow Conservatives to 'shoot the works in the Beauharnois investigation.'[38] This brought to the witness stand John Aird, Jr, who, according to the Beauharnois records and the word of Beauharnois promoters, had collected $125,000 for the Ferguson Conservatives.

Aird readily admitted that he had received $125,000 (120 $1,000 bonds, plus accumulated interest, plus a small cheque, bringing the total to exactly $125,000), but he claimed this sum had been a payment to him personally for service rendered to the Beauharnois company. He produced a letter from his Toronto bankers showing that he still had the 120 $1,000 bonds and that they had, therefore, never gone to the Ontario Conservative party. When asked what services he had rendered to earn the $125,000 Aird was vague. He did admit that he had spoken only once to Sweezey and never to anyone at Ontario Hydro or in the Ontario Conservative party organization. His only political activity, he claimed was that he had once driven a group of men digging a ditch at Mimico to a polling booth.[39] When pressed to explain exactly what he had done to earn the $125,000 Aird admitted: 'I cannot remember anything definite.' Both Sweezey and Griffith, who had made the payment, were emphatic in their statements that Aird had represented himself as an agent of the Ontario Conservative party, and the payment had been made as a political campaign contribution.

Aird's unbelievable testimony led one Liberal member of the Select Committee to some heated words: 'Q. Do you suggest that Mr. Sweezey was such an utter ass to pay $120,000 for anything of that kind? ... A. I do not know whether you would consider him an ass or not. He wanted something pretty badly.'[40]

Sweezey's evidence, of course, sharply contradicted that given by Aird. Sweezey, in fact, presented himself in a surprisingly candid manner. He readily admitted that he had bought political influence, and that he had spent large sums of money in order to obtain the crucial order in council. His general attitude was simply that he had been a politically naïve and innocent engineer who knew very little about politics and had followed the advice and guidance of his political mentors. Wasn't that the way things were usually done? He regarded the campaign contributions and other political payments as a form of tax which promoters like him had to pay to have the necessary things done in Ottawa, Toronto, and Quebec City.[41] The explanations given by Sweezey and Griffith about the $125,000 seemed far more persuasive than the story offered by John Aird, but Aird still had the bonds. They had not been turned over to the Conservative party of Ontario, and the committee therefore concluded that 'no evidence [was] before the Committee that would indicate that any of these bonds have reached any political organization, or any person authorized to receive campaign funds.'[42]

The Aird testimony created an atmosphere of 'sensation and suspicion' in the committee rooms and in the surrounding lobbies and hallways where assorted lawyers, politicians, and reporters jostled one another. At this point Mackenzie King became particularly concerned about the impression that might be created if information about the substantial donations of Dr McDougald to the P.C. Larkin fund in the Old Colony Trust, Boston, was also revealed.[43] On 15 July 1931 King wrote in his diary that 'he [McDougald] has so little sense & is so devoid of the ethical side of things that one dreads the outcome of any testimony he may give.'[44]

Two days later his worries were more clearly focused on McDougald's contributions to funds collected by P.C. Larkin to refurbish Laurier House and establish the trust fund in Old Colony Trust, Boston.

> I can see the Tory party intend to do their worst to destroy me, if they can – they will try to link up all this with McDougald & McDougald with myself. Fortunately I have been careful with McD. right along, but the thing that

distresses me greatly is the interpretation they will try to place on our association – on the voucher – but most of all any contribution he may have made to the L.H. Fund which they know of, I feel sure, & which will be completely misrepresented. The association of Haydon will also be magnified into one related to Beauharnois etc. All of this has made me very depressed & sick at heart.[45]

Mackenzie King regarded his suffering as 'a real Gethsemane thro' which one is being called upon to pass at this time.'[46] His peace of mind was further disturbed two days later when Sweezey was recalled and asked specifically about contributions he had made during the last federal election campaign. Sweezey replied cheerfully that between $600,000 and $700,000 had gone to the federal and Quebec Liberals, with much smaller sums going to individual candidates and to the Conservative party in Quebec. The next day King wrote:

This has been one of the hardest days of my life. I felt sick at heart & mortified at the revelations of yesterday reflecting as they do on the Administration which bears my name & on those who have been close political friends and associates ... It was very trying to go about with wealthy friends on such a day, to be arranging a dinner party with wines etc etc when I really should be in prayer, in sack-cloth & ashes were I to carry out the feeling I have.[47]

King spent Sunday 19 July at Kingsmere and noted: 'If ever in my life I felt the blessing of a quiet sabbath it was today.' But even in the peaceful atmosphere of Kingsmere the worries persisted. 'My fear has been McDougald might be questioned on these lines. [Larkin fund] as it [is] known on so many sides I have been assisted & by whom in many cases.' King added, however, that in this difficult time he had particularly felt the nearness of 'dear mother.' A dream in which deceased family members came to comfort him, provided further solace for the opposition leader's troubled soul.[48]

Mackenzie King's biographer states that there were widespread rumours that some unsavoury scandals were never made public because of a 'gentleman's agreement' between Bennett and Mackenzie King. He suggests that the discussion about whether to introduce the Bermuda voucher was the basis of these rumours.[49] It seems far more likely that McDougald's contributions to the Larkin fund and Sweezey's alleged $200,000 payment to Howard Ferguson were the subject of rumours in 1931 and 1932. The King diaries, and King's later actions, do not suggest he was directly involved in any 'gentleman's agreement.' But Bennett and the Conservatives almost certainly knew about the Larkin fund and decided it would not be appropriate to introduce that evidence. King, Andrew Haydon, and other prominent Liberals remained convinced that Howard Ferguson had been paid off. But Senator McDougald was not questioned about the Larkin fund, and later in the Senate inquiry a complete airing of the payment to Ferguson was effectively thwarted.

Senator McDougald gave his evidence to the parliamentary committee on 20 July. He was calm, collected, and gave straightforward answers, prompting one committee member to say McDougald had been their best witness. That evening, however, an 'immensely relieved' Mackenzie King noted that the Larkin fund, and hence 'the ignominy of the whole business in the eyes of those who do not understand,' had not been mentioned. He could therefore go to bed 'so grateful to the Almighty God for his protecting Providence. I pray it may continue.'[50]

King's troubles, however, were not quite over yet. On 21 July McDougald's Bermuda voucher was entered officially as evidence. Rather than appear personally before the committee to offer his explanation, King decided to make an official statement, as a matter of privilege, in the House of Commons. He toyed with the idea of making his statement before the voucher was officially entered as evidence[51] but instead decided to offer a more detailed and carefully prepared statement on the following day. He pointed out that

> any bills that were put into the Beauharnois company were not put in with my knowledge or with my consent; they were not put in by me or on my account, but were put in by Senator McDougald with respect to expenses which he himself had incurred ... I had no knowledge that Senator McDougald had settled the hotel account at Bermuda until I was about to pay my bill, when the clerk informed me that the Senator, before leaving, had paid the account ... During the entire trip to Bermuda I never discussed the question of Beauharnois either with Senator Haydon or with Senator McDougald, or with anyone else.[52]

These revelations really marked the end of the substantive testimony presented to the Select Committee. Several witnesses examined earlier, including John Aird, Jr, and R.O. Sweezey, were recalled for some additional questions, but the last week of July was devoted to the preparation of the committee's report. The chairman drafted the report, and then the entire committee went over that draft, paragraph by paragraph. Numerous alterations were made, but eventually each paragraph was unanimously approved by the committee members. This task done, the chairman proposed that the report be forwarded to the House of Commons with the unanimous committee recommendation that the House concur in it. The Liberal committee members wanted an opportunity to review the entire report with Mackenzie King before agreeing to endorse it, but the chairman 'made it abundantly plain that I consider it to be my duty to see that the report was a report from this committee and not influenced by any advice which might come from the leader of the opposition or others.'[53]

The official, or fourth, report of the Select Committee was tabled in the House of Commons on 28 July, and the motion for concurrence was debated on 30 July 1931. The twenty-six-page report provided a good deal of background and historical information about the project and proceeded to deal with specific issues and individuals. Senator McDougald and R.A.C. Henry were criticized particularly harshly for their involvement and actions with the Sterling Industrial Corporation. According to the report Senator McDougald's actions 'cannot be too strongly condemned,'[54] while R.A.C. Henry 'does not commend himself as a fit and proper person to continue in the management of Beauharnois.'[55] R.O. Sweezey and H.B. Griffith were condemned for the campaign contributions that were 'shamelessly, wastefully and needlessly made for the expressed purpose of obtaining favourable consideration of the company's proposals to the Government,' and the committee recommended that these men be required to repay personally any funds improperly taken from the company for political campaign contributions.[56] Senator Haydon's acceptance of the $50,000 fee, contingent on approval of the order in council, was 'strongly condemned,' while his and Senator Raymond's acceptance of campaign funds was criticized.[57] J.B. Hunter, deputy minister of public works, and K.M. Cameron, chief engineer of the department, were also severely criticized. The committee found that 'the evidence of neither of these officials appeared to be given in the manner which one might expect from Departmental Officials.'[58]

The committee also prepared detailed financial statements designed to determine what profits the promoters had taken and the sums still required to complete the work. With reference to the promotional profits, it was clear to committee members that alleged profits of $104 million were entirely fanciful. The committee, after detailed review of all the relevant financial statements, concluded that

the promoters of the Beauharnois Project involving the exploitation of a great natural resource have been able to secure to themselves a return of all money's advanced by them or any of them, a profit of $2,189,000 in cash and 1,000,000 Class A Common shares, which if saleable at the market quotation would at one time have been worth $17,000,000 and at today's quotations at $4 per share would be worth $4,000,000. This cash profit was paid out of the moneys borrowed by the Beauharnois Power Corporation Limited by the sale of its bonds.[59]

The Select Committee also addressed the two issues that originally had led to its establishment – that the Beauharnois company was proceeding without properly approved detailed plans, and that it was planning to divert much more than the original 40,000 cubic feet per second for which formal authorization had been obtained. These matters, however, were no longer in any dispute and merely had to be recorded. The more important concerns dealt with ways and means to correct these problems and to ensure completion of at least the first phase of construction. The committee specifically urged that the federal and Quebec governments resolve any outstanding constitutional differences 'so that the project may not be imperiled by delay.' In a vague recommendation the committee also urged that 'the Parliament of Canada take such action as may be within its power, and without prejudicing the rights of the Province of Quebec, to procure the development of this project in such a manner as will best serve the people of Canada.'[60] Robert Gardiner and at least one Conservative committee member favoured nationalization of the project, while other committee members favoured some form of federal assistance and supervision but continued private management. They all agreed, however, that the project should be completed and that the federal government should safeguard and preserve the rights of navigation.

The committee report was notable for some of the things it did not say. It did not find specific fault with Mackenzie King. Howard Ferguson also escaped any criticism, the committee finding no evidence that he had received any money from the Beauharnois promoters. They reported that there was no evidence to show that the $125,000 paid to John Aird, Jr, ever reached any political organization. Thus the politicians, other than the three senators, were largely absolved of anything more than a vague and general responsibility for an unsatisfactory state of affairs. The *Financial Times* summarized the case, stating that 'the report obviously condemns the conduct of those who operated the toll-gates on the progress of this great project rather than those who paid the tolls.'[61] To that assessment might be added the statement that the report condemned those who collected the tolls, but it did not condemn the politicians who became beneficiaries of some of the tolls collected.

The Select Committee report provided no help or relief for the two men who had really set events in motion. Narcisse M. Cantin and Frank Regan and the Transportation and Power Corporation did not get so much as a mention in the report, despite the fact that Regan continued to provide Gardiner with information and advice throughout the committee's July hearings.[62] Regan and Cantin, in fact, were experiencing heavy weather in their legal battles, as excerpts from a rather pathetic exchange of letters between the two men illustrates. On 1 November 1930 Regan wrote to Cantin: 'I require money to carry on a law office and it makes me sometimes wonder whether I am wise in undertaking such a tremendous burden when the financial support seems so vague and indefinite ... I must have some more money! I hope I am not offensive when I say this and say it the way that I do, but there is no question about my being unable to go on unless more financial support is given me.'[63] Cantin's reply to Regan's request for more money was not encouraging. It was indicative of Cantin's peculiar ideas and unhappy experiences with others he tried to involve in his dreams and schemes.

> Coming to the statement in your letter that you 'require money to carry on a law office,' 'I must have some more money,' [sic] no one better that I appreciate under what difficulties you have carried on the fight. I regret that I am not in a position to meet your very proper request just now ... My experience in financing the Great Lakes to Ocean Route waterway has been to show me as much difference in the mental and moral of the men who have assisted me financially as there is difference in the crispness and cleanliness of a thousand one-dollar bills collected at the beer counter of a Church bazar. Most of them hand it over for the beer they get or to satisfy their own personal gratifications while the few hand it over for the good the dollar will do in support of the deed. Of all the men who have given me $5,000 or more in the promotion of the project, only a very few have played fair towards their co-partners.[64]

The Select Committee report was debated in the House of Commons on 30 and 31 July 1931. Gordon introduced the report and made a brief speech, followed by a three-and-one-half-hour reply by Mackenzie King. The former prime minister denied that he had known anything of the Sterling Industrial Corporation or of political campaign contributions. He admitted, however, that the affair was a major embarrassment and humiliation for the Liberal party. 'Individual members of the Liberal party may have done what they should not have done. The party is not thereby disgraced. The party is not disgraced, but it is in the valley of humiliation. I tell the people of this country today that as its leader I feel humiliated, and I know my following feel humiliated. I told them so, that we are in the valley of humiliation.'[65] It was a difficult time for King, whose state of mind at the time the committee report was debated in parliament may be judged from his diary entry that day.

This has been one of the most trying if not *the* most trying days of my life, apart from those which have related to personal sorrow through illness or death of those I love. Through it all though I have felt a sense of the nearness of dear mother & also a detached attitude towards all that is transpiring ... Two small incidents meant much to me today. Little Pat [King's pet dog] came in the morning and licked my hand as it was stretched out of bed. It seemed to me he was speaking of mother being near. He has so reminded me of mother in all his illness, his great patience etc that it has been like her spirit sent to comfort. The other more strange. For luncheon Mary gave me fish, a slice almost the shape of what I saw in my dream on Tuesday when I thought of the nearness of mother & father. It was the colour. I thought of the 'burning bush', but there it was before me to sustain me before my ordeal.[66]

The parliamentary debate did not add much that was new or unknown and ended quickly after King's long speech. It was followed on 1 August 1931 by the introduction of new legislation to make arrangements for the completion, operation, and management of the Beauharnois project. With this legislation the focus of attention shifted from past misdeeds to the future development of the project. The revelations had been a considerable shock to many Canadians and had certainly enlivened the front pages of Canadian newspapers in what is normally a dull period with little political news. Canadians were apparently outraged, but perceptive newspaper reporters were inclined to think that the outrage was not deeply rooted. Hence it need not prove disastrous to any except the three or four individuals specifically condemned in the report.

> We all professed, of course, to be suitably outraged and there was considerable viewing with alarm to be seen in high places. But actually our main interest was comparable to that of the audience at a vaudeville show or movie. This was high entertainment, and though good form insisted that we must damn the culprits, shaking our heads and inquiring of each other what the world might be coming to, the actual, basic interest of the individual citizen was in the amusement value to be derived from reading the verbatim report of each day's evidence, with a feeling that he had been let down badly by the producers when there were lulls in the quality of the performance.[67]

After the brief debate on the Select Committee report the prevailing mood in both the business community and on Parliament Hill was well expressed in a major headline in the *Financial Times*: 'On with the Beauharnois Project.'[68] Before that could happen, however, at least the most obvious offenders in the Beauharnois scandal had to be suitably punished.

12

Cleansing the corporation

The revelations of the Beauharnois parliamentary inquiry led to an inevitable and understandable public and political demand that the chief offenders be suitably punished. Specifically, three senior executives of the Beauharnois companies had been declared by the parliamentarians to be unfit to continue in their positions. They were R.O. Sweezey, president, W.L. McDougald, chairman of the board, and R.A.C. Henry, executive vice-president and general manager. In addition, the inquiry had also found serious wrongdoing on the part of three senators, W.L. McDougald, Andrew Haydon, and Donat Raymond. The parliamentary committee recommended, and the public demanded, that the Beauharnois board rooms and the Canadian senate be purged or cleansed by the removal of these five persons from their positions of trust and authority. And there was considerable fuss and fury in the nine months following publication of the committee's reports, but in the end much less was done than had been anticipated.

R.O. Sweezey was the most prominent offender. The embattled Beauharnois president and many of his business colleagues, however, did not think he should be removed from his position or be prevented from further participation in the affairs of the Beauharnois companies. Shortly after receipt of the parliamentary inquiry report Sweezey wrote a pathetic letter to Prime Minister Bennett, begging to be allowed to stay.

Pardon my writing to you. For me it is unfortunate that I have not been permitted to speak to you. Yet, because of the importance of the Beauharnois project I feel that as the founder of the enterprise you may hear me ... In the engineering, economic and legal fields I knew where I was going, but in the political swamps I was simply beset on all sides and accepted guidance from those who claimed to be more experienced. For such mistakes I have had to accept responsibility without revealing particulars.

Today I see my project within eleven months of successful operation but I am personally threatened with extinction.

I have never been greedy on my own account and have worked four years without salary. Mistakes were made but not in the main features of the enterprise in which all my early conceptions have proved sound as to engineering and economic principles ...

I am full of boiling energy for this great enterprise. It is only beginning. Must I abandon a life work at a time when every one of us should put forth his supreme effort? ...

Will you permit me to remain on the board of my company? It is not lack of modesty that causes me to say that the company needs me. I wish I could have a talk with you.[1]

The prime minister knew that it would be politically difficult, if not impossible, to allow Sweezey to remain on the boards of the various Beauharnois companies. His reply was therefore brief and to the point. 'I have given the most careful and lengthy consideration to every angle of the situation since receiving your letter, and I think, under all the circumstances surrounding the Beauharnois project, it is perhaps better that you should retire from the Board. I dislike sending you a reply of this nature, but the above is my view of the situation as I see it.'[2]

When it became known in business circles that Sweezey's head was on the block, he received a surprising amount of support. One editorial, quoted approvingly by the *Financial Times*, defended him thus:

Sweezey, a man above reproach, so far as anybody knows, up till the time he got into Beauharnois ... found the sledding a little difficult in working out his power scheme. Being a first-class engineer, he knew the development was sound. It would pay handsomely. But he found out that there were bare spots on the sleigh haul – and the fellows standing around watching his efforts to get his load over these spots didn't offer to throw a little snow on the bare spots so his horses could handle the load. A man in a fix like that is generally willing to do business. He can either do that, or give up and return his team to the stable. A hustler usually doesn't give up. He'd sooner do a little honest log-rolling. If he has to pay he pays, and gets on with the job ... It is just as reasonable to abuse him [Sweezey] as it is to find fault with the missionary who has to buy his freedom from Chinese bandits ... Most of us will bargain with a burglar rather than face ruin.[3]

The *Kingston Whig-Standard* also took up Sweezey's cause, noting that he was a distinguished graduate and important fund-raiser for Queen's University, who 'out of his own brain conceived and by his genius and energy, has up to date carried through one of the greatest power developments in all the world.' The paper then went on to explain that 'this relatively young man, untrained in the wiles of politics, felt that it was either a case of "put up or shut up" and manifestly with millions already involved in the undertaking it was unthinkable that it would be "shut up."'[4] The *Financial Times* regarded the entire affair as a political rather than as an entrepreneurial scandal and urged that Sweezey's services be retained.

The project has been his in such a large sense and he has been so closely identified with its many developments and extensive ramifications that it is widely assumed that he will continue to play an important part in the carrying out of the whole undertaking. It has been pointed out that there would now be an opportunity for him to devote himself to the project itself rather than to those promotional activities which have been so much in the limelight and which belong to a phase of the undertaking now fortunately passed if not forgotten.[5]

Even some the company's bankers weighed in on Sweezey's behalf. They recognized him as a competent engineer whose continued professional services would expedite completion of construction. But they also recognized that there were serious problems in having Sweezey as a member of the board, and they sought to devise appropriate means to retain his professional and managerial services.[6]

The image of R.O. Sweezey as the innocent wayfarer going about his honest business when beset by political grafters who forced him 'to grease itching palms against his will'[7] had some credibility, and earned him considerable sympathy and support. In the end Sweezey was forced to resign as president, but he was not driven entirely out of the Beauharnois companies. He remained an active and respected member of the Montreal business community.

No such sympathy or support was forthcoming for his business associate, Senator W.L. McDougald. McDougald had denied any influence peddling or wrongdoing until incontrovertible evidence forced him to admit that his earlier statements had been 'ambiguous.'[8] The parliamentary inquiry had concluded that 'Senator McDougald's actions cannot be too strongly condemned.'[9] In the business community there was no disagreement with that political assessment and with the conclusion that McDougald should be prohibited from any further involvement in the dealings of the Beauharnois Power companies.

It would not be easy to get rid of the senator. McDougald held two of the Beauharnois Power Corporation's crucial five management preferred shares. R.A.C. Henry, McDougald's partner in the much-denounced Sterling Industrial Corporation, held a third. Between them these two men controlled all appointments to the Beauharnois Power Corporation's board of directors.

It seemed clear that, after the revelations made before the parliamentary inquiry, companies dominated by McDougald and Henry would not enjoy the confidence of the public, the politicians, or other businessmen. The two men probably could not bring the power project to a successful completion on their own. But they could refuse to co-operate in any future reorganization of the company. They still had the power to wreck it if they thought the punishment meted out to them was too severe.

A particularly troublesome point was the question of what should be done with the Beauharnois shares that McDougald and Henry had received for the Sterling Industrial Corporation. The prevailing and strongly held view among businessmen and politicians alike was that there had been little or no value in the Sterling company. The two men had used privileged information that had come to them through Henry's position in the civil service and through McDougald's role as chairman of the Montreal Harbours Board and as a member of the National Advisory Committee. He had deliberately kept his involvement in Beauharnois a secret until he and Henry had successfully forced the lucrative merger between the Sterling and Beauharnois companies. As a result, there was a widespread view that the Beauharnois shares issued to the two men to acquire their non-existent assets should simply be cancelled without any compensation. Some of the other share transactions had also been criticized, and some critics demanded that McDougald and Henry be deprived of all shares for which they had not actually paid. But the two embattled men refused to give up their management preferred shares if such action were contemplated. There was, consequently, great indignation among the politicans and the bankers when it was reported that 'The Senator is said to have offered to get out of the Beauharnois and to turn over his management stock to the banks. So far so good; but it is stated, he claims that his common stock should be bought out, and his price, according to reports, is a good one. Dr. McDougald may be able to make the company meet his terms.'[10]

The senator was a tough customer. Everyone connected with the Beauharnois companies wanted to get rid of him. In the end he was indeed forced out, but he and Henry were made to give up only the Beauharnois shares they had received for their interest in the Sterling Industrial Corporation. They were able to retain all their other Beauharnois share holdings and entitlements, mainly because of the controversial role played by R.A.C. Henry, the company's vice-president and general manager. Henry had been criticized almost as severely as McDougald, but like Sweezey, he was a highly competent and respected professional engineer whose continued guidance and advice was needed to complete construction. Lawyers pointedly warned the prime minister that if Henry was stripped of his holdings and forced out of the company, he would have nothing to lose by ruining it. The need of the company for Henry's services, and the difficulty in imposing harsh terms on him, led the lawyers to suggest that his lucrative employment contract be cancelled, but that he then be taken back at a reduced salary and in a lesser position but allowed to keep all his shares in the company except those connected with the Sterling acquisition.[11]

At first Henry balked at these terms. Prime Minister Bennett personally exerted considerable pressure on him and on the Beauharnois companies. When those efforts failed, the Department of Railways and Canals, where Henry briefly had served as deputy minister, was brought into the action. The specific and detailed plans for rail relocations and location of the main canal and relevant remedial works in the Beauharnois section needed immediate approval. The bureaucrats, almost certainly with political encouragement, refused to approve anything as long as Henry remained the general manager. Without appropriate bureaucratic approval construction would be disrupted, and the company would face almost certain ruin in which Henry, along with the other promoters, would lose his entire equity in the venture. It was a crude piece of brinkmanship, but it worked. On 20 October 1931 Henry capitulated with bad grace. He sent a formal note to the prime minister informing him that

I would hesitate to permit my personal interest in this great undertaking to interfere with the approval of the plans at Ottawa or with any other action on the part of the Government at Ottawa so necessary for the furtherance and continuance of the Beauharnois project, but, before agreeing to do as you suggest, I would like a definite statement from you in writing that approval of the plans will not be granted and that other necessary action on the part of the Government at Ottawa to permit completion of the project will not be taken, unless I make the concessions you suggest, – namely the surrender of certain shares and the cancellation and readjustment of my contract with the Beauharnois Power Corporations, concessions which, you will admit, involve great personal sacrifice.[12]

This action cleared the way for the removal of Sweezey, McDougald, and Henry from the boards of directors of the Beauharnois Power Corporation and its subsidiary companies. The minutes of the parent company report the matter thus:

At the request of Mr. R.O. Sweezey, the resignations of himself, Senator W.L. McDougald and R.A.C. Henry were then presented to the meeting. Mr. Sweezey requested that these resignations be acted upon, as he felt that their acceptance would facilitate the Company negotiations with the Dominion Government. After considerable discussion Mr. Sweezey and Senator McDougald withdrew from the meeting ... After further discussion it was moved ... that the resignations of Senator W.L. McDougald, R.O. Sweezey and R.A.C. Henry as members of the Board of Directors be accepted, and that no announcement of such resignation be made at the present time.[13]

Officially the three men were out of the Beauharnois companies, although Sweezey and Henry continued to work for the company and to guide the Beauharnois construction program much as they had before their resignations. McDougald and Henry had to give up, without compensation, the Beauharnois common shares they had obtained for their holdings in the Sterling Industrial Corporation, but they retained their other shares and bonds.

Sweezey and Henry could now carry on in their reduced role with the Beauharnois companies. For Senator McDougald, however, there were further and even more serious problems. The parliamentary inquiry report had documented and condemned his activities and those of two of his colleagues. The Commons did not, however, have authority to take any action against members of 'the other chamber.' That was a matter to be decided in the Senate.

Responsibility for further action in the Senate fell to Arthur Meighen, a former prime minister and newly appointed senator and Government Leader in the Senate. Meighen's appointment to the Senate on 3 February 1932, in fact, was partly due to the wish of Prime Minister Bennett that the Beauharnois matter be dealt with vigorously but prudently in the Senate. Bennett's and Meighen's objective was to condemn and punish the offending senators, but without at the same time bringing the entire free enterprise system or the Canadian political system into disrepute. They felt that every effort should also be made to ensure that any further inquiry in the Red Chamber not get out of hand or deteriorate into a general investigation of political campaign contributions and business practices.

Arthur Meighen's prowess as a forensic debater was well known, as was his passionate devotion to the parliamentary system of government and his equally passionate hatred of Liberal leader Mackenzie King. Meighen was also a successful lawyer and businessman who had been active in and understood the investment business. He had been recently appointed a commissioner of Ontario Hydro and could be counted on to defend the interests and reputation of G. Howard Ferguson. Prime Minister Bennett hoped Meighen and his colleagues would be able to impeach and remove the three offending Liberal senators, much as a skilled surgeon might excise a cancerous growth. But the operation had to be carefully pinpointed, lest rude socialist critics extend it recklessly to include appendages that were vital to both established political parties.

Meighen prepared himself carefully for the confrontation with Senators McDougald, Haydon, and Raymond. His first inclination was to impeach and permanently disqualify the three senators on the ground that they had been found guilty by the parliamentary committee of 'an infamous crime.' He quickly discovered the impeachment or expulsion of a Canadian senator is no simple matter. He received several contradictory legal opinions on the matter. One view was that impeachment of a senator by peers must proceed under the terms of British common law. That, unfortunately, was possible only following conviction in the courts for specific crimes. The three senators had been condemned by a parliamentary committee, but they had not been convicted in court for an impeachable crime. That being the case, one legal opinion obtained by Meighen stated,

No mere resolution of either or both Houses will be effective ... The B.N.A. Act itself provides as to how a vacancy can occur. The case [of the three senators] is not within it ... It is doubtful at least whether it [impeachment] does not require in Canada conviction exterior to Parliament, of crime ... Impeachment is the only possible (and it is *only possible*) remedy without recourse to Imperial legislation. It is *probable* that even impeachment is not available.[14]

Meighen did not accept this interpretation, and obtained a second and contrary legal opinion. Two lawyers were officially appointed as counsel for the Senate committee. They argued that Section 33 of the British North America Act might apply. That section provided that 'If any Question arises respecting the Qualifications of a Senator or a vacancy in the Senate, the same shall be heard and determined by the Senate.'[15] Meighen and his colleagues accepted this imprecise opinion but then had to decide on the most appropriate procedure whereby the qualifications of the three might be determined. It seemed most expedient to appoint a special Senate committee which would be specifically charged with responsibility for investigating and determining the significance of the findings of the Special Select Committee of the House of Commons. Such a senatorial committee was appointed on 11 February 1932. The terms of appointment did not make it clear, however, what, if any, remedies the committee could prescribe if the three were found guilty of improper conduct.[16]

Mackenzie King had, in the meantime, made some arrangements and preparations of his own. His diary entries indicate that the former prime minister was shocked at some of the revelations before the parliamentary committee, particularly those involving Senator McDougald, R.A.C. Henry, and the Sterling Industrial Corporation. And he obviously understood that the expensive gifts he had accepted from Senator McDougald, and the senator's substantial contribution to the trust fund in Boston, left him vulnerable. Fortunately, from his point of view, those matters had not been revealed in the parliamentary inquiry.

As the Senate inquiry approached, King again became apprehensive, and on 23 October 1931 he informed Senator McDougald that he 'wished to return to him the contribution he made to Mr. Larkin towards the fund for myself.'[17] At the same time he also urged McDougald to resign from the Senate and from his other official positions. Such action, King hoped, would head off further damaging revelations in the Senate inquiry and in another separate inquiry which was expected to investigate serious irregularities at the Montreal Harbours Board, also involving McDougald.[18]

A major confrontation between the two men came on 16 November 1931, when King made a special trip from Ottawa to Montreal to call on Dr McDougald. King brought along his personal cheque to repay McDougald the money he had paid to Larkin and also a draft letter of resignation from the Senate which he wanted McDougald to sign. A lengthy diary entry that evening describes the events of the day.

> Got off at Westmount and drove in a taxi to Dr. McDougald. It was a weird sort of drive. There was a mist – which developed into a heavy fog. I was shewn into the downstairs parlor, small room heavily panelled with paintings. Then the Dr. came & took me to their sitting room on the first floor. We talked for about an hour. I read over to him a letter I had spent part of the morning dictating, his resignation as a senator, based on his withdrawing from politics, [that he was] through with helping party in organization. He spoke of all he had done and of the hypocrisy of Raymond, Senator Wilson, Beique, Dandurand [word in round brackets not legible] & most of all of Geoffrion. It came as a bit of a blow to him to have it all put up so solidly. He resented Hepburn particularly, & spoke of the Liberals as a poor lot. I gave him the cheque covering his contribution to the Larkin fund, he said did I still think it was the best thing to do, & said it was like severing the last link. I told him it would make for more freedom on the part of each. He was anxious for me to stay for dinner. I dined with Mrs. McD. John & himself. There was much talk of the gossip and meanness of others. He spoke of being 50 & having had the worst year of his life this year. He drove with me to the station and on the way said definitely he wd resign for my sake, spoke of what he had done for the party, said I wd be PM in 2 years, that he would help to that end, but he hoped I wd remember him. It was curious to see this ambition for the future. I left with him the letter of resignation to Senate & to myself re Committee next week.[19]

It was a hard day for both men, but that night King had 'a wonderful vision' of his mother and family, whose significance he interpreted thus:

> My interpretation is, that the act of giving back to Dr. McD. what he had given to the Larkin Fund – separating myself from material wealth from that source was something which they [deceased members of his family who visited him in this vision] all were glad of that having changed my thoughts 'when the devil left him, angels ministered unto him'. What is most remarkable that

mother appeared as dead or dying in a dream I had when on the way to Bermuda & at Bermuda related to McD. and now it is light & life – when separating from him & that influence ... It is an immense relief to me to have that money given back to McD., to be under no obligation indirect or direct to him – & to have the assurance of his resignation which he says he will give for me.[20]

Senator McDougald, despite King's continued urging, did not resign from the Senate in November of 1931 and soon became the main target of the Senate inquiry. King, however, felt obvious relief that McDougald's money was no longer in the Boston trust fund.

The Special Senate Committee was appointed on 11 February 1932. Senator Charles E. Tanner, a former leader of the Conservative party of Nova Scotia, was appointed chairman. Four other Conservative and four Liberal senators were appointed members. This committee began its public hearings on 16 February, but its deliberations were severely hampered from the beginning.

Liberal senators, who had an overall majority in the Senate, chose to regard the inquiry as nothing more than a partisan tactic by their Conservative colleagues, making a divided committee report almost a certainty. Both parties, moreover, recognized that such a divided committee report would provide a poor basis for any subsequent motion to expel the three senators who had not been convicted in the courts of any specific crime. The fact that Arthur Meighen, as government leader in the Senate, adopted highly partisan tactics further undermined prospects for unanimity in the matter.

Senators from both parties also seemed determined to prevent any further disclosures about election campaign contributions. The Conservatives did not want their activities in that area to be examined, and the Liberals were intent on limiting the damage to what had already been revealed in the House of Commons inquiry. In the case of Senator Raymond this reluctance to wash dirty political linen in public was reinforced by serious constitutional considerations. Raymond had been one of the chief Liberal fund-raisers in Quebec for both the federal and the provincial parties. Anything that dealt in any way with Quebec provincial politics or campaign contributions was regarded as being entirely outside the jurisdiction of the Senate and its Special Committee. This attitude ensured that the Senate committee would learn nothing more about Senator Raymond's activities.

Senator McDougald, of course, could be and was questioned closely by his peers, but he revealed very little that was new or startling. He admitted what could no longer be denied as a result of the House of Commons committee's findings, but he denied or professed ignorance on all other matters. He had been in political and legal trouble often enough and had surrounded himself with very capable legal advisers. McDougald's basic strategy was to deny whatever could not be proved.

The situation was different and more tragic when the Senate committee sought to obtain evidence from Senator Haydon. The affable, refined, and intellectual Ottawa senator had fallen gravely ill. He had high blood pressure and had suffered a major heart attack in December of 1930. He had survived that incident, but his condition steadily deteriorated. Ill health had prevented him from testifying before the parliamentary inquiry, and there was fear that the strain of the hearings of the Special Senate Committee could prove fatal. Senator Haydon, moreover, was highly respected and well liked by his colleagues in both parties. He was described as 'sensitive and sympathetic to a degree, and in his relations with those who are not of his religious creed, he displays a breadth of mind, and a warmth of heart, that it would be well for all of us if we could imitate.'[21] Few senators wanted to hurt, much less kill, the likeable Haydon, and many later believed Senator Murphy when he alleged

> that it broke the hearts of the Liberals on the Committee to sign such a report, but that they had to sacrifice Haydon in order to save King! In other words, they knew that Haydon was innocent; but, with the amazing stupidity and lack of logic, as well as the lack of honesty, that characterizes so many people in their attitude towards a party and towards a Party Leader, they deliberately did a grievous wrong to an honourable and innocent man in order to shield one who did not deserve to be shielded.[22]

None of the senators wanted to push Haydon too hard. Illness did not, however, entirely shield Haydon from investigating senators, or those senators from Haydon's phenomenal political finesse. He was encouraged to prepare a carefully worded written statement. The Special Senate Committee then came to his residence on 15 March, listened to his presentation, and asked him a few questions. Doctors were in attendance and stopped the hearing after about fifteen minutes of questioning and long before all the necessary evidence had been obtained. Several days later the doctors allowed a small subcommittee to take additional evidence, again at Haydon's Ottawa residence.

The preparation of Senator Haydon's written and oral statements involved numerous meetings between Haydon, Mackenzie King, Senator McDougald, and an assortment of lawyers. The principal difficulty, or advantage, depending on one's point of view, with Haydon's memory and with his proposed statement was that they contradicted important denials that Senator McDougald had made. According to King, Haydon feared 'that he wd. have to say on the witness stand some things that might not be pleasant to McD.'[23] Once Haydon's statement was drafted, Senator McDougald's lawyers tried desperately to have it suppressed or changed, but King considered it 'an excellent statement. It will clear Haydon & the Govt.-may make it more difficult for Mcdougald, but it is his own fault.'[24]

Haydon, shrewdly calculating the possible political fall-out, included in his statement several specific references to the approximately $200,000 of Beauharnois money which he claimed had been paid to Howard Ferguson. This sum was in addition to the $125,000 paid to John Aird, Jr. Haydon's allegation was very unsettling to the Conservative senators, who 'refused to let his [Haydon's] statement be read or anything said of the payments to Aird, all this to shield Ferguson.'[25] Several urgent telegrams were immediately dispatched to London to obtain Howard Ferguson's reactions to Haydon's allegations. Ferguson labelled Haydon's statement as 'absolutely false and without a shadow of foundation,' but he booked passage from London immediately and at his own expense in order to appear in person before the committee.[26] The committee had to recess its hearings for a week while awaiting Ferguson's arrival from London. It heard his evidence on 6 April. He told committee members that 'I have never seen Mr. Sweezey but twice in my life.' Ferguson claimed to know nothing about campaign funds or how they were raised. After several pages of evidence, much of it taken up with discussions between lawyers, the committee chairman apologized to Ferguson for putting him to so much trouble. Ferguson replied that 'Like most decent fellows, after a long public career you are charged with all kinds of things. I may have been guilty of lots of things, but nobody has been able to besmirch my personal integrity.'[27]

R.O. Sweezey, then in the midst of negotiations with R.B. Bennett and others regarding refinancing of the Beauharnois companies, also issued a public statement claiming that Haydon's evidence regarding the $200,000 pay-off to Premier Ferguson was not true. A few months later Howard Ferguson noted rather complacently that 'I gather that the whole Hydro investigation has pretty well petered out ... The reaction will ensure to the advantage of the government. The extravagant language of the leaders will recoil upon their own heads.'[28] Howard Ferguson's bravado was impressive. But Senator Haydon's testimony worried all the members of the Senate committee. Mackenzie King noted in his diary that 'Many of our men are afraid of enquiry into Beauharnois further – Ferguson or otherwise – clearly the machine end is involved on both sides.'[29]

It was obviously time to bring the official hearings to an end and to get on with less dangerous or revealing matters. The Special Senate Committee adjourned on 18 March, the day after Haydon's testimony. It met once more to hear the evidence of Howard Ferguson, after which the committee again adjourned.

There was much political discussion regarding the wording of the final report of the Special Senate Committee. At least four separate drafts of the report were prepared. The second draft was perhaps the harshest. It recommended that Senators McDougald and Haydon 'be called to the bar of the Senate and be forthwith expelled from membership in it' and that Senator Raymond 'be called to the bar of the Senate and be severely censored by that body.'[30] In the final report, however, the senators simply expressed their agreement with the conclusions reached by the parliamentary committee. They further stated that 'Senator McDougald's actions were not fitting or consistent with his duties as a Senator,' and that Senator Haydon's conduct 'was unfitting and inconsistent with his position and standing as a Senator of Canada.' They found that Senator Raymond had accepted very large sums of money from the Beauharnois promoters, and then they urged that 'Senators of Canada should not place themselves in the position of receiving contributions from or being interested in an enterprise dependent on specific favour, franchise or concession to be made by a government.' But then they further softened their criticism of Senator Raymond, in deference to several of the French-Canadian members of the Senate committee. 'It is impossible for us to do otherwise than accept Senator Raymond's denial that influence directed toward affecting government policy was actively exerted by him.'[31]

The senators did not place similar confidence in Senator Haydon's claim that $200,000 had been paid to Howard Ferguson, in addition to the $125,000 admittedly paid to John Aird, Jr, in return for the Ontario Hydro contract. The report was explicit: 'Senator Haydon's evidence in this regard was not correct.' This conclusion, more than anything else, ensured that the Liberals would vote against the report and its findings, both in committee and when the matter was debated in the Senate. Such divisiveness stood in sharp contrast to the unanimous support given to the House of Commons inquiry report by all members of the committee.

The Special Senate Committee report, opposed by the Liberal members of the committee, was introduced and debated on 28 and 29 April 1932. Arthur Meighen took the lead, and his performance was vintage Meighen. The *Globe* reported it thus:

> Two Liberal Senators entangled in the Beauharnois mesh are going to the guillotine as surely as night follows day. Of that there cannot be the slightest doubt on the part of any one who heard tonight the devastating speech of Right Hon. Arthur Meighen, Government Leader in the upper House. It was an indictment of political wrongdoing, a condemnation of prostitution of public office for private gain, the like of which probably never has been heard in the legislative halls of Canada.[32]

In this case, however, Meighen's rhetoric had something in common with that of the clergyman who noted in the margin opposite a particular portion of his sermon 'Logic weak – Shout loud!' Meighen made a great speech, but he had also agreed to a quiet settlement.

Mackenzie King's reaction to the Senate report was rather characteristic. He complained that

> The effect of the report is to leave the impression that the passing of the O-in-C was contingent on these things which it was not. – Haydon seemed to me to be a little more upset today. I could see he was feeling the effect on his heart, tho' he is very philosophical – but it is political persecution – a damn scoundrel like Ferguson gets off as a saint by perjury & the *Globe* which should be the defender of Justice & fair play plays into Ferguson's hands & against the party which seeks to uphold the people.[33]

King also worried that 'Haydon's present condition is such that extreme action by the Senate might be followed by fatal results.'[34]

The report still left the door open for further action, including the expulsion of Senators McDougald and Haydon. There were no further formal proceedings in the Senate. Instead, an arrangement or understanding had been negotiated between the several leading politicians. McDougald, it was agreed, must resign his seat in the Senate immediately. McDougald finally agreed, provided all further inquiries into his conduct with regard to Beauharnois or the Montreal Harbour Commission were dropped. Nothing further was to be done regarding Senator Haydon, in view of his precarious health. King understood the arrangement thus:

> J.C. Cook called told me he had just left Meighen and Meighen had given him his word that if McD. resigned nothing further wd. be done re Haydon or Raymond. He wd. make a public statement to the press or the Senate that they did not intend to proceed in the condition Haydon is in. Haydon must agree however not to turn up & begin to raise a row in the Senate, at this or any subsequent session. As to Montreal Harbour etc. Cahan wd. give McD. an assurance on the part of the Govt.– Cahan acting for some [words illegible] firm involved – & he Meighen & Bennett wd. see that McD. was not pressed there.[35]

In order to lend greater credence to this arrangement, Meighen demanded expert information regarding Andrew Haydon's health. Two medical opinions were obtained. One of the doctors advised that 'It is unquestionably true that sudden physical or emotional strain might readily precipitate cardiac collapse and a sudden terminal event, an accident very common in this type of heart disease.'[36] The second doctor concurred. Haydon's heart could not stand the strain of expulsion proceedings. Subsequent events confirmed these medical opinions; Andrew Haydon's health continued to deteriorate and he died on 10 November 1932.

Meighen and Bennett faced considerable public criticism for not proceeding with the expulsion of all three senators, while many Liberals criticized King for not pushing much harder for a major inquiry into all political campaign contributions, particularly into the past activities of Howard Ferguson. All the federal political leaders held to the arrangement, however, using Haydon's precarious health as their justification for not proceeding further. Arthur Meighen did try to leave the door open for further action, just in case Haydon's condition improved: 'The information obtained as to Senator Haydon's condition is such that I could not make myself responsible for further drastic action and the result which might have followed in the not distant future. The statement I made was quite consistent with a reconsideration of the matter at a later date if circumstances warrant same.'[37]

Thus were the corporate and political organizations cleansed and the offenders punished. Sweezey, McDougald, and Henry were forced to resign from the board of directors of the Beauharnois companies. McDougald and Henry also had to surrender the Beauharnois shares they had received in return for their Sterling Industrial Corporation interests. Sweezey and Henry were allowed to continue their professional work with the Beauharnois Companies and subsequently pursued successful business careers. Henry later went on to a distinguished public career.

Senator McDougald was forced to resign his seat in the Senate. His colleague, Andrew Haydon, escaped further action in the Senate only because he was dying of heart disease, while Donat Raymond got away with nothing more than a reprimand, primarily because much of his activity concerned Quebec provincial politics which were beyond the jurisdiction of the Canadian Senate.

The removal or punishment of these five men cleared the way for further corporate reorganizations and financial arrangements which would permit completion of the first phase of construction and management of the powerhouse and canal at Beauharnois.

13

Protecting workers and investors

The removal or demotion of R.O. Sweezey, R.A.C. Henry, W.L. McDougald, Andrew Haydon, and Donat Raymond was a necessary prerequisite for the survival, reorganization, and future financing of the Beauharnois companies. Discussions about future organization and financing, however, began long before the punishment for the five men had been determined. The interests involved in those organizational and financial discussions were diverse and the resulting discussions lengthy, acrimonious, and frustrating for all concerned. They led eventually to the take over of the Beauharnois companies by Montreal Power. That was a result originally opposed by everyone except the Montreal Power interests, but failure to agree on any alternative solution inevitably led to the complete triumph of Montreal Power.

The $30 million (par value) 6 per cent collateral trust bonds issued by the parent Beauharnois Power Corporation in 1929 provided the necessary financing to pay for construction costs through 1929 and 1930. Those funds, however, were exhausted early in 1931, before the House of Commons Inquiry began. Sweezey's plan was to have the operating subsidiary company, the Beauharnois Light, Heat and Power Company, issue up to $20 million (par value) first mortgage bonds. The directors authorized the issuing of these bonds on 15 January 1931.[1] There were delays in bringing them out, and the Beauharnois managers negotiated an interim arrangement with a consortium of three banks, the Bank of Montreal, the Canadian Bank of Commerce, and the Royal Bank.

The three banks agreed to advance up to $6 million, pending sale of the first mortgage bonds which would, in the meantime, be pledged as collateral security for the bank loans. The Beauharnois Light, Heat and

Power Company agreed to pledge $150 (par value) first mortgage bonds for each $100 advanced by the banks. Any and all additional loans made and securities accepted would require the unanimous consent of the three banks.[2] None of the Beauharnois Light, Heat and Power Company's first mortgage bonds approved on 15 January 1931 was ever officially issued. Instead the company typed temporary first mortgage certificates. These 'typewritten' bonds were then pledged as collateral with the three banks.

The assisting banks advanced $6,495,000 to the Beauharnois Light, Heat and Power Company on this basis before the most damaging information was revealed in the House of Commons Inquiry in June and July of 1931. The revelations of large promoters' profits, questionable business practices, and huge political campaign contributions created immediate and great concern among the bankers, which precipitated a major financial crisis early in August of 1931, when the banks refused all further advances. Frantic meetings were immediately arranged, involving the prime minister, Secretary of State C.H. Cahan, the bankers, and the Beauharnois promoters and managers. Other equally urgent meetings took place between the Beauharnois promoters and Montreal Power officials. In addition, some preliminary but unsuccessful discussions with New York financial interests were initiated.[3] The key figure in all the reorganization proposals was the prime minister, who had a strong business background and took a personal interest in the problems of Beauharnois and of several other large but distressed corporations in the 1930s.

Everyone involved in the Beauharnois discussions agreed that construction should continue. The obvious problem was financing after the damaging parliamentary revelations, and in the generally depressed state of the stock market. The Beauharnois promoters first looked for help to Montreal Power, which already controlled about one-third of the shares issued by the Beauharnois Power Corporation, and at least $5 million of the company's collateral trust bonds.[4]

Montreal Power had the necessary resources to provide additional assistance. They knew that the Beauharnois project was technologically and financially sound. Only a few of its promoters and managers had been discredited. If the future management of the project were entrusted to administrators in whom the public had confidence, there was no reason why the proposed first mortgage Beauharnois bonds could not be issued and sold. At that very time, moreover, Montreal Power was busily negotiating management contracts with several other financially embarrassed public and private electrical systems. If Montreal Power could be persuaded to do the same for Beauharnois, that company's financial problems might be solved, and it could still retain its separate identity. A.F. White, vice-president and after Sweezey's resignation acting president of the Beauharnois companies, described the discussions with Montreal Power immediately after the parliamentary revelations thus.

We approached Montreal Light, Heat and Power Consolidated already interested in this company, with the suggestion that it take over the management and direction of the enterprise, as under these conditions we felt it would be possible during August and early September to sell First Mortgage Bonds. There was no suggestion that Montreal Light, Heat and Power should guarantee the bonds, but that Company itself enjoyed such excellent credit, that in our opinion a sale under its sponsorship would have been successful.[5]

This Montreal Power plan included an arrangement whereby the securities and investment firm of Wood, Gundy and Company, probably with a participation by the Montreal-based partnership of Holt and Gundy, agreed to underwrite a substantial portion of the proposed first mortgage bonds to be issued by the Beauharnois Light, Heat and Power Company. A conditional underwriting agreement with Gundy was discussed in August and signed in September of 1931. It was never implemented because Prime Minister Bennett still strongly opposed any arrangement under which the Beauharnois and Montreal Power management would have been effectively merged.[6]

Premier Taschereau of Quebec was also opposed to closer relations between Beauharnois and Montreal Power. One of the important considerations when the provincial government had granted Beauharnois its charter was that it should compete with or against Montreal Power. Some reports alleged that Taschereau had in fact demanded a firm promise from Sweezey that Beauharnois would never pass to Montreal Power.[7] Discussion of the first Montreal Power plan also came at a politically inconvenient time for Taschereau. A provincial election had been called for 24 August 1931. Damning the monopolistic practices of Montreal Power was standard political fare in Montreal. No new agreement between Montreal Power and Beauharnois could be approved until the provincial Liberals were safely returned to office.

Bennett and Taschereau disliked the Montreal Power plan, but they wanted Beauharnois construction to continue. In order to make that possible the prime minister agreed that the federal government would guarantee additional loans made by the three banks. The amount of collateral was, however, increased. Now $200 (par value) 'typewritten' bonds had to be pledged for each $100 advanced.[8] This was an unsatisfactory, uncertain, and temporary method of financing, but the construction crews remained at work.

The hope in August and September 1931 was that the management of the Beauharnois companies would be reorganized and that the market for bonds would strengthen. The informal government guarantees, based on private letters from the prime minister rather than on legislation, were designed only as an interim measure. But the government faced serious criticism for providing even that limited interim assistance.

Robert Gardiner and many other members of parliament from the prairies and Ontario believed the whole principle of private ownership of hydroelectric developments had been discredited by the scandal and should be replaced with a publicly owned and operated system. Specifically, they wanted the federal government to take over and operate the Beauharnois project. Premier Taschereau and the Quebec Liberals, however, adamantly opposed public ownership. They would not take over the project themselves and were determined to precipitate a major constitutional crisis if the federal government made any effort to nationalize the Beauharnois companies.[9] Ideological, political, and constitutional considerations made nationalization of Beauharnois difficult, and Prime Minister Bennett quickly rejected that option, explaining that

> The Dominion might take it over, although legal difficulties would arise, to which reference was made yesterday and in regard to which I wholly agree, of such a character that the inevitable result would be the stoppage of the enterprise. Mr. Woodsworth must realize clearly we could not by any declaration of this Parliament, unless Quebec acquiesced and became a partner with us, do what he suggests so far as the Dominion is concerned. As to the government of Canada taking the place of the shareholders of the Beauharnois Company, the lease from the Province of Quebec naturally provides that that province must concur in any alienation or transfer of that property and they would exercise their own discretion in that regard. But I have no reason to believe they desire the Dominion of Canada to undertake the operation of a hydroelectric plant in that province; neither have I any intention of asking the House for authority to do so.[10]

Even many supporters of publicly owned and operated hydroelectric plants had no desire to see the federal government, rather than provincial governments, become involved in activites which they also believed were matters under provincial jurisdiction.[11] The Beauharnois embarrassments rekindled the ongoing debate about the relative merits of public or private hydroelectric developments, but nationalization was not seriously considered, by either the federal or the Quebec provincial government. The discussion was sufficient, however, to draw a dire warning from the president of Montreal Power. 'This is not the time,' Sir Herbert Holt pontificated, 'for unsettling rumours. This is a time when we should all stand together to make our way out of the depression. Otherwise, prosperity will not return.'[12]

Canadians would not accept J.S. Woodsworth's recipe for economic recovery in 1931, but many were not yet prepared to endorse Herbert Holt's monopolistic tactics and practices. The Montreal Power president could wait. Sooner or later something always seemed to turn up in the entrepreneurial jungles of St James Street which allowed the strong and the successful to have their way with weaker and less successful rivals.

Prime Minister Bennett had two important objectives in mind when he agreed to guarantee Beauharnois's interim bank loans. He wanted construction to continue uninterrupted, thereby keeping thousands of men at work in a time of massive unemployment, and he wanted to protect the interests of bona fide investors who had purchased the Beauharnois collateral trust bonds. It would be a tremendous shock to the economy and to investor confidence if a massive project like Beauharnois went under without any regard for the thousands of small investors who had put their hard-earned money into the project.[13] Bennett's concern about the workers and bondholders, nevertheless, had to be tempered by all the other interests involved. The Beauharnois shareholders, the bankers, the power companies which would buy Beauharnois power, and the provincial governments of Ontario and Quebec, all demanded that their interests also be looked after in any Beauharnois reorganization.

The interim financial arrangements made in August 1931 gave the federal government time to clean up several matters. The first of these concerned PC 422 and the detailed plans that had never been filed. Bennett decided to wipe the slate entirely clean. All previous federal orders in council pertaining to construction or approval of Beauharnois construction plans were cancelled. New orders in council were then prepared which required not only the filing of detailed construction plans, but also the conveyance of full and complete ownership of the canal to the federal government. That canal, being built at company expense, would belong to the federal government but could also be used by Beauharnois without further charge to develop hydroelectric power. This decision clarified some of the constitutional and jurisdictional confusion that had beset the project from the start. But the conveyance of the $16 million canal to the federal government without further compensation did nothing to improve the company's ability to sell its first mortgage bonds.

Initially R.B. Bennett was determined that the federal guarantees of Beauharnois bank loans should not exceed $6 million since the $20 million of 'typewritten' bonds authorized at the January meeting of the Beauharnois directors would then be exhausted. Since the company had obtained approximately $6.5 million from the banks before the federal government became involved, the total indebtedness to the banks would therefore rise to slightly more than $12 million. That level of indebtedness was reached in January 1932, at which time Beauharnois officials also informed the government that they would need an additional $13 million to complete construction to the point where the first generators would produce electricity on 1 October 1932.[14]

The Beauharnois managers and the bankers argued that federal guarantees of at least $16 million could be justified in return for the conveyance of the canal to the federal government. Bennett balked at this suggestion. Instead he urged that the bankers take the lead in arranging a major reorganization of the Beauharnois companies. As early as October of 1931 he had written Morris W. Wilson, general manager of the Royal Bank of Canada, urging more aggressive action by the bankers.

It appears to me that the bankers, their associates and clients interested should, forthwith, prepare and present to the Government definite proposals with regard to the reorganization of the finances, directorate and management of the Beauharnois Light, Heat and Power Company, Limited, which they will undertake forthwith to carry into effect; and, if these proposals are deemed by the Dominion Government to give satisfactory assistance that the undertaking will be carried to a completion efficiently and satisfactorily, then the Dominion Government will be prepared to enter at once upon a discussion of the terms and conditions, with such limitations and reservations, as it may be deemed expedient to prescribe by Order in Council to ensure that Dominion rights and interests, in respect of such diversion of the waters of the River St. Lawrence, shall be properly conserved, and the rights of legitimate investors protected.[15]

The basic objective of any reorganization along the lines suggested by the prime minister was to have the banks take Beauharnois bonds and shares in payment for the mounting construction debts. In return the board of directors would have to be reorganized to give the banks appropriate representation. The banks, however, were not eager to invest equity capital in the project. Government-guaranteed loans suited them much better. In addition, all three banks had to agree to any changes, and the Bank of Montreal was, as usual, particularly prudent.

The cautious and unimaginative response of the banks frustrated and irritated Prime Minister Bennett a great deal. Consequently, in January 1932 he changed his mind and indicated that he would now entertain a solution that he had earlier rejected. In a series of meetings and an exchange of rather acrimonious letters between the prime minister, the bankers, and the Beauharnois directors, Bennett made it clear that the federal government would not provide further guarantees and that the Beauharnois companies should try to work out an appropriate plan of action with one of the other large power companies. He specifically mentioned Montreal Power, Shawinigan Power, Gatineau Power, and Southern Canada Power. If an arrangement with one of these companies was not possible, he thought the Beauharnois companies should be liquidated.[16]

The Beauharnois directors and bankers reacted angrily to these suggestions. In a letter approved by the entire board, pointed reference was made to Bennett's refusal in September 1931 to allow the company to work out a deal with Montreal Power. Shawinigan Power and Southern Canada Power had already indicated they were not interested in helping Beauharnois if that company turned over the canal to the federal government. Gatineau Power, a subsidiary of the International Paper Company, which was then engaged in a fierce newsprint pulp and paper fight with the Holt interests, expressed some interest if all relevant information were provided. The Holt interests, which controlled a minority of the Beauharnois stock, regarded this move merely as an attempt to obtain secret information about a competitor's operations.

That left Montreal Power. But Montreal Power officials claimed the situation had changed and deteriorated since September. They needed more time to prepare a new proposal. Quick help from any of the other power companies was therefore not available early in 1932.

The Beauharnois directors also pointed out that liquidation would inevitably lead to a halt in construction, throw thousands of workers out of jobs, and probably lead to a major financial panic and serious losses to the bondholders whom Bennett had promised to protect. Liquidation would solve nothing and make almost everything worse.[17]

Bennett's approach did, however, move the increasingly desperate Beauharnois directors to further action. Their money and credit were exhausted, but if construction was stopped, the project would not be ready to generate its first power on 1 October 1932. The company would then not be able to meet its contractual obligations to deliver power to Ontario Hydro and Montreal Power. Without such deliveries the entire security of the collateral trust bonds would be lost. And that, almost certainly, would not be only temporary. The power situation itself had changed significantly. The economic depression had led to numerous industrial plant closings with a resulting sharp reduction in hydroelectric requirements. Yet, across Canada facilities to generate an additional 546,650 horsepower were put into operation in 1931, and an additional 1.4 million horsepower, including the 500,000 at Beauharnois, were under construction.[18] Instead of a power shortage the country faced serious power surpluses. Under those circumstances failure to meet the terms of its contracts with Ontario Hydro and Montreal Power would be disastrous for Beauharnois. Ontario Hydro in particular, faced with a large power surplus, was looking for any proper pretext to cancel some of its power contracts.[19]

The first step in the reorganization of the Beauharnois board of directors came on 19 November 1931 when Sweezey, McDougald, and Henry resigned and transferred their management shares to the corporation's secretary. This move was followed on 7 January 1932 with a recommendation from the remaining directors that the entire board be reorganized. The directors recommended that a new board be appointed, consisting of eleven members, two to be named by the Quebec government, one by Montreal Power, two by each of the three banks, and two others not directly named by, but acceptable to and unofficially representing the interests of, the federal government. They suggested that this new board of directors should then prepare a plan for future financing.[20] In the meantime, the federal government should provide further guarantees, up to a $16 million limit.

While the prime minister was trying to persuade the banks to take Beauharnois bonds and shares for the guaranteed loans, and the remaining members of the Beauharnois board of directors were trying to reorganize and strengthen themselves, R.O. Sweezey was busily concocting his own reorganization plans and presenting these to the prime minister.[21]

All the financial rescue plans had some important elements in commmon. The first was that future financing would be based on first mortgage bonds of the Beauharnois Light, Heat and Power Company. The plans further provided for the exchange of first mortgage bonds for the debts and liabilities of the Beauharnois companies. The federal government, for example, was expected to take or subscribe $16 million of the first mortgage bonds, in return for which it would reimburse the banks for their guaranteed loans. The banks were expected to take at least $6 million of the bonds and, in return, cancel the $6 million loans not covered by the federal guarantees. The Quebec government was expected to take bonds in lieu of royalty payments for the water used by the company, and the holders of the 6 per cent collateral trust bonds were expected to forgo interest payments until construction was completed and thereafter to accept lower interest rates, more in keeping with the depressed financial conditions of the 1930s. Most plans required a new bond issue, and agreement of the holders of the 6 per cent collateral trust bonds to exchange them for new bonds bearing a lower rate of interest. While there was much haggling about precise figures and legal and financial details, the use of the first mortgage bonds to eliminate all or most of the current liabilities was generally accepted.

The real problem was where, when, and how to sell additional first mortgage bonds to raise new money needed to pay 1932 construction expenses. There was no public market for such securities in 1932. Initially most proposals suggested that the three banks and the company's shareholders should put up whatever additional funds were needed and take first mortgage bonds in return for the money advanced. The bankers were not interested, and most Beauharnois shareholders, with the notable exception of Montreal Power, could not raise the required funds. One or several of the larger investment houses might be in a position to buy the necessary number of first mortgage bonds, but in 1932 very few major investment firms could provide the funds required, and the few that could were inclined to set harsh terms. These few investment firms, moreover, were also closely linked with the Montreal Power interests. Thus, the provisional underwriting agreement with the firm of Wood, Gundy and Company could be renegotiated, but Gundy was Sir Herbert Holt's partner.

Beauharnois was still a prize that Holt and his associates wanted to pick up, but preferably with as few obligations and encumbrances as possible. Montreal Power and investors associated with them were the only ones willing to assist, but the terms of a Montreal Power sponsored or assisted Beauharnois rescue would be tough. Until everyone was desperate enough to turn to them, Sir Herbert Holt and his associates simply waited. In August of 1932, for example, Holt calmly informed the press that 'Our main interest is to see that the Beauharnois scheme shall be completed as efficiently and as economically as possible. Beauharnois is beyond question the greatest power site in the whole world.'[22]

In April of 1932 the situation had become even more complicated and serious. The half-yearly interest payment on the collateral trust fund bonds fell due, payable in either New York or Montreal and Toronto; $900,000 to $1 million was needed, depending on whether payment was made in Canadian or American funds. The collateral trust bonds once had a sinking fund, and sufficient money had been placed in an escrow fund to pay interest for the first two years. But the directors had 'borrowed' all the remaining money in the escrow fund and could not make the 1 April interest payment unless they borrowed the required amount from the banks.

Prime Minister Bennett refused to provide a federal guarantee for bank loans to pay bond interest. Without such a guarantee the banks refused to advance the money, and the company defaulted on its April interest payment. Bennett strongly urged the formation of a bondholders' protective committee which would have the power to take over or force the company into liquidation ninety days after a default in interest payments. Bennett hoped that, once formed, the bondholders' protective committee would accept responsibility for its own protection, relieving the government of that responsibility. It would not be that easy. A temporary committee of bondholders was formed on 22 April and this temporary committee, with the co-operation of the Beauharnois directors and bankers, began to work out some financial proposals.

The Beauharnois default on its bond interest payments also prompted Montreal Power to work out its own proposal for the rescue and virtual take-over of Beauharnois. The Montreal Power proposal called for the government to provide $16 million, the banks to increase their loans to $9 million, and the shareholders to put up $10 million all to receive first mortgage bonds in return for their contributions.

Montreal Power offered to underwrite the $10 million first mortgage bonds to be sold to the shareholders. They would only do so, however, if the number of Beauharnois class A common shares were reduced from 1.8 million to 180,000, giving each shareholder one share for every ten previously held. Each shareholder could, however, get his other nine shares back if he took up his proper allotment of the $10 million first mortgage bonds. Montreal Power, as the underwriter, would pay for any of the $10 million bonds not taken by the shareholders and, of course, receive the shares to which those shareholders would have been entitled if they had taken up their proper allotment. It was estimated that 90 per cent of the other shareholders would not be able to pay for their allotment of the new bonds. The proposal would, therefore, give Montreal Power more than 90 per cent of the shares of Beauharnois in return for their purchase of $10 million new first mortgage bonds.[23]

The Montreal Power proposal did not ignore the holders of the 6 per cent collateral trust bonds. They were asked to forgo all interest payments for six years, and then to receive only 5 per cent. Montreal Power was willing to agree, however, that half of the net earnings, after depreciation, in the years from 1938 onward, could be used to repay the bondholders for forgone interest. Many of the bondholders naturally regarded the payment of both interest and principal as a contractual obligation, but if the company could not pay and went into liquidation, it would be difficult to salvage anything. The bondholders therefore needed a protective committee which truly looked after their interests.

The temporary and unofficial committee of bondholders established in April of 1932 developed its own financial plan which was almost identical to that proposed by Montreal Power.[24] This action infuriated many of the smaller bondholders, who did not think the temporary committee represented their interests. The interests of the bondholders were diverse. Some were large institutional investors who also held large blocks of Beauharnois common shares. Some were closely associated with Montreal Power, while others had only very small holdings. And a few bondholders, such as the ubiquitous Frank Regan, had personal grievances which they wanted the committee to champion. Those who owned no common shares were interested in getting as much as possible for their bonds, even if that left very little or nothing for the shareholders. Those with large holdings of common shares naturally had a different view of the matter. The first temporary committee of bondholders was dominated by those who also had large share holdings.

After this committee announced its financial plan, a group of dissident bondholders, mostly from Toronto, began to meet on their own. Headed by I.E. Weldon, these dissidents were determined to press for better terms than those offered by Montreal Power and by the temporary bondholder committee. The temporary bondholder committee, however, had included at least one individual, a man named Frank Somerville, who was hostile to the Montreal Power interests. He later complained that in the meetings of the temporary bondholder committee some heavy-handed tactics had been used.

While our Committee was in session at Ottawa Mr. Godin [Herbert Holt's former private secretary and a director of the Beauharnois companies] was called on the telephone when he was before us making that offer which we conveyed to you and he informed us that the message received over the telephone was an intimation from the Canadian General Electric that their bill must be paid at once or they would cease to continue the work. This was, no doubt, dictated by one, Mr. Holt, who I believe is a Director in that Company.[25]

The first direct confrontation between the rival groups of bondholders came at an official meeting on 10 June 1932 when a new and offical bondholders' protective committee was to be named. At that meeting several officials of the Beauharnois companies gave lengthy and detailed reports. Subsequently the bondholders proceeded to the election of their first official and legal protective committee. As might be expected, serious trouble erupted immediately. The temporary bondholder committee suggested that the official bondholders' protective committee consist of seven members and then nominated a full seven-member slate which did not include the disgruntled Frank Somerville or any of the Toronto dissidents. There were immediate and vociferous objections, and a counter-proposal was made to increase the membership of the committee to twelve. The meeting had to be recessed as the disputants considered their positions. After the recess unanimous agreement was reached that the committee should be increased to twelve. But then, apparently to the surprise of the dissidents and perhaps even in violation of the understanding arrived at during the recess, another complete slate, now consisting of twelve members, was put forward. The recess had apparently been used by those presenting the first slate to find five additional members. The Toronto dissidents who had been left off the first slate, and hoped to be included if the committee was enlarged, were again shut out.[26]

The vote itself was also controversial. The packed slate was approved, but the majority was achieved in a dubious manner. R.O. Sweezey was the holder of a large block of bonds, but these had been pledged as collateral to several banks. At the meeting the Royal Bank dictated how Sweezey's bonds should be voted. Frank Somerville informed the prime minister that $15,480,000 worth of bonds was represented at the meeting, and that about $9 million was voted in favour of the stacked slate. $2.9 million of those $9 million was Sweezey's bonds, voted against his will by the Royal Bank to which he had pledged the bonds as collateral.[27]

The same disgruntled bondholders claimed the leaders of this coup were Montreal Power people, supported by Dominion Securities, who represented and owned 80 per cent of the entire outstanding common share issue. This seemed to be an attempt by the shareholders to control the bondholders' protective committee. The atmosphere was described thus:

> Their [the Montreal Power and Dominion Securities] actions may be worthy of an Al Capone but certainly not worthy of honest dealing and common decency. I have voiced, on more than one occasion while on the Provisional Committee, that the bondholders own the property and that the shareholders receive whatever in the opinion of the bondholders would be a fair thing. As you know, one million shares were purchased by the promoters for $1,000,000 after they had taken $2,189,000 of the bondholders' money out of the treasury to purchase for $1,000,000 these shares.[28]

It was evident that the shareholders would get nothing if dissident bondholders such as Frank Somerville controlled the bondholders' protective committee. It was equally evident to Somerville and his associates that their interests would not be adequately protected by the committee that had been elected. He therefore wrote to the prime minister that 'It is quite evident to me that the bondholders must look to you [Bennett] for protection.'[29] That role, however, was precisely what Bennett was hoping to avoid.

Frank Regan's insistent and frequently repeated demands that his client's interests be safeguarded in any Beauharnois reorganization further muddied the waters. If Bennett intervened on behalf of the disgruntled bondholders, Regan would insist that he also intervene on behalf of the Cantins.[30]

The disagreements among the bondholders inevitably led to the formation of a second bondholders' protective committee.[31] This so-called Toronto committee was led by I.E. Weldon, and it began work on a plan whereby the bondholders, with the aid of further federal guarantees, would raise the necessary money to complete the project.[32] Under this proposal all the common shares would go either to the federal government or to the bondholders, with no compensation of any kind for the previous shareholders. The bitter disputes also immediately and seriously depressed the value of the bonds. Most of them had been bought at or near the par value of $100. They had fallen to $40 by March 1932, and plummeted to $22 immediately after the divisive meeting of the bondholders in June.[33]

R.B. Bennett, whether he liked it or not, was left to deal with the problems of a Beauharnois reorganization. The Montreal Power interests seemingly had effective control of the official bondholders' protective committee, but their proposals had roused a vociferous opposition. The political hostility to Montreal Power's monopoly, combined with the anger of numerous small bondholders, was too much for Bennett to face in 1932. So he continued to do what he had unwillingly started in April 1931. He provided further letters guaranteeing Beauharnois bank loans. He wanted to ensure that the project would be completed at least to the point where the contracted power to Montreal Power and Ontario Hydro could be delivered. Fortunately construction was fortunately proceeding according to schedule. If there was no financial interruption, the first generators would be ready to deliver power on the contracted date of 1 October 1932. Long-term solutions to Beauharnois's financial problems would be deferred until the plant was actually in operation. Montreal Power would have to wait several months longer before the situation became desperate enough for their financial proposals to be accepted.

Politically and financially Beauharnois had become a nightmare. Technologically it was still a dream that was gradually coming true. The first four turbines, generating 50,000 horsepower each were tested in mid-September of 1932 and performed to perfection. They were ready to be turned on and to generate hydroelectric power to meet the requirements of the contracts with Ontario Hydro and Montreal Power on 1 October 1932, as were the two auxiliary turbines which provided the power necessary to drive all the major works of the new plant.[34]

The income from the two power contracts strengthened the position of the Beauharnois bondholders. But there was still a good deal of work to be completed, and the remaining six turbines had to be installed if the increased power deliveries envisioned under the two contracts were to be met. R.A.C. Henry estimated in December 1932 that he would need another $4,808,248 for construction purposes in 1933.[35] A total of $51,423,502 had already been spent, and an estimated $16 million more was needed before all the turbines would be in operation in 1937.[36]

Prime Minister Bennett was emphatic in December 1932. He had helped bring the project to the point where the first turbines were in operation. The federal government would provide no further guarantees. There was, consequently, a renewed flurry of proposals and counter-proposals for the reorganization and refinancing of the Beauharnois companies. All this activity came to a head in March 1933 when the official bondholders' protective committee reached agreement with Montreal Power for a modified reorganization plan.

The proposed new plan still required the exchange of ten old Beauharnois Power Corporation shares for one new share. It also provided for the creation of 590,000 new Beauharnois Power Corporation shares, but 150,000 of these new shares were to be distributed among the bondholders on the basis of five shares for each $1,000 bond. The remaining 440,000 would go to those who ultimately bought first mortgage shares to be issued by Beauharnois Light, Heat and Power Company. The new proposal called for the issue of $40 million first mortgage bonds. Of these bonds $24,148,000 was to be used to pay off the company's federally guaranteed and unguaranteed indebtedness at the banks, $1,352,000 was to go to the Quebec government as payment for water leases and rentals, while $13.5 million would be underwritten by Montreal Power. These bonds, with bonuses of the 440,000 common shares referred to above, first would be offered, at par, to collateral trust bondholders. Any of the first mortgage bonds and accompanying share bonuses not taken up by the collateral trust bondholders would be taken by Montreal Power. The package also provided for the refinancing of the 6 per cent collateral trust bonds. These were to be replaced, on the basis of one old bond for 1.2 new 5 per cent collateral trust bonds. The new bonds would pay no interest until 1938 and 5 per cent thereafter.[37]

The anticipated net result of this proposed reorganization was that it would give Montreal Power control of 51.18 per cent of the common shares of the Beauharnois Power Corporation. Montreal Power would still underwrite first mortgage bonds to cover the remaining construction costs, while the federal government, the banks, and the Quebec government had to take Beauharnois bonds to meet their guarantees, loans, and water leases, respectively. This modified Montreal Power proposal still roused much opposition. R.O. Sweezey was particularly concerned about the number of new shares that would go to the underwriters, as opposed to the number that would go to bondholders. He continued to pester Bennett with his own financial proposals but in the end received a stern rebuff from the harassed prime minister. 'The Beauharnois debenture holders have appointed a committee to deal with the matter of reorganization. Under these circumstances, your duty is to deal with them in matters of this kind, rather than me.'[38]

I.C. Weldon and the members of his Toronto committee were also strongly opposed to the new Montreal Power proposals and offered a plan of their own. In an effort to gain support for their plan Weldon and his committee members prepared a formal address to the Senate and House of Commons, charging that 'the proposed contract with the Montreal Light Heat and Power Co. is exceedingly inequitable to us and we are utterly opposed to it, except as a last resort to save us from losing the money we have already contributed.'[39] At least two or three other financial plans were proposed by various interested parties,[40] but Bennett and most of the parliamentarians had had enough of the incessant wrangling. They refused to intervene. To a question in the House of Commons Bennett replied that 'having protected security holders to the extent of enabling them to protect themselves [he] did not consider [the federal government] responsible for determining as to the disposition of the plan of reorganization.'[41] As a result, directors of the Beauharnois Power Corporation approved the new scheme of reorganization on 16 March 1933, and an appropriate contract with Montreal Power was signed.[42] The bondholders gave their final approval on 3 May 1933.

I.E. Weldon remained hostile and bitter to the end. After it was all over, he wrote an indignant letter to the editor of the *Toronto Star* to protest and publicize the means whereby Montreal Power had achieved its control over Beauharnois.

I came back from the Beauharnois Bondholders meeting in Montreal thoroughly convinced that these debenture holders were getting a raw deal indeed. It would look from the report of the meeting, as though all these Bondholders were eager to accept the proposition of the Montreal Light, Heat and Power Co. As a matter of fact no other proposition had been put to the debenture holders.

The Executive Committee who really represented the holders of common stock and not Bondholders were in control of the finances of the Company, and of the lists of the debenture holders, and the Executive Committee made every effort in getting proxies in favour of the offer of the Montreal Power. Every local Bank Manager seemed to be using every effort to get the people in his locality to sign proxies in favour of the Executive Committee, and the Executive Committee in its turn, had been appointed by the same people who put over so many 'lame ducks' a few years ago – P. Burns, Robert Simpson, Abitibi, Consolidated Investment Trust and so on ad nauseum and then some. ... Sweezey is the largest debenture holder in Beauharnois. On Sunday last he told me here in Toronto that he would be able to vote his debentures any way he chose. The day before the meeting, however, the Banks told him exactly how he would vote his debentures, or intimated that he might not own the debentures long. Of course, Sweezey had to submit to this as he could not afford to become impoverished over the matter. The whole deal stinks.[43]

The 1933 reorganization gave the Beauharnois companies the funds needed to bring all ten 50,000 horsepower generators into operation. The contracts with Montreal Power and Ontario Hydro guaranteed an annual income sufficient to pay all operating costs and fixed charges. R.B. Bennett could claim that he had kept his promise that the federal government would ensure completion of the first phase of the project and protect bona fide investors. The shareholders had not lost everything, as many thought they should. The bondholders had to make concessions on interest payments, but the value of their bonds eventually rebounded. When taking into account the disasters that befell so many North American corporations during the 1930s, the outcome seemed reasonable.

14

Postscript and conclusion

The affairs of the Beauharnois companies proved to be only a temporary embarrassment for most of those involved. Some unsavoury aspects of Canadian political and entrepreneurial life had been revealed, but they did not result in any fundamental changes. After 1933 Beauharnois still provided fodder for some political sniping, another financial reorganization, and minor political and personal adjustments. But when the last of the huge Beauharnois turbines were finally turned on in 1961, generating 2 million horsepower of electricity, it was once again 'a dream come true.' The nightmare of the scandal of 1931 and 1932 was not mentioned.[1]

The 1933 reorganization of the Beauharnois companies was expected to remove the matter from further political trouble. Other more pressing economic and political concerns dominated the political agenda, and the two major federal political parties were not interested in fundamental political reforms which would threaten their future campaign funds.

Beauharnois did, however, figure in one more political skirmish. The Ontario Liberal leader, Mitchell F. Hepburn, saw in the Beauharnois revelations an opportunity to attack and perhaps defeat the Conservatives, who had become more defensive after the departure of 'Boss Ferguson' for Canada House in London. In 1932 Hepburn complained loudly enough about numerous alleged irregularities in Ontario Hydro that the government of Premier Henry agreed to appoint a royal commission. The terms of reference of this royal commission were carefully restricted, and all efforts to introduce evidence about a $200,000 Beauharnois contribution to Premier Ferguson were systematically ruled out of order by the chairman. He and his fellow commissioners were empowered to investigate only 'the possible relationship of the payment to John Aird Jr., to the purchase of power from the Beauharnois interests,' and several controversial matters relating to other power contracts.[2] This excessive caution probably raised more suspicions than it quieted, and the Beauharnois affair became a factor in the defeat of the Ontario Conservatives in 1934. After the election, Hepburn set up a new inquiry in which more information was made public. The payment to John Aird, Jr, was discussed again, but no proof could be found that an additional payment of $200,000 had been made to Premier Ferguson.

Mitch Hepburn made effective political use of the revelations in the House of Commons, the Senate, and the first Ontario investigations. During the 1934 provincial election campaign he promised to repudiate Ontario Hydro's power contracts with Beauharnois and several other private companies. He alleged that bribery and fraud were involved in the negotiation of those contracts. The promise to repudiate was appealing to many in Ontario. It would correct a morally dubious transaction with the private power interests, and it would solve an immediate practical problem. The economic recession had led to sharply reduced industrial power requirements, and Ontario had a surplus of electric power in 1934.[3]

Hepburn's colourful and flamboyant 1934 election campaign was successful, and he was sworn in as premier of Ontario on 10 July 1934. He moved somewhat cautiously, but relentlessly, against the power companies, and on 6 December 1935 legislation repudiating Ontario Hydro's power contract with Beauharnois and three other private electrical companies was proclaimed law. Repudiation of the contract, of course, destroyed a substantial part of the security of the $36 million (par value) 5 per cent collateral trust bonds issued to replace the $30 million (par value) 6 per cent collateral trust bonds. J.S. Norris, the president of Montreal Power and also elected president of the Beauharnois Power Corporation after the 1933 reorganization, consequently reported to his directors that

> Pending re-sale of the power summarily cut off by the untoward act of the Ontario Legislature, the Company will for all practical purposes be dependent for revenue upon its contract with Montreal Light Heat and Power Consolidated, the net revenue from which, with the utmost economy in operation, will be insufficient to meet the full interest charges on the outstanding First Mortgage Bonds of Beauharnois Light Heat and Power Company regardless of depreciation and amortization.[4]

The bondholders were again encouraged to form a protective committee to safeguard their interests. The first official action, however, was a suit brought before the Supreme Court of Ontario for the restoration of the Ontario Hydro contract. Beauharnois won the early legal battles, but Ontario Hydro was eventually given leave to appeal the case to the Judicial Committee of the Imperial Privy Council.[5] Before the case could be heard in London, Ontario Hydro and Beauharnois Light, Heat and Power renegotiated their disputed contract. The delivery dates were set back by five years and the price was reduced from $15 to $12.50 per horsepower. The price of Beauharnois Power delivered to Montreal Power was also reduced to $12.50 per horsepower at the same time.[6]

The altered prices and delivery schedules of the Beauharnois power contracts did not provide sufficient funds to meet the obligations of the 5 per cent collateral trust bonds. Yet another scheme of reorganization was worked out and approved in 1938; it offered Montreal Power bonds and junior Beauharnois Light, Heat and Power Company securities in exchange for the 5 per cent collateral trust bonds. The 1938 reorganization also provided for the winding-up of the Beauharnois Power Corporation and the surrender of its charter. The charters of the Beauharnois Construction Company, the Beauharnois Land Company, the Beauharnois Railway Company, and the Beauharnois Transmission Company had already been surrendered following the 1933 reorganization. After the 1938 reorganization only the Beauharnois Light, Heat and Power Company remained in operation. All its shares, which had been owned by the Beauharnois Power Corporation before the 1938 reorganization, were transferred to Montreal Power.

The repudiation of the Beauharnois power contracts had another important effect. Application was made for authorization to export surplus power to the United States. Such exports had always been firmly opposed by Premier Taschereau, but the difficult circumstances of the 1930s forced him to change his policy.[7] Similarly, when Ontario Hydro renegotiated its power contracts, it sought authority to export its surplus power to the United States. The long-term result was that all the power generated at Beauharnois was exported to the United States. That was not what R.O. Sweezey had had in mind when he first took an interest in the project, and he protested vigorously.[8]

The political and financial disruptions significantly changed the Beauharnois project but did not prevent its completion. The first four main turbines and the two auxilary units, as already indicated, were put into service in September, and power deliveries began on 1 October

1932. The remaining six main turbines of the first construction phase were added before the end of the decade.[9]

Before the first ten turbines, each capable of generating 50,000 horsepower of electricity, were completed, work was begun on additional units. World War II created major new power demands, and two additional units were added during the war. Two more were placed in production in 1949, twelve in 1953, and the final ten in 1961.[10] This brought the plant to its full capacity with thirty-six main turbines and two auxiliary units, utilizing the entire flow of the St Lawrence, except for the water required to operate the St Lawrence Seaway canal and the water used by the other, less efficient, but still operational power plants in the Soulanges Section.

Construction of the powerhouse was as good as R.O. Sweezey had promised. Three of the original four main turbines were still in operation in 1982, and, after fifty years, the resident engineer placed a dime on the top ledge of one of these turbines to demonstrate the absence of any serious vibration which would move the dime from the spot where it had been placed. In the spacious visitors' reception area an impressive film, based in part on the excellent photographs taken by the American consulting engineers, explained important aspects of the construction of the power plant.[11]

Despite the technological quality of construction and the financial strength of Montreal Power, the Beauharnois works are no longer privately owned and operated. The Liberal administration of Louis-Alexandre Taschereau, which was strongly committed to free enterprise, came under increasing attack as the depression of the 1930s worsened. In 1935 the provincial party was reduced to a minority. A reform-minded Liberal faction had broken away to form Action Nationale, whose leader was Paul Gouin, the son of a former Quebec premier, federal cabinet minister, and major shareholder in a number of private power and paper enterprises. Action Nationale helped to defeat the provincial Liberals in 1936 and bring to power the provincial Conservative party led by Maurice Duplessis, who then formed his own Quebec nationalist party, the Union Nationale.

A provincial commission was established in 1934 to study the hydroelectric power situation in Quebec. This commission recommended the nationalization of the monopolistic, privately owned and highly profitable hydroelectric companies. Montreal Power and its affiliates refused to co-operate in any way, or to provide any information requested by the provincial commission. The substantial profits of the private companies, particularly of Montreal Power, were nevertheless a source of much controversy, which turned decisively against the private power interests during World War II. The illness and death in September of 1941 of Sir Herbert Holt, patriarch of the Montreal Power colossus, further changed the situation and expedited nationalization on terms dictated by the provincial government. The Quebec legislature passed an act in May 1941 empowering the provincial government to acquire in whole or in part the undertakings of a number of privately owned power companies.[12] The private interests fought back ferociously, but in 1944 a commission was created to take possession and operate the facilities of Montreal Power and its subsidiaries, including the Beauharnois Light, Heat and Power Company.[13] The shareholders received compensation as determined under expropriation procedures established for that purpose.

The defeat of the Quebec Liberals and later the nationalization of the Montreal and Beauharnois power companies by a another Liberal administration were at least partly rooted in the earlier troubles. It had seemed in 1931 and 1932 that the Beauharnois scandal had left the Quebec government relatively unscathed. Taschereau's biographer suggested that the Quebec premier was 'lightly duped' by the promoters and unfairly criticized for his role in the company's affairs.[14] Specifically, the premier was not told 'when Herbert Holt insinuated himself into the Beauharnois organization.' Premier Taschereau had, however, been able to shield himself behind arguments about provincial rights. He was never compelled to give evidence about his role in Beauharnois, and Senator Donat Raymond successfully resisted all pressure to reveal anything about provincial election campaign funds. The events of 1931 and 1932 nevertheless created public perceptions of Liberal corruption which contributed to the subsequent electoral reverses of the Taschereau government in 1935 and 1936. A biographical sketch of the Quebec premier rather accurately summed up his public image.

He is also known to newspapers as The Grand Seigneur of Quebec, and takes quite a kindly interest in the welfare of simple old habitants like Sir Herbert Holt and Mr. George Montgomery ... He lives in Quebec on a street called Grande Allée, but is never quite as far from Montreal's St. James Street as these geographical circumstances would indicate ... He regards Mr. Lapointe [Mackenzie King's Quebec lieutenant] as a thoroughly impractical politician and Mr. Lapointe looks upon him as a misplaced Conservative, both of which opinions are probably quite right. His political attitude may be described as pro-Liberal but anti-King.[15]

The Beauharnois scandal and the subsequent defeat of Premier Taschereau did not lead to a reform of Quebec provincial politics. Maurice Duplessis, once firmly in control, proved himself as adept in the exercise of political patronage and corruption as his predecessors. Duplessis's term in office was interrupted from 1939 until 1944 by a Liberal administration led by J.A. Godbout in which some reforms were undertaken, but the exigencies of war limited what could be done at that time. The Duplessis government after 1944 developed relations with the large corporations that were similar to those of the Taschereau government.

The other apparent winner in 1931 and 1932 was Sir Herbert Holt and Montreal Power. The political and financial embarrassments of the Beauharnois Power interests allowed Montreal Power to move in and gain effective control of the power situation in the entire Montreal area. That monopoly and the lucrative profits earned by Montreal Power, however, also contributed to the increasing and ultimately successful agitation for the nationalization of the entire Montreal Power empire. After Montreal Power took over the Beauharnois companies, there was no authority, other than the provincial government, which could effectively challenge it, and political pressure on provincial legislators to challenge Montreal Power seemingly became irresistible. In the end even the solidly entrenched Montreal Power proved to be something less than an immovable object.

Most of the businessmen directly associated with the Beauharnois project did not suffer unduly after it came under the control of Montreal Power. R.O. Sweezey was, and remained, a highly respected and exceptionally able engineer and promoter. He stayed with the Beauharnois project until the first eight main turbines and the two auxiliary turbines were installed and operating satisfactorily. He also remained active for many years in several large pulp and paper ventures and promoted or served as an engineering consultant for other large hydroelectric and mining ventures in western Canada. Before becoming involved in the Beauharnois promotion, he had been a partner with Sir Herbert Holt in several pulp and paper ventures, and after 1934 he again served on the boards of several Holt-dominated companies. His mansion of Pine Ledge, just east of Kingston overlooking a bay in the St Lawrence, became the scene of extravagant social functions, which involved many influential academic friends from Queen's University and the Royal Military College, as well as political and business friends from Ottawa, Toronto, and Montreal. He died on 13 May 1968 in Montreal, but the obituaries written more than thirty-five years after the event still referred at length to his association with the Beauharnois scandal of 1931.

Sweezey's friend and colleague R.A.C. Henry did even better. The Montreal Power managers recognized his engineering, political, and managerial abilities. They cut his salary to bring it into line with salaries of their other senior managers, but they retained his services.[16] Then, during World War II, Henry was appointed executive assistant to C.D. Howe, minister of transport and of munitions and supply. In 1944, when Howe became minister of reconstruction, Henry was named his deputy minister and served in numerous top-level wartime posts. In 1949 he returned to private practice and ended his professional career as one of the senior consulting engineers of the St Lawrence Seaway Authority. He organized and supervised the staff that prepared the plans for a new 2.2 million horsepower project in the International Section of the St Lawrence River, upstream from the Beauharnois development. His obituaries described him as one of Canada's most distinguished and able engineers and civil servants but made no mention whatever of his involvement in the Beauharnois scandal.[17]

Things did not go nearly as well for Sweezey's competitor and antagonist N.M. Cantin and his lawyer Frank Regan, who had provided the information which led to the scandal. Cantin, Regan, and the Transportation & Power Corporation struggled on until 1940, when the company underwent bankruptcy proceedings. It was sold by the liquidator in bankruptcy court for $15,000. The purchaser was none other than the Beauharnois Light, Heat and Power Company.[18]

Sweezey's other early rival and later adviser and agent, Winfield Sifton, died before the required federal order in council was approved. Sweezey for a time paid Sifton's widow a small allowance but refused to pay the $50,000. Winfield Sifton's heirs sued both the Beauharnois Power Corporation and Sweezey personally and ultimately carried the case against Sweezey to the Judicial Committee of the Imperial Privy Council. They won their case in February of 1938, whereupon Sweezey turned to the Beauharnois Power Corporation, claiming he had acted only on behalf of that company. The Beauharnois directors, who had offered the Siftons a 50 per cent settlement before they appealed the case to the Privy Council, refused to help Sweezey after the Privy

Council decision. The Sifton heirs eventually got their $50,000 from Sweezey.[19]

The three Liberal senators directly implicated in the scandal did not fare well. The fate of Senator Andrew Haydon was particularly tragic. His health continued to deteriorate in 1932, despite the political agreement whereby further proceedings in the Senate were halted after Senator McDougald's resignation. By the end of October of 1932 Haydon's condition was so serious that Mrs Haydon told Mackenzie King that she hoped 'he might not linger longer, that he suffers great pain at times with his legs, has even bitten his fingers with the pain.'[20] King thought this 'a sad end, a tragic close to a life that had many great qualities, and of one who was a true & devoted & faithful friend.'[21]

Senator Haydon died on 10 November 1932. Mackenzie King's reaction was a curious combination of guilt, caution, and sanctimoniousness.

> I had not thought it wise to issue a tribute in the morning fearing arousing political controversy of a spiteful kind, but later Joan again fortunately phoned me after reading others in the Citizen saying she thought I should. I was glad she said so, & find it difficult to understand why I should have let my caution & sensitiveness combine to the extent it did to cause me to hesitate. I prayed for guidance to say the right thing, and after dinner wrote out a few paragraphs, feeling there was not enough of the personal sense of loss expressed in it. Just why I could not go farther it seemed difficult for me to understand. It may have been some guidance, or being held to earth. However, I felt I would do this side as it should be done at a meeting of the party caucus on Wednesday. Haydon's spirit stands out in the tribute paid him. I used the word 'martyrdom' designedly in what I wrote. I shall always regret not having said what I wanted to in the H. of C. about his being the soul of honour, & which would have been said but for Bennett's threat. It may have been a bluff of his intention as I gathered it from his words to come out with something unknown if I spoke re Haydon.[22]

The next day King went to the Haydon residence to view the body and described his reactions thus 'After dinner called at the Haydon's, & saw dear Haydon lying in his coffin, his face was very noble, a fine scholarly head, so peaceful, not a look of scorn or disappointment but just as one who had come through great tribulation & won his perfect peace.'[23]

Haydon's funeral was held on 12 November and the entry in King's diary for that day brings the various elements of the sordid relationship between the prime minister and the Beauharnois senators into sharp focus.

After lunch I called for Lapointe and we drove together to Haydon's house on the Driveway to be present at the funeral as pall bearers ... Dr. McDougald was inside, in the dining-room with a few of the friends, & pall bearers. It seemed to me like Mephisto coming out of a church to see him leave the room. Haydon's whole life would have been different but for his [McDougald's] selfishness, and the Senate wd. never have taken the action they did against Haydon as well as him, had he resigned when he should have, & when he told me he would ... His doing nothing for Haydon since when he promised me he wd. with the money he had contributed to Mr. Larkin's fund for me & which I returned to him is despicable and a part of his meanness.[24]

King thought 'the church buried Haydon as one of their saints. He merited all.'[25] But his own conscience continued to bother the Liberal leader all day. That evening, however, he had a moving spiritual experience which he described thus: 'It was Haydon & mother bringing comfort and assurance to my heart & evidence of his survival. When I left and walked around the driveway & was communing with Haydon aloud, I felt as it were someone pressing my right shoulder. I said yes Andrew I know it is you continue to press & I could feel the pressure as of a bag of air – a spiritual body, against my shoulder.'[26]

Wilfrid Laurier McDougald, alias Mephisto in Mackenzie King's fevered brain, also suffered major health problems during and after the Beauharnois investigations. He was forced to resign his chairmanship of the Montreal Harbour Commission and to relinquish any active role in the Liberal party of Canada, but he hoped eventually to be forgiven and reinstated. In 1935 he wrote to the recently re-elected Mackenzie King that 'I have been most careful, in every way, to comply with your wishes since 1930 in protecting and safeguarding the interests of yourself and the Liberal Party and in the words of Mr. Lapointe, "layed low."'[27] In the same letter, however, McDougald indicated that he seriously considered seeking a nomination and running in the 1935 election in order to gain personal vindication. He then gave his own assessment of the scandal of 1931 and 1932.

It was a matter of high satisfaction to myself and doubtless to yourself as well, that no point whatever, was made in the campaign by the Tory leaders and press, of any material phase of the circumstances which were made so much of in 1931 and 1932. It must now be evident that these matters completely lacked verity and vitality; that the single aim and purpose was to destroy the Liberal Party and its Leaders, and to eliminate me, even though a humble figure in the ranks of the Party; yet one who, as they evidently thought, had been an efficacious instrument in advancing the interests of the Party.[28]

The former senator in 1935 still expressed his continued friendship and affection for Mackenzie King, but a letter to the prime minister in 1938 took on a more hostile tone. McDougald complained that the prime minister would not see him in person and then expressed particular bitterness over the fact that King had not yet reappointed him to the Senate. He insisted that King had made such a promise to him personally and separately to his son and wife. McDougald thought the perfect opportunity for such an appointment had come in 1938: 'By every rule of the game: District, Religion and Service to Party, I am entitled and qualified and therefore now count on you to fulfill your promise to me and see that I get it [the Senate seat vacated by the death of Senator Tobin]. If I get no response to this request from you I shall be definitely convinced that there is no gratitude or sincerity in the great Liberal Leader.'[29]

The former Montreal medical doctor, businessman, and senator was not, of course, reappointed to the Canadian Senate. Even if McDougald did not grasp the situation Mackenzie King certainly understood that such a reappointment was politically impossible. If the Liberal leader could scarely bring himself to issue a public tribute on the death of Senator Haydon, whom he regarded as a real saint, he would never reappoint the man whom he considered little better than the devil himself. The relationship between the prime minister and the former senator nevertheless remained fairly cordial. The letter of 1938 was an exception. There was no final and dramatic break between the two men until McDougald died in Montreal on 19 June 1942, at the age of sixty, after a lengthy illness. He had never fully recovered his health after 1932.

The individual who probably came off best in the whole Beauharnois affair was John Aird, Jr. He kept the $125,000 that R.O. Sweezey had paid him, on the understanding that the money was a political contribution to the Ontario Conservative party. That party, as already indicated, denied any knowledge of political campaign funds, and attempts by some Beauharnois bondholders to sue Aird for the return of the funds were never followed up. Aird's personal finances were reviewed in some detail by the 1934 Ontario royal commission. The suspicion was that Aird had kept the bonds he got from Sweezey but had paid the appropriate amounts to the Conservative party from another account. There were several large withdrawals from other Aird accounts, but Aird said they paid for some investments in California. The royal commission did not have access to Aird's California accounts.

The Beauharnois incident, and several others in connection with the affairs of Ontario Hydro, cast something of a cloud over the business career of the younger Aird. But the Aird family was well established in Toronto, Sir John Aird serving as general manager and then president of the Canadian Bank of Commerce. John Black Aird, a grandson of Sir John Aird, and a nephew of John Aird, Jr, had an exceptionally successful legal and business career, which culminated in his appointment as lieutenant-governor of Ontario in 1980. Peter C. Newman regarded the Aird family as one of Toronto's most distinguished and John Black Aird as one of Ontario's more successful lieutenant-governors 'whose presence at social occasions lends a touch of class, a hint of representative royalty.'[30]

A discussion of those involved in the Beauharnois affair can properly end with the remarkable career of William Lyon Mackenzie King. In 1931 and 1932 King, by his own admission, walked the Valley of Humiliation. Revelation of huge campaign contributions made at a time when the federal cabinet was considering Beauharnois's development plans, seriously embarrassed the Liberal party and its leader, but at least Senator McDougald's contributions to the Laurier House fund were not made public.

Mackenzie King was probably not aware of the size of the Beauharnois election campaign contributions, and his decision to approve the required order in council was made only after lengthy and careful reviews of all the relevant circumstances. There was no direct link between the prime minister's decision to approve the order in council and any financial contributions made to the Laurier House fund or to Liberal party campaign fund-raisers. There were, however, important indirect links which probably determined that the decision was favourable. Sir Clifford Sifton was an influential member of the Cabinet Advisory Committee which, after considerable controversy, recommended approval of the Beauharnois plans. Both Haydon and McDougald were close to the prime minister and used their influence to secure approval of the Beauharnois plans, as did several others who were not personal friends of the prime minister but who enjoyed considerable political influence. A detailed review of the chronology of events, and the influences brought to bear at critical times, leads to one inescapable conclusion. Without the use of political influence the Beauharnois promoters would not have had a full and sympathetic hearing, and their plans would not have been approved on time. Mackenzie King and his cabinet colleagues decided the case on its own merits, not as a result of a direct bribe. But they seriously considered the merits of the case as quickly as they did only because of the political influence and pressure that was exerted.

The Beauharnois affair revealed important facts about the Canadian political system. Promoters and lobbyists cannot rely solely on the merits of their proposals to obtain prompt legislative or bureaucratic approval of their legitimate projects. The politicians were too busy and politically preococupied to set aside their immediate political, constitutional, and bureaucratic problems to appreciate, without the assistance of lobbyists, the merits of an important and innovative new proposal. Means had to be found to focus their attention. Without an effective lobby the cabinet headed by Mackenzie King was far too cautious to approve proposals such as those advanced by the Beauharnois promoters.

The bureaucrats presented an equally serious problem. Their role was essentially negative or, in the more acceptable vocabulary of the day, regulatory. They saw themselves as guardians who had to make sure that all legislative and political requirements were met before a project received their approval, and they demonstrated a remarkable willingness to interpret laws and regulations in narrow, legalistic, and sometimes stupid ways. They seemed unconcerned if the conditions they set made it impossible for the promoters to proceed. Visionary entrepreneurs saw them as nothing more than obstacles to be overcome or circumvented.

Major developmental projects, such as the Beauharnois Power development, faced an array of political, bureaucratic, technological, financial, and administrative problems. The Beauharnois promoters were able to solve the technological, financial, and administrative problems with relative ease. They got into trouble when dealing with the political and bureaucratic problems, which they solved by co-opting senior bureaucrats and making generous campaign contributions to the politicans. An effective political lobby had to be mounted if the necessary political and bureaucratic authorizations were to be obtained.

There was a time when Canadian governments themselves initiated and promoted major new economic developments such as railways, canals, and postal and shipping facilities. In the twentieth century, under the Liberals, the Canadian government turned increasingly to regulation of private ventures rather than to the initiation of public ventures. Prime Minister Wilfrid Laurier, for example, did not think the government could administer any large business venture effectively. Political rather than sound business considerations had made an entrepreneurial shambles of ventures such as the Intercolonial Railway. Laurier unwittingly proved his point when his government became involved in the National Transcontinental Railway fiasco. Governments such as Laurier's could not properly initiate and manage major business projects. Experience had also demonstrated, however, that unregulated and uncontrolled free enterprise could lead to serious abuse and exploitation, particularly in industries where natural monopolies prevailed. So Canadian governments tried to regulate privately promoted ventures. Bureaucrats like J.B. Hunter flourished in offices that had once been occupied by visionaries like Sandford Fleming.

The Beauharnois scandal demonstrated the problems facing a private venture which was dependent on government regulatory agencies. It seemed necessary to resort to dubious means in order to capture and retain the attention and approval of politicians and bureaucrats. But the system could be made to meet the needs of both the entrepreneurs and the politicians. The entrepreneurs in this case needed government water leases and approval of their plans. The politicians needed resources to wage their electoral battles. The leaders of both major Canadian political parties recognized the need for political contributions from large corporations. They knew that those corporations would have important dealings with governments and would expect favours in return for their contributions. Those contributions paid the bills.

The precise ways in which political parties obtained campaign funds from corporate donors varied somewhat. The Ontario Tories, according to Sweezey and Griffith, had fixed toll-gating fees. They demanded 50 cents in campaign contributions for every 1,000 horsepower of electricity purchased by Ontario Hydro. That was an unusually rigid assessment. Party fund-raisers, nevertheless, had well-defined ideas of what they regarded as an appropriate donation for a corporate friend. The Liberals, again according to Sweezey and Griffith, came to collect once, and then, as their need increased, they came again. Sweezey was sufficiently concerned about the future of his project that he agreed to buy a little more political 'gratitude.'

Neither the Liberals nor the Conservatives wanted fundamental change or reform. So they conspired to ensure that details of the entire system of financing election campaigns would not be revealed. That system was not challenged. Only the apparent excesses of the Liberals in 1930, which had become public knowledge as a result of Frank Regan's revelations to R.B. Bennett and Robert Gardiner, were investigated. Bennett was happy to see the Liberals embarrassed, but he had no desire whatsoever for more general inquiries about campaign funds.

The Liberals also displayed little remorse or regret for what they had done. They were chagrined because they had been caught, while Howard Ferguson, who, they thought, was every bit as guilty as they were, was more successful in burying his secrets. They were also frustrated that nothing was revealed about the sources from which the federal Conservatives had obtained funds. It was widely believed that much of the Conservative war chest came from Sir Herbert Holt's companies.

The real lesson the federal Liberals learned from the entire affair was that they must be more careful in the future. Specifically, arrangements were made to separate or insulate the political leaders from the more unsavoury aspects of politics. In the future Liberal leaders must know as little as possible about campaign funds, and there must be no incriminating documentation. Howard Ferguson was the model to be emulated. The corporations and other major interests would continue to make campaign contributions and seek government favours in return. The leaders must not know the details.

There is an old saying that he who would sup with the devil must have a long spoon. In 1930 the Liberals had used a spoon that was too large, with a handle that was too short. After 1930 they did not change their dining habits, but they equipped themselves with a longer spoon. The most detailed study which examines Liberal party finances and organization concluded that 'the Liberal party, especially under King's leadership, was haunted by the spectre of the Beauharnois affair, and found considerable political utility in a formal separation of the fund raising apparatus from the parliamentary leadership of the party.'[31] In a major article *Maclean's* raised the question 'After Beauharnois – What?' The article stated emphatically that 'The

Liberal and Conservative parties alike have become pensioners of selfish interests. If they are to become real instruments of public welfare, drastic changes must be made in our election laws.'[32] No such drastic changes in Canada's election laws were made then or since. Both major political parties made some internal arrangements to establish greater distance between their party leaders and campaign funds, but the political system that created the Beauharnois scandal was not reformed in any fundamental way.

A thoughtful journalist who compared the actions of the Beauharnois promoters with those of other Canadian businessmen concluded that

> If the public has been shocked by the Beauharnois revelations on campaign funds, the cause must surely be nothing more than the amount of the contributions. No one with any knowledge of politics can be unaware that such contributions are among the normal expenses of most large corporations, and that they are given with the expectation of favours in return. Only, those favours generally take the form of tariff increases. In all other aspects the Beauharnois is on the same footing as other capitalist enterprises, and the same things can be said in its behalf. It had the noble aim of developing the resources of Canada. It was to employ – and actually did employ – several thousand Canadian workmen. It was incidentally going to cost the general public a large amount of cash. The chief difference is that its product was not subject to tariff protection. The concessions it desired were different and more direct; the ultimate effect on the public would be the same.[33]

The Beauharnois scandal is a story of Canadian entrepreneurship and politics and of the relationships between politicians, businessmen, bureaucrats, and investors. It is a fairly typical story, save for two things. The size of the contributions made to the 1930 Liberal election campaign were unusually large, and, thanks to the unrequited efforts of thwarted rivals, the facts became known to the public.

Notes

The following abbreviations are used in the notes:

AO Archives of Ontario, Toronto
DU Duke University Archives, Durham, NC
FT *Financial Times*
FP *Financial Post*
HQA Hydro-Québec Archives, Montreal
Inquiry Evidence
Transcripts of Hearings of the Special Committee on Beauharnois Power, published as part of Appendix 5, *Journals of the House of Commons*, Session 1931
Inquiry Report
Fourth Report of the Special Committee on Beauharnois Power, published as part of Appendix 5, *Journals of the House of Commons*, Session 1931
NAC National Archives of Canada, Ottawa
OHA Ontario Hydro Archives, Toronto
Ontario Inquiry
OHA, Transcript of Hearings, and Report of the Royal Commission Appointed to Inquire into Certain Matters Concerning the Hydro-Electric Power Commission ...
QUA Queen's University Archives, Kingston, Ontario
Senate Evidence
Transcripts of Hearings of the Special Senate Committee on Beauharnois, published as part of an appendix of *Journals of the Senate*, Third Session, Seventeenth Parliament, 1932

Senate Report

Report of the Special Senate Committee on Beauharnois, published as part of an appendix of *Journals of the Senate*, Third Session, Seventeenth Parliament, 1932

CHAPTER 1 A spectacular beginning

1 *Ottawa Evening Citizen*, 14 Oct. 1929. Other accounts of the official opening are available in the *Montreal Gazette*, 14 Oct. 1929; *New York Times*, 14 Oct. 1929; QUA, Sweezey Papers, Box 2, File 3D; and DU, Lee Papers, Box 9, Memorandum of Operations of Beauharnois Construction Company, for week ending 14 Oct. 1929.
2 *Ottawa Evening Citizen*, 14 Oct. 1929; and *Montreal Gazette*, 14 Oct. 1929
3 The flow of water in the St Lawrence varies seasonally, but engineering studies indicated that at its lowest point there was a flow of approximately 185,000 cubic feet per second, while flows of more than 330,000 cubic feet per second had been recorded during the spring and summer run-offs. The mean flow of the river was 250,000 cubic feet per second. NAC, RG 11, Vol. 4223, File 8044, 'Report Showing Studies, with Plans, of Control and Remedial Works in Soulanges Section of St. Lawrence between Lake St. Francis and Lake St. Louis to protect River Navigation and to maintain present water levels at the Head of Cedars Rapids in connection with Proposed Diversion of 40,000 cu. ft. per second from Lake St. Francis.'

In 1928 the hydraulic turbine horsepower installed in all of Canada was 5,349,232. QUA, Sweezey Papers, Box 2, File 3A, pamphlet entitled *Beauharnois*, and published by the Dominion Securities Limited, 1929
4 Ibid.
5 *Montreal Gazette*, 14 Oct. 1929
6 QUA, Sweezey Papers, Box 2, File 3D
7 *Montreal Gazette*, 14 Oct. 1929
8 DU, Lee Papers, Box 8, pamphlet entitled *Beauharnois* and published by the Beauharnois Power Corporation Limited, Montreal, 15 Sept. 1930
9 *Montreal Gazette*, 14 Oct. 1929
10 DU, Lee Papers, Box 8, *Beauharnois*
11 QUA, Sweezey Papers, Box 2, File 3D
12 *Ottawa Citizen*, 14 Oct. 1929
13 Biographical information on R.O. Sweezey is drawn from QUA, Sweezey Papers, Box 2, File 3D, Autobiographical Note; ibid. Box 2, File 5, press clippings, including Sweezey's obituaries; and Dr T. Dickinson, 'Sweezey's

Beauharnois, touching upon the romantic and personal side of the greatest industrial enterprise ever projected in this Dominion,' *FT*, 1 Nov. 1929
14 QUA, Sweezey Papers, Box 2, File 3D, Autobiographical Note
15 Ibid., Box 2, File 5, press clipping entitled 'Sweezey of Beauharnois,' by Leslie Roberts
16 Ibid., Box 2, File 3D. Autobiographical Note
17 The methods of the Royal Securities Corporation are discussed in Armstrong and Nelles, *Monopoly's Moment*
18 *Inquiry Evidence*, 636
19 Christopher Armstrong, 'Making a Market: Selling Securities in Atlantic Canada before World War I,' *Canadian Journal of Economics* 13 (August 1980)
20 Royal Military College Archives, *Annual Report of the Commandant. Royal Military College of Canada for the year 1917*. The *Royal Military College of Canada Review*, November 1923, refers to R.O. Sweezey, Esq. as a former associate professor of surveying. The *Royal Military College Syllabus of the Course of Instruction* (Ottawa: Government of Canada Printing Bureau 1915) makes it clear that land and railway surveys were the primary focus of prewar courses. Sweezey helped broaden that spectrum considerably.
21 Dickinson, 'Sweezey's Beauharnois'
22 Biographical information on Wilfrid Laurier McDougald is drawn from his obituary in the *Montreal Gazette*, 20 June 1942; J.K. Johnson, ed., *The Canadian Directory of Parliament, 1867–1967* (Ottawa: Public Archives of Canada 1968), 405; Neatby, *King*
23 NAC, King Diary, 2 Dec. 1924
24 NAC, McDougald Papers, W.L.M. King to McDougald, 10 Aug. 1922
25 Ibid., 30 Dec. 1926, 7 March 1927, and 20 Nov. 1927. In each of these letters King thanks McDougald for gifts.
26 NAC, King Diary, 19 Sept. 1929
27 Biographical information on Andrew Haydon is drawn from obituary and funeral reports in the *Ottawa Evening Citizen*, 10, 11, and 14 Nov. 1932; Johnson, *Canadian Directory of Parliament*, 264; Neatby, *King*
28 *Ottawa Evening Citizen*, 10 Nov. 1932
29 Ibid., 11 Nov. 1932
30 Ibid., 14 Nov. 1932
31 Ibid., 10 Nov. 1932
32 Biographical information on Donat Raymond is drawn from his obituary notice in the *Montreal Gazette*, 6 June 1963; and Johnson, *Canadian Directory of Parliament*, 483

33 Biographical information on R.A.C. Henry is drawn from NAC, RG 32, Vol. 125, R.A.C. Henry personnel file, four folders.
34 Biographical information on Sir Herbert Holt is based on a variety of primary sources in Ireland, England, and Canada, which I consulted in the preparation of an as yet incomplete biography of this Canadian capitalist.
35 QUA, Sweezey Papers, Box 2, File 3D, documents entitled 'Thoughts for Saturday, October 12th,' and 'Programme, Saturday, October 12th, 1929'
36 DU, Lee Papers, Box 8, Pamphlet entitled *Down the Canal: A Pictorial Presentation of the Beauharnois Power and Navigation Development* (Montreal: Beauharnois Power Corporation Limited 1931)
37 Ibid.

CHAPTER 2 Success in Quebec

1 A detailed report prepared by Henry Holgate in 1915 and another prepared by Surveyor and Frigon in 1916, both dealing with the hydroelectric potential of the Soulanges Section are available in NAC, RG 11, Vols 4222 to 4226, File 804-1
2 John H. Dales, *Hydroelectricity and Industrial Development: Quebec 1898–1940* (Cambridge, Mass.: Harvard University Press 1957), 108
3 QUA, Sweezey Papers, Box 2, File 3D, Autobiographical Note
4 DU, Lee Papers, Box 8, *Beauharnois*
5 NAC, RG 11, Vol. 4222, File 804-A. *Report to the Chief Engineer of Public Works on the application of the Beauharnois Light, Heat and Power Company to divert water from Lake St Francis*, by Surveyor and Frigon, Consulting Engineers, 11 March 1916
6 QUA, Sweezey Papers, Box 2, File 3A, *Beauharnois*
7 NAC, RG 11, Vol. 4223, File 804-1-A. Report by Henry Holgate, 31 May 1915
8 The names of the subsidiary Great Lakes and Atlantic Canal and Power Company and of the parent Transportation and Power Corporation are used interchangeably in the documentation. The relationship between the various Cantin companies is given in NAC, King Papers, 129975–84, J.W. Harris to J.B. Hunter, 22 Oct. 1928
9 *Inquiry Evidence*, 637
10 Dickinson, 'Sweezey's Beauharnois'
11 HQA, Beauharnois Power Syndicate Stock Book. The dates given in this stock book are misleading. They show when the stock was officially issued, rather than when it was subscribed and paid for.
12 *Inquiry Evidence*, 641

13 Ibid., 439–40
14 HQA, File 7105-9, Memorandum of suggested method of dealing with the assets acquired by R.O. Sweezey from W.H. Robert et al. by the agreement of 3 Feb. 1927.
15 M. Grattan O'Leary, 'Holt vs. Jones. Twin word sketches of the principals in a colossal struggle for control of Canada's most stupendous asset – hydro-electric power,' *Maclean's*, 15 March 1929
16 R.O. Sweezey to J. Alderic Raymond, 14 Oct. 1926, as quoted in *Inquiry Evidence*, 638
17 Ibid., 787
18 Ibid., 788–9
19 Ibid., 646
20 For an informed, candid, and perceptive discussion of Premier Taschereau's personal views of Beauharnois see NAC, King Papers, 129987–8, Andrew Haydon to Mackenzie King, 1928
21 *Inquiry Evidence*, 638
22 Ibid.
23 NAC, King Papers, 134885–6, L.-A. Taschereau to King, 18 Dec. 1928.
24 *FT*, 30 March 1928
25 HQA, Minute Book of the Beauharnois Light, Heat and Power Company, Meeting of Directors, 13 June 1927
26 *Inquiry Evidence*, 647
27 HQA, Minute Book of the Beauharnois Light, Heat and Power Company, Meeting of Directors, 13 June 1927
28 *Inquiry Evidence*, 442–3
29 HQA, File 7105, Memorandum entitled 'Beauharnois Syndicate Profits'
30 HQA, Beauharnois Power Syndicate Stock Book. A complete list of shareholders in the first and second Beauharnois syndicates is given in *Inquiry Report*.

CHAPTER 3 Political intrigue in Ottawa

1 *Inquiry Evidence*, 648
2 Ibid.
3 NAC, Sir Clifford Sifton Papers, Memorandum showing the advantages that the Ottawa River has over the St. Lawrence River, more especially in regard to Hydro-Electric Power Development [1924]. See also NAC, Clifford Sifton Jr. Papers
4 NAC, Clifford Sifton Jr. Papers, Transcript of Evidence in the Privy Council, on appeal from the Court of King's bench for the Province of Quebec, No. 14 of 1937, between Clifford Sifton et al. ... and Robert Oliver Sweezey

5 *Inquiry Evidence*, 681–2
6 NAC, Clifford Sifton Jr. Papers, Transcript of Evidence
7 *Inquiry Evidence*, 649
8 Ibid.
9 Ibid.
10 Ibid., 625, 915
11 NAC, King Diary, 20 and 21 Jan. and 1 Feb. 1928
12 M. Grattan O'Leary, 'The Scramble on the St. Lawrence,' *Maclean's*, 1 May 1928; E.C. Drury, 'The St. Lawrence Question,' ibid., 1 and 15 Feb. and 1 Mar. 1929
13 'Press Debates St. Lawrence Project,' ibid., 15 May 1928
14 NAC, King Diary, 3 Jan. 1928
15 A duplicate copy of the official deposit slip from the Old Colony Trust Company, Boston, dated 29 Dec. 1927, is available in NAC, McDougald Papers
16 NAC, King Diary, 8 Jan. 1928
17 The Old Colony Trust Company deposit slip for $15,000, dated 1 Oct. 1928, by Senator McDougald on account for W.L.M. King, is also available in NAC, McDougald Papers
18 NAC, King Diary, 14 Jan. 1929. The diary entry for 16 Aug. 1928 gives the amount of another donation to the Old Colony Trust fund, together with the name of the donor. An examination of the numerous references to the McDougald contribution in the diary entries in November 1931 clearly indicates that King knew and worried about the McDougald contributions, eventually driving to Montreal to return the money.
19 *Inquiry Evidence*, 656
20 NAC, RG 11, Vol. 4223, File 8044, Application of the Beauharnois Light, Heat and Power Company, 17 Jan. 1928
21 NAC, King Diary, 6 Jan. 1928
22 Ibid., 20 Jan. 1928
23 Ibid., 3 Jan. 1928
24 Ibid., 5 May 1928
25 Ibid., 11 July 1928
26 Ibid., 14 Dec. 1928
27 Ibid., 13 Dec. 1928
28 Ibid., 20 Jan. 1928
29 Ibid., 21 Jan. 1928. King's objective was 'to gain time by this reference.'
30 Ibid., 26 June 1928
31 M. Grattan O'Leary, 'Holt vs Jones'

CHAPTER 4 Bewildered bureaucrats and a divided cabinet

1 NAC, RG 11, Vol. 4225, File 804, J.W. Harris, Transportation and Power Corporation, to J.B. Hunter, Deputy Minister of Public Works, 22 Oct. 1928; NAC, King Papers, 129975–84
2 *Inquiry Evidence*, 566
3 Ibid., 575
4 *FT*, 4 Jan. 1929
5 NAC, King Papers, 130056–7, Andrew Haydon to King, 3 Dec. 1928
6 NAC, King Diary, 11 Dec. 1928
7 Ibid., 18 Dec. 1928
8 NAC, King Papers, 141858, Senator Donat Raymond to King, 25 Jan. 1929
9 Ibid., 141858, undated letter from Raymond to King. The context clearly indicates that the letter was written early in January 1929.
10 *FT*, 4 Jan. 1929
11 NAC, King Diary, 13 Dec. 1928
12 Ibid., 14 Dec. 1928
13 Ibid., 21 Dec. 1928; NAC, King Papers, 143898–900, J.H. Spence to King, 12 Jan. 1929
14 NAC, King Diary, 25 Dec. 1928
15 Ibid., 14 Jan. 1929
16 Ibid.
17 *Inquiry Evidence*, 575
18 Complete documentation on the hearings is in NAC, RG 11, Vol. 4225, File 804-1-C
19 *FT*, 8 Feb. 1929
20 Ibid., 18 Jan. 1929
21 NAC, King Diary, 25 Jan. 1929
22 NAC, King Papers, 137689–91, Aimé Geoffrion to King, 25 Jan. 1929
23 Ibid., 138529–34 and 141858, F.P. Jones to King, 25 Jan. 1929 and Donat Raymond to King, 25 Jan. 1929
24 *FT*, 4 Jan. 1929
25 NAC, King Diary, 25 Jan. 1929
26 Ibid.
27 Ibid., 5 Feb. 1929
28 Ibid., 6 Feb. 1929
29 *House of Commons Debates*, 1929, 11, 8 Feb. 1929
30 Ibid., 262–6, 19 Feb. 1929
31 NAC, King Diary, 19 Feb. 1929

32 *House of Commons Debates*, 1929, 349, 21 Feb. 1929
33 NAC, King Diary, 25 Feb. 1929
34 Ibid., 27 Feb. 1929
35 *House of Commons Debates*, 1929, 440, 25 Feb. 1929
36 NAC, King Diary, 2 March 1929
37 Ibid., 6 March 1929
38 Ibid., 8 March 1929

CHAPTER 5 Sir Herbert Holt insinuates himself

1 Canada, PC 422, 8 March 1928, clause 11
2 NAC, RG 11, Vol. 4225, File 804-1-D, J.S. Norris, Vice-President, the Cedars Rapids Manufacturing and Power Company, to the Minister of Public Works, 27 March 1929
3 *Inquiry Evidence*, 646; NAC, King Papers, 138529–34, F.P. Jones to King, 25 Jan. 1929
4 Ibid.
5 M. Grattan O'Leary, 'Holt vs Jones'
6 House of Lords Record Office, Beaverbrook Papers, Series A, Box 72, Beaverbrook to Holt, 3 Dec. 1928 and Holt to Beaverbrook, 4 April 1928; ibid., Series A, Box 55, Dudley Oliver, Bank of Montreal, to Beaverbrook, 10 May 1929
7 *FT*, 10 May 1929
8 *Inquiry Evidence*, 678; HQA, Minute Book of the Beauharnois Light, Heat and Power Company, Meeting of Directors, 15 January 1931.
9 *Inquiry Evidence*, 381
10 *FT*, 26 July 1929
11 Ibid., and 2 Aug. 1929
12 *Inquiry Evidence*, 373–84, 487 and 684; QUA, Sweezey Papers, Box 2, Memorandum of Agreement ... 26 July 1929 ... between Frank P. Jones ... and Robert Oliver Sweezey
13 *Inquiry Evidence*, 678
14 The two companies reached an agreement in principle late in July of 1929. A formal agreement was signed on 19 November 1929, but it was approved by the boards of directors of the two companies only in January of 1931. See HQA, Minute Book of the Beauharnois Light, Heat and Power Company, meeting of Directors, 15 Jan. 1931. A copy of the agreement is attached to these minutes.
15 NAC, King Papers, 141358, Donat Raymond to Mackenzie King [Jan. 1929]
16 Vigod, *Quebec Before Duplessis*, 168, 247

17 *FT*, 23 Aug. 1929
18 QHA, Minute Book of the Beauharnois Light, Heat and Power Company, Meetings of Directors, 5 Aug. and 25 Oct. 1929
19 DU, Lee Papers, Box 8, W.S. Lee, 'Beauharnois Development of the Soulanges Section of the St. Lawrence River,' paper presented at the summer convention of the AIEE, Chicago, Ill., 26–30 June 1933
20 Ibid., Box 2, 'Quebec Aluminum Company, Limited'
21 Ibid., Box 9, F.H. Cothran to W.S. Lee, 26 July 1929

CHAPTER 6 Ontario Tories make a deal

1 NAC, King Papers, Ferguson to King, 19 Nov. 1928
2 OHA, *Ontario Inquiry*, Transcript of Hearings, 439; NAC, Magrath Papers, Vol. 5, Memorandum re Quebec Power Contracts
3 HQA, Minute Book of the Beauharnois Light, Heat and Power Company, Meeting of Directors, 5 June 1929
4 OHA, *Ontario Inquiry*, supporting document entitled, 'Report re Power Supply for the Niagara System contracts with the Gatineau Power Company, the Beauharnois Light, Heat and Power Company, the James MacLaren Company, and the Chats Falls Power Company, 7 Dec. 1931, 14
5 Oliver, *G. Howard Ferguson*
6 OHA, *Ontario Inquiry*, Hearings, 832–74
7 *Inquiry Evidence*, 654
8 *Senate Inquiry*, xxviii; OHA, *Ontario Inquiry*, Hearings, 89
9 OHA, *Ontario Inquiry*, Hearings, 89
10 Ibid., 1806–7
11 Ibid., 917
12 Ibid., 1022
13 Ibid., 1040–4
14 Ibid., 990
15 Ibid., 975
16 Ibid., 958
17 Ibid., 999
18 Ibid., 1768
19 Ibid., 1084–92
20 Ibid., 917–1094
21 Ibid., 'Report re Power Supply'
22 Ibid., Hearings, 939, 948
23 Ibid., 972
24 Ibid., 975

25 Ibid., 976
26 Ibid., 1822
27 Ibid., 822
28 Ibid., 1959
29 Ibid., 918
30 Ibid., 770–4

CHAPTER 7 A 'poison pill' and collateral trust bonds

1 HQA, Minute Book of the Beauharnois Power Corporation, 1–20, By-Laws of the Beauharnois Power Corporation Limited
2 Ibid.; *FT*, 23 Aug. 1929
3 HQA, Minute Book of the Beauharnois Power Corporation, Meetings of Directors and Management Preferred Shareholders, 30 Sept. and 31 Oct. 1929, and Stock Register of the Beauharnois Power Corporation
4 Ibid., Meetings of Directors and Management Preferred Shareholders, 30 Sept. and 31 Oct. 1929
5 Ibid., Meetings of Management Preferred Shareholders, 5 Nov. and 20 Dec. 1929
6 *Inquiry Evidence*, 654
7 Ibid.
8 NAC, RG 11, Vol. 4226, File 804-1-A, Statement filed in lieu of Prospectus
9 QUA, Sweezey Papers, Box 2, has numerous documents dealing with the legal and administrative arrangements for the issuance of the 6 per cent collateral trust bonds.
10 *FT*, 6 March 1929
11 Ibid., 12 Sept. 1930
12 Ibid., 6 Dec. 1929

CHAPTER 8 Realizing the dream

1 T. Dickinson, 'Sweezey's Beauharnois'; *FT*, 1 Nov. 1929, and 17 Oct. 1930
2 DU, Lee Papers, Box 9, F.H. Cothran to W.S. Lee, 26 July 1929
3 Ibid., Box 8, manuscript entitled 'Down the Canal: A Pictorial Presentation of the Beauharnois Power and Navigation Development,' published 31 Jan. 1931 by the Beauharnois Power Corporation Limited; published article by W.J.W. McNaughton entitled 'Beauharnois: A Dream Come True. La Réalization d'un Rêve'; published article by W.S. Lee entitled 'Beauharnois Development of the Soulanges Section of the St. Lawrence River,' presented at the summer convention of the AIEE, Chicago, Ill., 26–30 June 1933

4 Ibid., pamphlet entitled *Physical Facts and Financial Figures on Beauharnois*, published 8 Dec. 1930 by the Beauharnois Power Corporation; Lee, 'Beauharnois Development of the Soulanges Section'; QUA, Sweezey Papers, Box 1, published article by W.S. Lee, 'Beauharnois Harnesses St. Lawrence for 2,000,000 h.p.,' *Electrical World*, 14 Nov. 1931
5 QUA, Sweezey Papers, Box 1, Lee, 'Beauharnois Harnesses St. Lawrence.' The final cost of constructing the first phase was $80 million.
6 Robert F. Durden, *The Dukes of Durham, 1865–1929* (Durham, NC: Duke University Press 1975), 191–3; DU, William Robertson Perkins Papers, Box 11, File entitled 'Haskell, George D. v. Alcoa – Alcoa Chronology'
7 QUA, Sweezey Papers, Box 1, Lee, 'Beauharnois Harnesses St. Lawrence.' The article provides a detailed discussion of the technical aspects of the project.
8 DU, Lee Papers, Box 9, F.H. Cothran to W.S. Lee, 26 July 1929
9 Ibid., Memorandum of Operations on the Beauharnois Development to Aug. 10, 1929, dated 12 Aug. 1929
10 Ibid., Memorandum of Operations of Beauharnois Construction Company for week ending October 14, 1929
11 Ibid., Memorandum of Operations ... for week ended 5 April 1930
12 *FT*, 8 Aug. 1930
13 DU, Lee Papers, Memorandum of Operations ... for the week ending 19 April 1930. A detailed technical explanation of the cause of the accident is given in this memorandum.
14 *FT*, 8 May 1930
15 Ibid., 4 April, 6 June, 25 July, 8 Aug., 19 Sept., 5 and 26 Dec. 1930, 13 and 27 March 1931 provided detailed construction progress reports.

CHAPTER 9 Helping political friends

1 NAC, King Diary, 24 Jan. 1930
2 *Inquiry Evidence*, 352
3 Ibid.
4 NAC, RG 11, Vols 4222 to 4226, File 804–1
5 *Inquiry Evidence*, 68
6 Ibid., 67
7 Ibid., 69
8 Ibid., 302
9 NAC, King Diary, 8 and 10 April 1930
10 *Royal Gazette and Colonist Daily*, Hamilton, Bermuda, 15 and 22 April 1930
11 Ibid., 21 April 1930

12 NAC, King Diary, 19 April 1930
13 Ibid., 22 April 1930
14 Ibid., 27 April 1930
15 *House of Commons Debates, 1930*, 1313, 2383–423, 2797
16 NAC, King Diary, 28 May 1930
17 Ibid., 1 June 1930
18 *Inquiry Evidence*, 824
19 Ibid.
20 Ibid., 823
21 Ibid., 833–4
22 Whitaker, *The Government Party*, 12–13
23 J.M. Beck, *Pendulum of Power: Canada's Federal Elections* (Scarborough, Ont.: Prentice-Hall 1968), 196

CHAPTER 10 The revenge of a thwarted rival

1 AO, Cantin Paper, MSS 6111
2 NAC, King Papers, 129975–84, J.W. Harris, Transportation and Power Corporation, to J.B. Hunter, Deputy Minister of Public Works, 22 Oct. 1928
3 *FP*, 15 Aug. 1931
4 Ibid.
5 NAC, Bennett Papers, 49130–3, Frank Regan to Bennett, 15 May 1930
6 Ibid., 513299–301, Regan to A.D. McRae, 15 July 1930
7 *House of Commons Debates*, 1930, 1313, 7 April 1930
8 NAC, Bennett Papers, 49137, Statement in lieu of Prospectus, 2 Dec. 1929. This was part of a package of material sent by Regan to the prime minister.
9 Ibid., 49130–3, Regan to Bennett, 15 May 1930
10 Ibid., 49134, R. Gardiner to Bennett, 22 May 1930; *House of Commons Debates*, 1930, 2395, 22 May 1930
11 *House of Commons Debates*, 1930, 2383–95, 22 May 1930
12 Ibid., 2403, 22 May 1930
13 Ibid., 2410–11, 22 May 1930
14 NAC, King Diary, 22 May 1930
15 *House of Commons Debates*, 1930, 2797, 29 May 1930
16 NAC, Bennett Papers, 513295–6, Frank Regan to General McRae, 10 July 1930
17 Ibid., 513293, A.D. McRae to Frank Regan, 11 July 1930

CHAPTER 11 The scandal revealed

1 AO, Cantin Papers, Box 1, File 1, Frank Regan to Col. W.H. Price, 23 June 1930

2 Ibid., Box 3, File E, Frank Regan to W.H. Price, 15 Oct. 1930
3 Ibid., W.H. Price to Frank Regan, 17 Oct. 1930
4 Ibid., Frank Regan to Col. W.W. Denison, 21 Oct. 1930
5 Ibid., Frank Regan to E.J. Garland, 26 Nov. 1930
6 Ibid.
7 Ibid., Robert Gardiner to Frank Regan, 21 Nov. 1930
8 Ibid., Frank Regan to Robert Gardiner, 4 Dec. 1930
9 Ibid., Charles Murphy to Frank Regan, 6 Dec. 1930
10 *House of Commons Debates*, 1930, 1740, 19 May 1931
11 Ibid., 867, 990, 1087, 1228, 1575, 1679: 22, 27, 29 April and 4, 14, 18 May 1930
12 AO, Cantin Papers, Box 3, File E, Frank Regan to Narcisse M. Cantin, 30 July 1930
13 QUA, Sweezey Papers, Box 1, *The Beauharnois Inquiry by a Special Staff Writer of The Evening Telegram* (hereafter referred to as *Telegram Reports*) Toronto, 6
14 *House of Commons Debates*, 1931, 1744, 19 May 1931
15 Ibid., 1737–8, 19 May 1931
16 Ibid., 1740, 19 May 1931
17 NAC, Bennett Papers, 510667–9, W.H. Price to Bennett, 22 April 1931
18 NAC, King Diary, 10 June 1931
19 *Journals of the House of Commons*, 1931, 353, 418: 15, 19 June 1931
20 *Telegram Reports*, 5
21 Ibid., 7–8
22 *FT*, 3 July 1931
23 Ibid., 26 June 1931
24 *Telegram Reports*, 13
25 Ibid., 14
26 Ibid.
27 Ibid., 16
28 Ibid.
29 *Inquiry Evidence*, 374–83. Jones was not entirely wrong about the profits of the co-operative grain and elevator companies. The Saskatchewan Co-operative Elevator Company, for example, sold its initial shares in 1911 for $7.50 each. These shares were purchased in 1925 by the recently organized Saskatchewan Wheat Pool for $155.70 each, in a transaction in which both the purchasers and the sellers were co-operating farmers.
30 NAC, King Diary, 10 July 1931
31 *Journals of the House of Commons*, 1931, 518, 536: 13, 14 July 1931; *Journals of the Senate*, 1931, 257–62

32 NAC, Bennett Papers, 514284–9, Henry Timmis to Bennett, 10 June 1931
33 Ibid., 514290–1, C.H. Cahan to Bennett, 13 July 1931, together with a copy of the expense claim submitted by Senator McDougald.
34 NAC, King Diary, 13 July 1931
35 Ibid.
36 Ibid.
37 *Telegram Reports*, 33
38 Ibid., 35
39 *Inquiry Evidence*, 849
40 Ibid., 854
41 Ibid., 638, 649–68, 822–3
42 *Inquiry Report*, xxii
43 There is some ambiguity regarding the exact amount involved. Neatby, *King*, 383, mentions the sum of $15,000. King, in his diary, does not mention a specific sum, but the bank deposit slips in NAC, McDougald Papers, document two deposits totalling $25,000.
44 NAC, King Diary, 15 July 1931
45 Ibid., 17 July 1931
46 Ibid.
47 Ibid., 18 July 1931
48 Ibid., 19 July 1931
49 Neatby, *King*, 374
50 NAC, King Diary, 20 July 1931
51 Ibid., 21 July 1931
52 *House of Commons Debates*, 1931, 4029, 22 July 1931
53 Ibid., 4374, 30 July 1931
54 *Inquiry Report*, 643
55 Ibid., 631
56 Ibid., 639
57 Ibid., 634–8
58 Ibid., 643
59 Ibid., 644
60 Ibid., 644–5
61 *FT*, 31 July 1931
62 AO, Cantin Papers, Files B, E, H, and N
63 Ibid., Box 3, File E, Frank Regan to Narcisse Cantin, 1 Nov. 1930
64 Ibid., 11 Nov. 1930
65 *House of Commons Debates*, 1931, 4709, 30 July 1931
66 NAC, King Diary, 30 July 1931
67 Roberts, *So This is Ottawa*, 191–2
68 *FT*, 31 July 1931

CHAPTER 12 Cleansing the corporation

1 NAC, Bennett Papers, 513533–6, R.O. Sweezey to Bennett, 12 Sept. 1931
2 Ibid., 513537, Bennett to Sweezey, 15 Oct. 1931
3 *FT*, 20 Aug. 1931, quoting an editorial from the *Sault Ste Marie Star*
4 Ibid., 18 Sept. 1931, quoting from the *Kingston Whig-Standard*
5 Ibid., 14 Aug. 1931
6 NAC, Bennett Papers, 512235–43, Aimé Geoffrion to Bennett, 17 Sept. 1931
7 *FT*, 28 Aug. 1931
8 Ibid., 24 July 1931
9 *Inquiry Report*, xxx
10 *FT*, 29 Jan. 1932
11 NAC, Bennett Papers, 512235–43, Aimé Geoffrion to Bennett, 17 Sept. 1931
12 Ibid., 512277, R.A.C. Henry to M.W. Wilson, General Manager, Royal Bank of Canada, 20 Oct. 1931
13 HQA, Minute Book of the Beauharnois Power Corporation, Meeting of Directors, 19 Nov. 1931
14 NAC, Meighen Papers, 91231–2.
15 Ibid., 91667–70, J.A. Mann and A.L. Smith, Counsel for the Senate Committee, to Charles E. Tanner, Chairman, Beauharnois Senate Committee, 12 April 1932
16 *Senate Report*, 22
17 NAC, King Diary, 23 Oct. 1931
18 Ibid., 15, 21 Oct. and 14 Nov. 1931
19 Ibid., 16 Nov. 1931
20 Ibid., 17 Nov. 1931
21 NAC, Bennett Papers, 419141–5, Senator Charles Murphy to Senator G. Lynch-Staunton, 30 Dec. 1931
22 Ibid.
23 NAC, King Diary, 12 Feb. 1932
24 Ibid., 2 March 1932
25 Ibid., 3 March 1932
26 AO, Ferguson Papers, Ferguson to Senator Tanner, Chairman, Investigating Committee
27 *Senate Evidence*, 259
28 AO, Ferguson Papers, Ferguson to Miss Saunderson, 3 June 1932
29 NAC, King Diary, 16 March 1932
30 NAC, Meighen Papers, 91345–61, Draft of Synopsis for Report of Senate Committee, 28 March 1932
31 All quotes from the *Senate Report*
32 *Globe*, 29 April 1932

33 NAC, King Diary, 23 April 1932
34 Ibid., 29 April 1932
35 Ibid., 30 April 1932
36 NAC, Meighen Papers, 91387–90, R.S. Stevens to John P. Edds [sic], 30 April 1932, and J. Fenton Argue to John P. Ebbs, 30 April 1932
37 Ibid., 91423, Meighen to Randall Davidson, 6 May 1932

CHAPTER 13 Protecting workers and investors

1 HQA, Minute Book of the Beauharnois Light, Heat and Power Company, Meeting of Directors, 15 Jan. 1931
2 Ibid.; NAC, Bennett Papers, 512229–33, Jackson Dodds to Bennett, 9 and 14 Sept. 1931 and Bennett to Jackson Dodds, 16 Sept. 1931
3 *FT*, 7 Aug. 1931
4 Lists of shareholders and bondholders are in NAC, Bennett Papers, 514431–525; HQA, Beauharnois Power Corporation Documents, File 6300-13
5 NAC, Bennett Papers, 512717–21, Minutes of the Bondholders' Protective Committee meeting held 10 June 1932 to whom White made his report
6 *FT*, 7 Sept. 1931
7 Ibid.
8 NAC, Bennett Papers, 512230, Jackson Dodds to R.B. Bennett, 9 Sept. 1931
9 *Montreal Gazette*, 27 July 1931; NAC, Bennett Papers, 514306, 'Noel' to 'Maurice,' 27 July 1931
10 *FT*, 7 Aug. 1931
11 NAC, Bennett Papers, 510667–9, W.H. Price, Attorney General of Ontario, to Bennett, 22 April 1931
12 *FT*, 14 Aug. 1931
13 Ibid., 7 Aug. 1931
14 HQA, Minute Book of the Beauharnois Power Corporation, Meeting of Directors, 7 Jan. 1932; NAC, Bennett Papers, 512425–7 and 512415–23, Memoranda of representations by the three banks to the Prime Minister, 11 and 15 Feb. 1932
15 NAC, Bennett Papers, 514579–84, Bennett to M.W. Wilson, 3 Oct. 1931
16 HQA, Minute Book of the Beauharnois Power Corporation, Meeting of Directors, 29 Feb. 1932, at which a letter from Bennett to Jackson Dodds was read and discussed
17 NAC, Bennett Papers, 512474–6, A.F. White, Acting President, on behalf of the Directors of the Beauharnois Light, Heat and Power Company, to R.B. Bennett, 29 Feb. 1932
18 *FT*, 18 March 1932

19 Ibid., 7 Aug. 1931

20 HQA, Minute Book of the Beauharnois Power Corporation, Meeting of Directors, 7 Jan. 1932, at which a letter from M.W. Wilson to Bennett outlining this proposal was approved.

21 NAC, Bennett Papers, 513716–18, 713729–34, Sweezey to Bennett, 7 and 14 March 1932

22 *FT*, 14 Aug. 1932

23 Ibid., 28 April 1932

24 Ibid., 13 May 1932

25 NAC, Bennett Papers, 513944, F. Somerville to Bennett, 14 June 1932

26 Ibid., 512717–21, Minutes of Meeting of the Holders of Thirty-Year 6% Collateral Trust Sinking Fund Bonds, held at Windsor Hall, Windsor Hotel, Montreal, Canada, the 10th day of June 1932

27 Ibid., 513941–8, F. Somerville to Bennett, 14 June 1932

28 Ibid., 513942

29 Ibid.

30 HQA, Minute Book of the Beauharnois Power Corporation, Meeting of Directors, 9 June 1932; NAC, Bennett Papers, 512717–21, Minutes of Meeting of the Holders of the Thirty Year 6% Collateral Trust Sinking Fund Bonds. Frank Regan spoke at length at both of these meetings.

31 NAC, Home Bank Records, Vol. 166, File entitled 'Beauharnois – Correspondence, 1931–1936,' I.E. Weldon to S.A. Morrison, 11 June 1932

32 Ibid., Unsigned petition to R.B. Bennett, 20 April 1933

33 *FT*, 11 March and 10 June 1932

34 'Beauharnois Development. 228,000 hp of final 2,000,000 hp now in operation. Many interesting features to major engineering project, constructed on dry land,' *Electrical News and Engineering* 41, no. 20 (15 Oct. 1932), 25–36

35 NAC, Bennett Papers, 512907–1, R.A.C. Henry to Bennett, 29 Dec. 1932

36 *FT*, 16 Dec. 1932

37 HQA, Minute Book of the Beauharnois Power Corporation, Meetings of Directors, 16 March, 6 April, 4 May, 9 and 23 June, 7 July, and 19 Oct. 1933; *FT*, 24 Feb., 31 March, and 7 April 1933; NAC, Bennett Papers, 513048–76, T.A. Russell, Chairman of the Collateral Trust Bond Committee, to Bennett, 15 March 1933, with numerous supporting documents

38 NAC, Bennett Papers, 513029, Bennett to Sweezey, 11 Feb. 1933.

39 NAC, Home Bank Records, Vol. 166, file entitled 'Beauharnois – Correspondence, 1931–1936,' Address to Members of the Senate and House of Commons, 1 May 1933

40 *FT*, 24 Feb., 31 March, and 7 April 1933

41 Ibid., 31 March 1933

42 HQA, Minute Book of the Beauharnois Power Corporation, Meeting of Directors, 16 March 1933

43 NAC, Home Bank Records, Vol. 166, file entitled 'Beauharnois – Correspondence, 1931–1936,' I.E. Weldon to the Editor of the *Toronto Star*

CHAPTER 14 Postscript and conclusion

1 QUA, Sweezey Papers, Box 1, copy of an article by W.J.W. McNaughton, 'Beauharnois. A Dream Come True / La Réalization d'un Rêve,' published in the *Canadian Geographical Journal*

2 OHA, *Ontario Inquiry*

3 AO, Hepburn Papers, Boxes 185, 239–42, deal with the Hydro Electric Power Commission contracts, and include correspondence from Beauharnois security holders. See also OHA, Proceedings of the Select Legislative Committee Investigating Hydro Power Contracts and Hydro Administration, 1938

4 HQA, Minute Book of the Beauharnois Power Corporation, Report of the President and Directors, 17 Feb. 1936

5 HQA, Minute Book of the Beauharnois Light, Heat and Power Company, Meetings of Directors, 28 Jan., 20 May, 22 July, and 21 Oct. 1937

6 HQA, Minute Book of the Beauharnois Power Corporation, Annual Meeting of Shareholders, 16 Feb. 1938

7 *FT*, 7 April 1933

8 NAC, Bennett Papers, 513533–6, Sweezey to Bennett, 12 Sept. 1931

9 *Visites des installations d'Hydro-Québec* (Montréal: Hydro-Québec, été 1982); *Beauharnois 1,574,260 kilowatts* (Montréal: Hydro-Québec 1981)

10 QUA, Sweezey Papers, Box 1, McNaughton, 'Beauharnois. A Dream Come True / La Réalization d'un Rêve'; Hogue et al., *Québec: Un siècle d'électricité*

11 Personal visit to the site by the author in 1982

12 HQA, Minute Book of the Beauharnois Light, Heat and Power Company, Meeting of Directors, 19 May 1941

13 Hogue et al., *Québec: Un siècle d'électricité*

14 Vigod, *Quebec before Duplessis* 168, 247

15 R.T.L., 'Taschereau,' *Maclean's*, 1 Feb. 1934

16 HQA, Minute Book of the Beauharnois Power Corporation, Meeting of Directors, 16 Nov. 1933

17 NAC, RG 32, Vol. 125, R.A.C. Henry personnel file

18 HQA, Minute Book of the Beauharnois Light, Heat and Power Company, Meeting of Directors, 18 March 1940
19 Ibid., Meeting of Directors, 15 May 1939
20 NAC, King Diary, 1 Nov. 1932
21 Ibid.
22 Ibid., 10 Nov. 1932
23 Ibid., 12 Nov. 1932
24 Ibid.
25 Ibid.
26 Ibid.
27 NAC, McDougald Papers, McDougald to King, 31 Oct. 1935
28 Ibid.
29 Ibid., 27 June 1938
30 Peter C. Newman, *Debrett's Illustrated Guide to The Canadian Establishment* (Toronto: Methuen 1983) 72
31 Whitaker, *The Government Party*, 405
32 'After Beauharnois – What?' *Maclean's*, 15 Oct. 1931
33 'Party Funds,' *Canadian Forum*, Sept. 1931

Bibliography

PRIMARY SOURCES

1 National Archives of Canada (NAC)

MG 26, I/Arthur Meighen Papers
MG 26, J/W.L. Mackenzie King Papers
MG 26, J-13/W.L. Mackenzie King Diary
MG 26, K/R.B. Bennett Papers
MG 27, II, C-1/Charles Fitzpatrick Papers
MG 27, II, D-15/Sir Clifford Sifton Papers
MG 27, II, D-18/Thomas White Papers
MG 27, III, B-1/C.H. Cahan Papers
MG 27, III, B-4/Lomer Gouin Papers
MG 27, III, B-7/R.J. Manion Papers
MG 27, III, B-8/Charles Murphy Papers
MG 27, III, B-9/H.H. Stevens Papers
MG 27, III, B-10/Ernest Lapointe Papers
MG 27, III, B-11/J.L. Ralston Papers
MG 27, III, C-4/Agnes MacPhail Papers
MG 27, III, C-24/W.L. McDougald Papers
MG 27, III, C-28/Andrew Haydon Papers
MG 28, II-11/Home Bank Records
MG 28, III-7/Kerry & Chace Ltd Records
MG 28, III-35/Blake & Redden Papers
MG 29, A-32/C.E.L. Porteous Papers
MG 30, A-16/J.W. Flavelle Papers
MG 30, A-26/D.W. McLachlan Papers
MG 30, A-51/James H. Dunn Papers

MG 30, A-105/Clifford Sifton [Jr] Papers
RG 2/Privy Council Office Records
RG 11 /Public Works Records
RG 12/Transport Records
RG 14/Parliament (Sessional Papers)
RG 15/Interior Records
RG 19/Finance Records
RG 32/Public Service Commission
RG 43/Railways and Canals Records
RG 51/International Joint Commission
RG 55/Treasury Board Records
RG 89/Water Resources Branch Records

2 Archives of Ontario (AO)
MU 6111, 6119, 6120, 6160/Narcisse M. Cantin Papers
MU 1020, 1027, 1028/G. Howard Ferguson Papers
RG 3/G. Howard Ferguson Papers
RG 3/George S. Henry Papers
RG 3/Mitchell F. Hepburn Papers

3 Archive Nationale du Québec
Louis-Alexandre Taschereau Papers
Records of the Department of Streams and Forests

4 Hydro-Québec Archives, Montreal (HQA)
Minute Book of the Beauharnois Power Corporation
Minute Book of Beauharnois Light, Heat and Power Co.
Minute Book of Beauharnois Construction Co.
Minute Book of Beauharnois Transmission Co.
Minute Book of Beauharnois Railway Co.
Minute Book of Beauharnois Land Co.
Minute Book of Beauharnois Electric Co.
Minute Book of Montreal Light, Heat and Power Consolidated
Minute Book of Cedars Rapids Manufacturing and Power Co.
Minute Book of Bond and Share Co. Ltd
File 7105 (nine subfiles) 'Organization Beauharnois Syndicate'
File 6300-13 'Shareholders of Beauharnois Power Corp. Ltd'
Beauharnois Power Syndicate Stock Book
Beauharnois Power Syndicate stock transfer books
Beauharnois Electric Company Ltd Stock Ledger
File 3800-2 'Jurisdiction over Water Powers and Navigation'
Cecil A. Ellis, *Report upon the Financial Affairs of Montreal Light, Heat and Power Consolidated and its Component Companies,*

and upon Capital Invested in its Various Properties as at April 14th, 1944 (Montreal, 12 November 1946)

5 Hydro-Electric Power Commission of Ontario Archives (Ontario Hydro Archives) (OHA)

Transcript of Hearings, and Report of the Royal Commission Appointed to Inquire into Certain Matters Concerning the Hydro-Electric Power Commission of Ontario, Namely: (a) The Mississippi and Madawaska Purchase. (b) The Possible Relationship of the Payment to John Aird, Jr., to the Purchase of Power from the Beauharnois Interests. (c) Purchase of the Assets of the Dominion Power and Transmission Company, 1932 (referred to in the footnotes as *Ontario Inquiry*)

Proceedings of the Select Legislative Committee Investigation Hydro Power Contracts and Hydro Administration, 1938

6 Queen's University Archives (QUA)

Robert Oliver Sweezey Papers

Thomas A. Crerar Papers

7 House of Lords Record Office, London, England (HLRO)

Lord Beaverbrook Papers

8 Duke University, William Robertson Perkins Library, Manuscript Department (DU)

William States Lee Papers

William Robertson Perkins Papers

9 Royal Military College of Canada, Arts and Special Collections Division

Annual Reports of the Commandant, Royal Military College of Canada, 1914–22

10 Bermuda Archives

Journals of the House of Assembly

The Royal Gazette and Colonist Daily

11 Parliamentary records

Debates of the House of Commons

Journals of the House of Commons, particularly the transcripts and reports (four) of Hearings of the Special Committee on Beauharnois Power Project, published as Appendix 5, *Journals of the House of Commons*, Session 1931. The report is also published in *Journals of the House of Commons*, 1931, 618–44.

Sessional Papers of the House of Commons

Proceedings of the Select Standing Committee of the House of Commons on Banking and Finance, 1934

Debates of the Senate

Journals of the Senate, particularly the transcripts and reports of Hearings of the Special Senate Committee on Beauharnois, published as an appendix of *Journals of the Senate*, Third Session, Seventeenth Parliament, 1932 (referred to in the footnotes as *Senate Inquiry* and *Senate Report*, respectively)

Sessional Papers of the Senate

Statutes of Canada

12 Newspapers, magazines and journals

Canadian Forum

Electrical News and Engineering

Financial Post (*FP*)

Financial Times (*FT*)

Journal of the Canadian Bankers Association

Maclean's Magazine

Monetary Times

Montreal Gazette

Montreal Star

Ottawa Evening Citizen

Queen's Quarterly

Royal Gazette and Colonist Daily (Bermuda)

Saturday Night

Toronto Globe

Toronto Star

Toronto Telegram

Transactions of the Canadian Society of Civil Engineers

SECONDARY SOURCES

1 *Books*

Armstrong, Christopher, *The Politics of Federalism: Ontario's Relations with the Federal Government, 1867–1942* (Toronto: University of Toronto Press 1981)

Armstrong, Christopher and H.V. Nelles, *Monopoly's Moment: The Organization and Regulation of Canadian Utilities, 1830–1930* (Philadelphia: Temple University Press 1986; pbk ed., Toronto: University of Toronto Press 1988)

Bauer, J. and N. Gold, *The Electric Power Industry* (New York 1939)

Black, Conrad, *Duplessis* (Toronto: McClelland and Stewart 1974)

Bouchard, T.-D., *La domination des trusts électriques* (St Hyacinthe, Qué.: Imprimerie Yamaska 1934)

Bright, Arthur A., Jr, *The Electric-Lamp Industry: Technological Change and Economic Development from 1800–1947* (New York: Macmillan 1949)

Chandler, Alfred D., Jr, *The Visible Hand: The Managerial Revolution in American Business* (Cambridge, Mass.: Harvard University Press 1977)

Dales, John H., *Hydroelectricity and Industrial Development in Quebec, 1898–1929* (Cambridge, Mass.: Harvard University Press, 1957)

Dannatt, C. and J.W. Dalgleish, *Electric Power Transmission and Interconnection* (New York 1930)

Denis, L. G. and A. V. White, *Water Powers of Canada* (Ottawa: Conservation Commission 1911)

Denison, Merrill, *The People's Power* (Toronto: McClelland and Stewart 1960)

Electricity. The Magic Medium / L'électricité cette prodigieuse énergie (Thornhill, Ont.: Institute of Electrical and Electronics Engineers Inc. 1985)

Graham, Roger, *Arthur Meighen: A Biography*, Vol. 3, *No Surrender* (Toronto: Clarke Irwin 1965)

Granatstein, J., *The Politics of Survival: The Conservative Party of Canada, 1939–1945* (Toronto: University of Toronto Press 1969)

Hannah, Leslie, *Electricity Before Nationalization* (Baltimore: Johns Hopkins University Press 1979)

– *Engineers, Managers and Politicians* (Baltimore: Johns Hopkins University Press 1982)

Hogue, Clarence, André Bolduc, et Daniel Larouche, *Québec: Un siècle d'électricité* (Montréal: Libre Expression 1979)

Houston, Edwin, *A Dictionary of Electrical Words, Terms and Phrases* (New York: Johnston 1888)

Hughes, Thomas P., *Networks of Power: Electrification in Western Society, 1880–1930* (Baltimore and London: Johns Hopkins University Press 1983)

Hunter, Louis C., *Waterpower: A History of Industrial Power in the United States, 1780–1930* (Charlottesville: University Press of Virginia)

Hutchison, Bruce, *The Incredible Canadian: Candid Portrait of Mackenzie King, His Works, His Times and His Nation* (Toronto: Longmans, Green 1952)

Landes, David, *The Unbound Prometheus: Technological Change and Industrial Development in Western Europe from 1750 to the Present* (Cambridge, Mass.: Harvard University Press 1972)

LaTerreur, Marc, *Les Tribulations des Conservateurs au Québec de Bennett à Diefenbaker* (Sherbrooke, Qué.: Presses de l'Université Laval 1973)
Leduc, R.P. Augustin, *Beauharnois: Paroisse Saint-Clement, 1819–1919, Histoire réligieuse: Histoire civile, Fêtes du Centenaire* (n.p.:n.p. 1920)
Linteau, P.-A., René Durocher, and J.-C. Robert, *Histoire du Québec contemporain: De la Conféderation à la crise 1867–1929* (Montréal: Boréal Express 1979)
Marr, W.L., and D.G. Patterson, *Canada: An Economic History* (Toronto: Macmillan 1980)
Marshall, H., F.A. Southard, and K.W. Taylor, *Canadian-American Industry* (New Haven, Conn.: Yale University Press 1936)
McKenty, Neil, *Mitch Hepburn* (Toronto: Ryerson 1967)
Neatby, H. Blair, *William Lyon Mackenzie King, 1924–1932: The Lonely Heights* (Toronto: University of Toronto Press 1963)
Nelles, H.V., *The Politics of Development: Forest, Mines and Hydro-electric Power in Ontario, 1849–1941* (Toronto: Macmillan 1974)
Neufeld, E. P., *The Financial System of Canada* (Toronto: Macmillan 1972)
Oliver, Peter, *G. Howard Ferguson, Ontario Tory* (Toronto: University of Toronto Press 1977)
Passer, Harold C., *The Electrical Manufacturers, 1875–1900* (Cambridge, Mass.: Harvard University Press 1953)
Plewman, W.R., *Adam Beck and the Ontario Hydro* (Toronto: Ryerson 1947)
Quinn, Herbert F., *The Union Nationale: Quebec Nationalism from Duplessis to Lévesque* (Toronto: University of Toronto Press 1979)
Roberts, Leslie, *These Be Your Gods* (Toronto: Musson 1929)
– *So This is Ottawa* (Toronto: Macmillan 1933)
Safarian, A.E., *The Canadian Economy in the Great Depression* (Toronto: McClelland and Stewart 1970)
Sinclair, Charles Henry, *Industrial Geography of the Beauharnois Canal Zone* (n.p.:n.p. 1954)
Stephens, George W., *The St. Lawrence Waterway Project* (Montreal: Louis Carrier and Company 1929)
Uppenborn, F., *History of the Transformer* (London: Spon 1889)
Urquhart, M.C. and K.A.H. Buckley, *Historical Statistics of Canada* (Toronto: Macmillan 1965)

Vigod, Bernard L., *Quebec before Duplessis: The Political Career of Louis-Alexandre Taschereau* (Montreal and Kingston: McGill-Queen's University Press 1986)

Whitaker, Reginald, *The Government Party: Organizing and Financing the Liberal Party of Canada, 1930–1958* (Toronto: University of Toronto Press 1977)

White, A.V., *Power Possibilities on the St. Lawrence River* (Ottawa 1918)

Wright, C.P., *The St. Lawrence Deep Waterway: A Canadian Appraisal* (Toronto 1935)

2 *Scholarly articles*

Armstrong, Christopher and H.V. Nelles, 'Contrasting Development of the Hydro-Electric Industry in the Montreal and Toronto Regions, 1900–1930,' *Journal of Canadian Studies* 18 (1983), 5–27

Biss, I., 'Recent Power Legislation in Ontario,' *Canadian Journal of Economics and Political Science* 2 (1936), 212–14

– 'Recent Power Legislation in Quebec,' *Canadian Journal of Economics and Political Science* 3 (1937), 550–8

Brady, A., 'The Ontario Hydro-Electric Power Commission,' *Canadian Journal of Economics and Political Science* 2 (1936), 331–53

Christie, C.V., 'The Cost of Hydro-Electric Power,' *Engineering Journal* (April 1924), 177–80

Davies, P.T., 'Cost of Electric Power,' *Engineering Journal* (August 1925), 337-43

Dirks, Patricia, 'Dr. Philippe Hamel and the Public Power Movement in Quebec City 1929–1934: The Failure of a Crusade,' paper presented at Canadian Historical Association annual meeting, June 1979

Durocher, René, 'Taschereau, Hepburn et les relations Hydro-Québec 1934–1936,' *Revue d'histoire de l'Amérique française* 24 (December 1970), 341–55

Heinzmann, Ralph, 'The Political Culture of Quebec,' *Canadian Journal of Political Science* 16 (March 1983), 3–59

Hughes, E.D., 'Industry and the Rural System in Quebec,' *Canadian Journal of Economics and Political Science* 4 (1938), 341–9

Lawson, A.J., 'Generation, Distribution and Measurement of Electricity for Light and Power,' *Transactions of the Canadian Society of Civil Engineers* (1890), 179–237

Lewis, B.W., 'Public Policy and Growth in the Power Industry,' *Journal of Economic History*, Supplement 7 (1947), 47–55

Prentice, J.S., 'Canada's Objection to the Exportation of Hydro-Electric Power,' *Journal of Political Economy* (1928), 592–624

Roberts, Leslie, 'The Silent Senator,' *The Canadian* 72, no. 6 (Dec. 1929), 46–7

Wilson, J., 'Hydro Development in Province of Quebec,' *Electrical News and Engineering* 60 (15 February 1949), 70–1, 79

Index